YALE HISTORICAL PUBLICATIONS

Leonard Woods Labaree, *Editor.*

MANUSCRIPTS AND EDITED TEXTS

XX

Published under the Direction of The Department of History

From the Income of

The Frederick John Kingsbury Memorial Fund

Wakeman Bryarly

AS A MAJOR IN THE RUSSIAN ARMY AT THE TIME
OF THE CRIMEAN WAR

TRAIL TO CALIFORNIA

THE OVERLAND JOURNAL OF
VINCENT GEIGER AND WAKEMAN BRYARLY

EDITED WITH AN INTRODUCTION

BY

DAVID MORRIS POTTER

Assistant Professor of History in
Yale University

NEW HAVEN

YALE UNIVERSITY PRESS

LONDON · HUMPHREY MILFORD · OXFORD UNIVERSITY PRESS

1945

PREFACE

T HE diary of Vincent E. Geiger and Dr. Wakeman Bryarly
is one of some fifty manuscript overland journals which
form a part of the William Robertson Coe Collection of
Western Americana. The manuscript portion of this collection,
touching almost every aspect of the history of the West, was presented to the Yale University Library by Mr. Coe in 1943.

In view of the variety and richness of the Coe Collection, no single
manuscript can effectively represent the whole. The Geiger-Bryarly
diary, however, may be at least suggestive of the quality of these
manuscripts, and it is for that reason, in part, that it is here published.

Altogether, multitudes of Gold Rush emigrants planned to keep
journals, and a surprising number adhered to their purpose. Consequently, scores of such day-by-day accounts have turned up, re-
cording journeys, throughout the forties and fifties, by way of Cape
Horn, Panama, Mexico, the Gila River route across the southern
United States and northern Mexico, and the Oregon and California
Trail over the South Pass and down the Humboldt. So many of these
diaries have found their way into print that it is possible to list more
than twenty of them for the single season of 1849 by way of the
South Pass route alone. Their very abundance might seem to render
the publication of still another superfluous. However, the diary begun by Vincent Geiger at St. Joseph, Missouri, and continued by
Wakeman Bryarly from the North Platte until the arrival in California, is characterized by certain features which lend to it a very
distinctive value.

In order to appreciate that value, it should be recognized that
many of the extant journals, although important for research purposes, make dull reading because they are mere notations of route
and mileage; while others, which display more literary ambition,
sometimes become effusive and sententious. By contrast, the Geiger-
Bryarly record is remarkably straightforward and articulate, detailed and explicit, and its occasional amateurish qualities compensate for themselves by revealing the personalities of the writers.
Although the journal frequently fails of literary correctness, it is

never perfunctory, but always maintains spontaneity and enthusiasm which make it consistently readable.

Wholly apart from the literary consideration, however, it is important that Geiger and Bryarly were travelling with a particularly well-organized party—one of the few which did not disintegrate to some degree during the journey. The methods and the success of this party, by comparison with others, tend to illuminate certain problems of the overland journey, and I have attempted to develop some of these aspects of their experience in my editing of the text. This quality of significance in the record, together with that of vitality in the narrative, seems amply to justify publication.

In dealing with the Gold Rush, one certainly does not find a neglected subject. In fact, its human and picturesque elements have so universally appealed to the imagination that the "Forty-niner" has taken a prominent place in the gallery of American historical types, and certain features of the Rush have almost become folk knowledge. The excitement of free gold, lying loose in the stream beds; the exuberance of "Oh Susannah"; the recklessness of gunplay, gambling, and "Hangtown Gals" in the mining camps; the epic length of the journey to the diggings; the hardships and dangers of mountain, desert, and plain—these ingredients form a pageant familiar to most Americans.

However, the very vividness of the pageant, the adaptability to technicolor, have sometimes prevented students from appreciating that the odyssey of the gold-seekers was more than a spectacle. The fascination of dramatic episode has overshadowed some of the aspects that are broader in their meaning. Without attempting to develop fully these broader aspects, it may be pertinent, here, to mention two of the elements in the story of the Gold Rush which seem to me to warrant attention and to invite a more analytical treatment of this movement, which is so often exploited for its theatrical values alone.

First, the mass movement to California represented the climactic manifestation of an American pioneer impulse to overrun the continent and to subdue it. In response to this impulse, the continuous westward surge had gathered momentum for two centuries, but in 1849 it reached a culmination as emigrants moved in unprecedented swarms. The discovery of gold was the superficial cause for their restlessness, but whatever may explain it fundamentally, the money value of the gold in prospect certainly cannot. Economic determinism is as inadequate to explain the Forty-niners as it is to account for the Crusades. Regardless of its cause, however, an overpowering compulsion enlisted men in this hazardous journey, drove them to the limits of human capacity in its prosecution, and enabled them to achieve the symbolical mastery of the American West.

Americans had always harbored a desire to see what lay "on the other side of the hump," and they had always been willing to move beyond the rim of settlement to satisfy that desire, but now they were avid to view every landmark described by Bryant and Frémont from the "coast of Nebraska" to the Golden Gate, and they unhesitatingly left the outposts of settlement two thousand miles behind. They had traditionally relished their enterprise spiced with adventure, and even with danger, but now they were bent upon "seeing the elephant" himself, that is, of surmounting every hazard which lurked in the wilderness of the Rocky Mountains and the Humboldt Desert. Since their exploit, elemental nature has never been quite so awesome, and the calling of the pioneer has lacked its epic flavor.

Second, not only was the Gold Rush the climactic event in the advance of the pioneers, it was also one of the last, and in some respects one of the greatest achievements of pre-Industrial America. Even as the Gold Rush took place, the machine was rapidly subduing the settled portions of the country. Most of the gold-seekers were carried to their starting place in Missouri by the power of steam applied to iron locomotive or to river boat. Geiger and Bryarly used both. These new forces were even then marching with seven-league boots, and just twenty years later, they spanned the nation with its first transcontinental railway. Both Geiger and Bryarly, by a coincidence, died in that year of the triumph of the machine. But in 1849, the only significant products of the machine age beyond the Missouri were firearms. Except for these, the land west of the river fell many centuries, technologically, behind the region to the east. Every aspect of the overland journey, therefore, was a reflex of animistic rather than mechanistic factors. The prime movers which propelled the emigration were not engines, but mules and oxen. The fuel which they required was no product of mine or refinery, but the native vegetation. These facts are, no doubt, obvious, but note how they shaped the emigration. The time of departure was not the time when the emigrants were ready to leave and the weather would

be pleasant, but when the spring grass became sufficient for the
animals—and the migration of '49 was delayed more than two weeks
because of the lateness of the season. The route followed was neither
that of the shortest distance nor of the easiest grades, which the
railway seeks, but of maximum forage and maximum proximity to
water. It is no accident that most of the California Trail has now
been abandoned, and that the South Pass is traversed only by enthusiastic antiquarians. The rate of travel was not the one most
acceptable either to man or beast, but the one which would get
them into California before snow closed the mountain passes. Thus
the Argonauts ended their journey, as they had begun it, in response
to the rhythm of the seasons. And if most of them were really not
Argonauts at bottom, but farmers' boys out on an adventure, the
routine of the camp, with cattle grazing, cowbells sounding, and, on
occasion, scythes swinging to provide hay for the barren stretches,
was no great divorcement from the experience of an agrarian age.

My conviction of the importance of aspects like these has governed
my treatment of the Geiger-Bryarly journal. Regarding it as more
than the record of a colorful episode, I have tried, with some probing
and analysis, to focus upon some of the more neglected aspects of
the Gold Rush. For instance, enough is already known of the hardships of the journey, and the routes have been most exhaustively
worked out. But there is surprisingly little information about the
structural organization and the formal constitutions of the overland
companies; the rules drawn up by the emigrants were spontaneous
applications of self-government, demonstrating American resource-
fulness in that field, but they have not been publicized, as have mining codes, cattlemen's associations, or other instances of self-government. Similarly, it is generally known that the large companies
broke up, that they overloaded their wagons and later had to throw
goods away, and that many of them ran out of food; but very little
has been said about the economy of overland travel—about the actual load which could be carried, about the type of draught animal
which was most efficient, about the proper ratio of men to animals
and to wagons, about the reasons for success or failure. Or again,
the accounts of the Gold Rush as a pageant usually show that the
trek westward was dangerous, and they dramatize the skulking
redskin; in fact, the mortalities were highest at the outset of the
journey, and the Indian menace, from an actuarial standpoint, was
negligible.

The fact that these points, and others like them, have been developed, does not mean that I have attempted an exhaustive study, but only that I have consistently sought to present the specific experience of other emigrant groups. To that end, I have undertaken to compare the Geiger-Bryarly journal with a large series of other diaries for the same season and the same general route. Altogether, 21 such diaries in printed form have been utilized, and 12 more in manuscript in the Coe Collection have also been included in the study. From these 33 diaries, comparisons have been drawn to apply to many aspects of overland travel. These comparisons occur throughout the introduction and the footnotes to the text, and they are basic to the study. If, in places, they detract from the "glamour" of the Gold Rush, it is hoped that they compensate for this by recognizing it as a phenomenon of genuine historical importance, and not merely as a colorful episode, useful principally for dramatic relief in the more serious historical record.

In editing the manuscript, my purpose has been to preserve the original text intact, and, at the same time, to present it in the clearest possible form. In the interest of clarity I have made all date lines, and the daily statements of distance traversed, uniform throughout. I have also cast the text into paragraphs and spelled out certain abbreviations. Where the original capitalization and punctuation were conducive to easy reading, I have avoided tampering with them, but where clarity was gained by altering them, I have done so. In view of the conditions under which the diary was written, it would seem pedantic to preserve every lapse in punctuation and every contraction used in writing. Where a word, a letter, or the like, was inadvertently omitted, or is needed to clarify the meaning, I have inserted it, using brackets as a means of informing the reader as to what has been done. But false spellings, grammatical errors, and capitalizations which imply emphasis are not corrected, and the text here printed attempts to provide a verbatim reproduction of the original journal.

In tracing the adventurous careers of Wakeman Bryarly and Vincent E. Geiger, I have been fortunate in receiving hearty co-operation from widely scattered sources. In this respect, no one has offered assistance more generously or provided the information I needed more effectively than William B. Marye, Corresponding Secretary of the Maryland Historical Society, and nephew by marriage of Wakeman Bryarly. In addition to the many items of fact which he provided, Mr. Marye also made arrangements with D. Sterett Gittings, of "Roslyn," Baltimore County, for the reproduction of Dr. Bryarly's portrait, which is the frontispiece of this book, and with Miss Victoria Gittings for the abstracting of important documents relating to Bryarly. These two members of the Gittings family are nephew and niece, respectively, of Dr. Bryarly, and Miss Victoria Gittings deserves especial thanks for having preserved materials that might otherwise have been lost, relating to her uncle. I am also indebted to the late Wakeman Munnikhuysen of Bel Air, Maryland.

My knowledge of the early life and family background of Vincent Geiger I owe entirely to John W. Wayland, of Madison College, Harrisonburg, Virginia. As an act of sheer personal kindness, Professor Wayland searched the Augusta County records thoroughly. I can hardly state my thanks in adequate form. On the Mexican War phase of Geiger's life, Philip M. Hamer, Director of Reference Service at the National Archives, consulted the records there and wrote me fully of the findings. Miss Mabel Gillis, State Librarian, similarly, made available to me transcripts of a number of valuable source items in the California State Library. Charles H. Ambler of West Virginia University, and Lieutenant Millard K. Bushong of the United States Military Academy also assisted me in my research on the Charlestown Company.

Staff members at the Library of Congress, at the New York Public Library, and at the Yale University Library, have all been consistently helpful. At the Yale Library, personal mention is the least that I can offer in appreciation of the encouragement and cooperation of James T. Babb, and of the aid, at difficult points in the manuscript, of Zara Jones Powers.

Turning from the research to the actual preparation of the book, I wish to thank Edward Eberstadt, Adviser to the Coe Collection, for generous criticism and suggestions, as well as for making the unique Isham journal available. I am obligated to Mrs. Ridgely Hunt for the care with which she has twice typed part of the manuscript and once typed all of it. And finally, I offer my thanks to Leonard W. Labaree, editor of this series, for his many thoughtful suggestions as to the treatment of the material and for his vast patience in scrutinizing every detail of the manuscript.

Timothy Dwight College,
Yale University.

CONTENTS

Map of the Route precedes index.

INTRODUCTION

DURING the three centuries of westward expansion across the United States, probably no single episode involving large numbers of people stands in such dramatic relief as the Gold Rush to California in 1849. This great mass-migration burst resistlessly through the last and most formidable barriers of the North American continent, and made the Pacific Coast an American shore in the national as well as the geographical sense. It is true of course, that intrepid individuals had already traversed the Oregon and California Trails, but it was the season of '49 which showed America in motion and the western movement at its climax.

The only perfectly contemporaneous and authentic records of this epic migration are the journals which a few of the Forty-niners kept while they were in transit. Many, to be sure, intended to keep diaries, but the rigors of the trip left most of them without energy for any non-essential pursuit. A few, however, persevered, and, no matter how gruelling the experience, wrote their account of it at the end of every day. Such journals as these are all-important. They are to the Gold Rush what the sagas were to the Vikings, or the *Chansons* to the Age of Chivalry. This book is principally the text of one of these Gold Rush journals, kept by two men, Dr. Wakeman Bryarly and Vincent E. Geiger.

Neither Bryarly nor Geiger was born in the American West, nor did either of them die there. Bryarly, a native of Maryland, died, prosperous and respected, near his birthplace; Geiger, by contrast, became a fugitive with a charge of murder on his head, and died in a country remote from his native Virginia. Yet despite the diversities of their lives and despite their limited residence in the West, both men illustrated and, in a measure, embodied the history of that region. In both there appeared that quality of restlessness always identified with the American frontier. Bryarly and Geiger alike volunteered in the Mexican War, and after that, their zest for adventure was not appeased by their participation in the Gold Rush. After the journey overland and the excitement of life in early California, neither of them could resume the quiet, prosaic ways of the society from which he had come. Physically, theirs was a relatively transient presence in the Western region, but the West was, nevertheless, to absorb, transform, and shape the lives of this Marylander and this Virginian far more than either of them realized when, as companions in travel, they wrote of their daily experiences on the journey across the Plains and over the Western mountains.

The elder of the two, by three years, was Wakeman Bryarly. He was born in October, 1820, in Harford County, Maryland,[1] the son of Dr. Wakeman Bryarly, Sr., and his wife Priscilla, daughter of Parker Hall Lee and Elizabeth (Dallam) Lee, also of Harford County.[2] The senior Bryarly was a prominent physician who had taken his M.D. degree at the University of Pennsylvania in 1805, and had subsequently practiced at Bel Air and Ensor in Maryland.[3] He died prior to August, 1821,[4] when his infant son was less than ten months old, but apparently the medical tradition in the family was strong, and the Lees were in position to help maintain it, for young Wakeman, in due time, enrolled in the Washington Medical University in Baltimore, from which he was graduated as a Doctor of Medicine in 1840.[5] For the next seven years apparently, he re-

1. Date of birth, Oct. 13 [?], 1820, is a part of the inscription on Bryarly's tombstone in Greenmount Cemetery, Baltimore. This inscription was very kindly copied, and other information provided by William B. Marye, Corresponding Secretary of the Maryland Historical Society. Place of birth given in Eugene F. Cordell, *The Medical Annals of Maryland, 1799–1899* (Baltimore, 1903), p. 337.

2. For the parentage of Bryarly, I am indebted to his late great-nephew, Wakeman Munnikhuysen of Bel Air, Md., and to William B. Marye. Mr. Marye also provides the information on the maternal grandparents, and informs me that the license for the marriage of Wakeman Bryarly, Sr., and Priscilla Lee was dated Jan. 30, 1816.

3. Cordell, *Medical Annals of Md.*, p. 337. Also see, in the Library of Congress, "An inaugural essay on the *Lupulus Communis* of Gaerther; or the common hop. By Wakeman Bryarly . . . Philadelphia: Printed for the author by John H. Oswald. 1805." This essay is further described as "an inaugural dissertation for the degree of doctor of medicine . . . University of Pennsylvania, on the 5th day of June, 1805."

4. Wakeman Bryarly made a will on Nov. 17, 1820 (one month after the birth of his son), which was proved Aug. 7, 1821. In it he named two children, Elizabeth and Robert. This Robert was probably Robert Wakeman, who, being called after his father, became the Wakeman Bryarly of this diary.

5. Cordell, *Medical Annals of Md.*, p. 337; John R. Quinan, *Medical Annals of Baltimore from 1608 to 1880* (Baltimore, 1884), p. 68. Bryarly wrote a paper on acupuncturation, presumably as a dissertation for his degree, in the year 1840. The Washington Medical College or University, as it was hopefully called, in the expectation of developing a liberal arts faculty, was an important Maryland institution in the first half of the 19th century. Organized in 1827 in Baltimore as the medical department of Washington College, Pennsylvania, it

mained in Baltimore as a practicing physician. Certainly that was his status in 1842, for when the boiler of the steam packet *Medora* exploded in April of that year, Bryarly was listed as one of the numerous physicians who went to the aid of the injured.[6] In 1846, he received an appointment as one of the city's first vaccine physicians. In 1847, he became a Demonstrator in Anatomy at the medical school from which he had taken his degree seven years before.[7] Apparently he was advancing in his profession, but before he had completed his first year as an instructor of medical students, the Mexican War intervened to offer him more adventurous pursuits.

The summer of 1847 found the war in its second year and the offensive well advanced. After landing at Vera Cruz, General Scott had pushed inland, won an engagement at Cerro Gordo, and occupied the town of Puebla, just outside the Valley of Mexico. Despite these successes, however, the Army had to reckon with the expiration of service of troops who had enlisted for only one year. To offset such losses, the Administration continued to encourage recruiting of new volunteer units. One such contingent, the District of Columbia and Maryland Regiment of Volunteers, was being recruited in Baltimore and Washington. Bryarly volunteered for service in this regiment, and was accepted with rank as Assistant-Surgeon.[8] The regiment embarked from Fort McHenry in July, and reached Vera Cruz in August. By that time, Scott had advanced to the environs of Mexico City, and he occupied that capital on September 14, at which time Bryarly's regiment was just beginning an advance into the interior. Thus the District of Columbia and Maryland Regiment

received an independent charter from the Maryland Legislature in 1833, and it was subsequently granted the formal name Washington University. In 1838, probably while Bryarly was a student, the college moved from its original location on Holliday St., near the Old City Hall, to a new building on North Broadway. See Thomas A. Ashby, ''The Progress of Medicine in Maryland,'' in Clayton C. Hall, ed., *Baltimore, Its History and Its People* (New York, 1912), I, 595.

6. J. Thomas Scharf, *The Chronicles of Baltimore, etc.* (Baltimore, 1874), p. 506.

7. For these two appointments see Cordell, *Medical Annals of Md.*, p. 337, and Quinan, *Medical Annals of Baltimore*, p. 68. In 1846 each ward of the city of Baltimore had a vaccine physician who received a stipend of $50 per annum and was required to report the number of persons vaccinated, refusing vaccination, or having small pox.

8. See List of Officers of the District of Columbia and Maryland Regiment of Volunteers, in John R. Kenley, *Memoirs of a Maryland Volunteer. War with Mexico in the Years 1846–7–8* (Philadelphia, 1873), pp. 481–484.

arrived too late for the main action, but it did experience sharp fighting at the strategic National Bridge crossing of the Antigua River. After holding this position against guerrillas for two months, the regiment was moved to Jalapa for garrison duty, and there it remained until June, 1848, when it began the journey back to the United States. After returning by way of New Orleans, the Mississippi River, and Pittsburgh, the regiment received an honorable discharge for all its members on July 24, 1848.[9]

The war which carried Bryarly into the heart of Mexico had also given Vincent Eply Geiger his first major adventure. Geiger was a native of Virginia,[10] probably of Augusta County in the Shenandoah Valley, for his family had lived there as early as 1797. He was born between November, 1823, and January, 1824,[11] one of at least three sons of George Geiger and his wife Susan, daughter of Vincent Tapp, also of Augusta County.[12] Both parents died, apparently, before he was twenty-one.[13] As a young man in Staunton, he seems to have been rather active, but not outstandingly successful, in business affairs. [14] His family connections were good, but he had acquired no significant stake in society, and had given no hostages to fortune, when he, too, felt the call of the Mexican War. He enlisted at Staunton on November 27, 1846, in the Augusta County Company of the

9. Kenley, *Memoirs of a Maryland Volunteer,* pp. 279, 286, 300–308, 318–332, 362–398, 481.

10. Geiger's nativity specified in the *Register of Officers and Agents, Civil, Military, and Naval in the Service of the United States on the Thirtieth September, 1859* (Washington, 1859), p. 95.

11. Geiger stated on Nov. 30, 1854, that he was thirty years old (statement in an application for bounty land for service in the Mexican War. Application in National Archives was found for me by Philip M. Hamer, Director of Reference Service). This indicates that he was born between Nov. 30, 1823 and Nov. 30, 1824. On Jan. 13, 1845, Geiger had attained the age of 21 (shown by the fact that on that date he was a grantor—and therefore legally of age—in an indenture. Augusta County Records, examined for me by John W. Wayland of Madison College, Harrisonburg, Virginia). This indicates that he was born before Jan. 13, 1824.

12. The relationships of the father and brothers are shown by Augusta County Records, Will Book 21, pp. 221–222, in which George Geiger gives bonds to pay dues from an estate to his sons, Vincent E., George H., and Franklin F. The mother and maternal grandfather are shown by a grant by Geiger of his equity in Vincent Tapp's estate. County Records, Deed Book 65, p. 370.

13. On Jan. 22, 1844, he was described as the orphan of George Geiger. On June 13, 1845, Susan (Tapp) Geiger was listed as deceased. Augusta County Records: Will Book 26, p. 171; Deed Book 65, p. 370.

14. On June 13, 1845, he assigned his share of Vincent Tapp's estate to a third party. In March and Sep. 1848, he purchased certain lands which were being sold for delinquent taxes. Deed Book, Vol. 65, p. 370; Vol. 68, pp. 78–86.

First Regiment of Virginia Volunteers, and he was commissioned a Second Lieutenant.[15]

Perhaps, at the time of receiving his commission, Geiger dreamed of winning further advancement by valor in the field, but the Virginia Volunteers were destined to see more service than glory. They were assigned to Zachary Taylor's Army, which had shown itself a most aggressive unit, invading Northern Mexico, winning a series of engagements, and capturing Monterrey and Victoria before the Virginia Volunteers had marched to Old Point Comfort to embark. Meanwhile, however, President Polk had concluded that the Whigs were more dangerous than the Mexicans, and he had effectively reduced Taylor's force to an "Army of Observation." As a consequence, Taylor fought but one more important action, the Battle of Buena Vista, and it came in February, 1847, nearly a month before the Virginia recruits were unloaded from their transports on the Texas coast.[16] Consequently, Geiger's experience was essentially that of a member of an army of occupation. In March, soon after his arrival, he was left sick in Monterrey, but he had rejoined his company and was on active duty during June and July. Again, in August and September, he was ill—sick in quarters—but during November and the first five months of 1848 he commanded his company, probably while the other officers took their turns being ill.[17] In August, 1848, after nearly two years of service without a single engagement, the regiment returned to Virginia. On August 11, Staunton gave a banquet in honor of her martial sons.[18]

Less than a month apart, Geiger and Bryarly had returned to civilian life in a republic that still believed in feasting its martial

15. Geiger's enlistment and rank is shown by a card file made up from muster rolls, originally for the Adjutant-General's Office but now in the National Archives. Philip M. Hamer, of the National Archives, has examined these records for me. For an account of the Augusta County Company, mentioning Geiger, see J. Lewis Peyton, *History of Augusta County, Virginia* (Staunton, 1882), p. 219. The Augusta County Company was commanded by Captain Kenton Harper, and the First Regiment by Col. John Francis Hamtramck.

16. Peyton, *Hist. of Augusta County*, p. 219, speaks of the regiment taking shipping for Corpus Christi, but gives no date. *Niles' Register*, Jan. 16, 1847, shows that the regiment was still in Virginia on that date, while *ibid.*, April 10, 1847, quotes the Washington *Union*, March 29, as saying that the volunteer regiments of Nov. 1847, had certainly reached Matamoros [not Corpus Christi] before March 23. Since Geiger was in Monterrey before the end of the month, he had probably landed at Matamoros, which is much closer.

17. All information from Adjutant-General's File (now in National Archives) as shown in note 15. For prevalence of illness, *Niles' Register*, July 31, 1847.

18. Peyton, *Hist. of Augusta County*, pp. 223–224.

heroes and leaving them, thereafter, to shift for themselves. The world after the Mexican War was not recognized as being a post-war world. Yet that war, like the greater ones, entailed problems of adjustment, and left thousands of men who must have found the normal routine of life humdrum and confined by contrast with the novelty and unrestraint of campaigning with a volunteer regiment.

If the two recently discharged veterans now cast about for some means to avoid return to the anatomy class of Baltimore or the rustic life of Augusta County, the answer for them, and for others like them, had already been provided, while they were still in Mexico learning that the duration is always longer than the war. In January, 1848, two months before the United States acquired formal title to California, Jim Marshall had discovered yellow metal in the tailrace at Sutter's Mill. He had taken the particles to Captain Sutter, who weighed them, calculated their specific gravity, touched them with nitric acid, and checked their qualities against an account in the *American Encyclopaedia*. When, at the end of this analysis, he pronounced them gold,[19] it was a crucial event in the personal lives of Geiger, Bryarly, and a hundred thousand other oblivious Americans.

News of the discovery was for a time suppressed, and it spread only slowly. Even after all California learned the secret and rushed to the diggings, the "States" remained in ignorance. It was not until August, 1848, that any Eastern paper carried news of the discovery. One of the very early reports appeared in the Baltimore *Sun* on September 20, and Bryarly may have read this historic piece of journalism.[20] Other reports followed fast, and the season of 1848, which yielded $10,000,000 worth of nuggets, lost nothing in the recounting. In December, President Polk told Congress of accounts "of such an extraordinary character as would scarcely command belief were they not corroborated by authentic reports." By the end of the year, the gold fever was raising more of a furor than the Mexican War had caused. Every part of the country was pre-

---

19. Hubert Howe Bancroft, *History of California* (San Francisco, 1888), VI, 32–39.

20. Ralph P. Bieber, ed., *Southern Trails to California in 1849* (Glendale, Cal., 1937), pp. 19–26, 65–90; Bancroft, *Hist. of Cal.*, VI, 114. Bancroft declares the Baltimore *Sun* article to have been the first widely copied report, but Bieber shows that this report had appeared previously in the Washington *Union*.

paring to contribute its quota to the new volunteer army of Forty-niners. Even on the island of Nantucket, one-fourth of the voting population was drained away by the gold fever.[21] Few communities were swept so clean as this, but wherever men congregated, California dominated their discussions. This was true, no doubt, in Baltimore and around Staunton, but the impetus which swept Geiger and Bryarly into the Gold Rush originated in the little community of Charlestown, in what is now West Virginia.

EARLY in January, 1849, a small group of men held a meeting in the law office of Benjamin F. Washington, in Charlestown, Virginia. These men, like similar groups throughout the country, had been caught up in the excitement of the Gold Rush, and they now met for the purpose of organizing a company of gold-seekers from the region around Charlestown. The affiliation of B. F. Washington with them indicated that their project carried weight, for the young lawyer belonged to a family of importance in that part of Virginia, and he had already risen to a place of leadership in the Democratic party in the state.

It was perhaps suggestive of their readiness to assume leadership, that these men planned an unusually close-knit organization in which the officers would have large responsibilities. Instead of forming a mere aggregation of travelling companions, each with his own supplies, weapons, and means of transportation, they had determined to create a co-partnership in which each member would pay $300 for the purchase of mules, wagons, foodstuffs, weapons, and even a large stock of additional supplies to be shipped around Cape Horn to await the company in California. Moreover, the members would not separately seek gold, each one for himself, but would pool the proceeds of their mining and divide the accumulated wealth equally at the end of their period of association.

This plan to adopt a thoroughly collectivist organization for such a supremely individualistic type of activity as the Gold Rush is one of the notable features of the Charlestown Company's history, and will require further examination later on. However, that organization had not been developed at the time of the meeting in Washington's office, and the work of that meeting dealt primarily with

---

21. Samuel Eliot Morison, *The Maritime History of Massachusetts, 1783–1860* (Boston, 1921), p. 333. Also see Bancroft, *Hist. of Cal.*, VI, 110–125, on the effect of the gold news in the States.

questions as to the supplies which might be needed, the actual cost
per member for the journey, the number of members who should
be admitted to the co-partnership, and the procedure of organization. Some of the organizers had already secured detailed information as to the costs of various items of food or equipment, and also
as to distances. With this information, they had computed the prob-
able expenses closely, and were confident of the soundness of their
estimate of $300 per member. They also had distinct ideas as to the
number of members whom it would be advantageous to include, and
they set the quota at sixty. The principal task, however, was to convert these plans into reality. Accordingly, they voted to hold a
general meeting for purposes of organization on January 22, and
to require a preliminary payment of $110 from each member by
February 10. The funds thus accumulated would pay, they anticipated, for such supplies as were to be sent in advance by sea. Clearly,
the inner circle of organizers knew what they wanted, and intended
to put their plans into effect.[22]

The public response at the meeting of January 22 showed the
success of the preliminary arrangements. Men crowded into the
room of meeting until it was densely packed, and before this audi-
ence, the committee on membership reported that the quota of sixty
members had been filled and that fifty other applicants, "worthy in
every way," had of necessity been rejected. Another committee reported on a constitution for the company, but no action was taken
on the document, presumably because the final list of members
eligible to act on a constitution could not be determined until the
first payments had been made. However, plans for the journey were
discussed; it was agreed that the company should furnish each man
with a knapsack for his clothes, and should limit him to a maximum
of fifty pounds of such apparel. It was also estimated that the company would collect about $18,000 from its sixty members and
would spend some $7,000 in the East and some $10,000 in the West,
holding $1,000 as a reserve.[23]

Formal organization and the first payment by members took
place at the Odd Fellows' Hall in Charlestown on February 10.
The quota of members was now increased to seventy (it was finally

---

22. Account of first meeting on Jan. 9, from Jan. 16th issue of *The Spirit of
Jefferson*, a weekly newspaper published at Charlestown. *Ibid.*, Feb. 13, spoke
of the prominence of Benjamin F. Washington.

23. *Spirit of Jefferson*, Jan. 30, 1849.

fixed at seventy-five at a meeting on March 3), and the Company elected its officers. Benjamin F. Washington was chosen President of the Company; Robert H. Keeling, Smith Crane, and Joseph E. N. Lewis were elected first, second, and third Commanders respectively; the Treasurer's post was assigned to E. M. Aisquith,[24] while the offices of Quartermaster and of Secretary went to Nat Seevers and J. Harrison Kelly. Having thus formally organized, the Company proceeded to adopt various motions on matters of business. For instance, it created a committee to consult with a certain metallurgist of Frederick County on the techniques of mining; it authorized the purchase of thirty rifles and forty double-barrelled shot guns; it named a committee to procure supplies (but did not create committees for the purchase of mules and of wagons until later); and, upon the motion of the President it elected Dr. Wakeman Bryarly, Surgeon of the Company.[25]

The most important business of this meeting, however, was the final adoption of a constitution. This document, containing twenty articles, was published in the columns of the county weekly,[26] and has therefore survived. It invites analysis, partly because only a very few of the written agreements governing the gold-rush companies have come to light and partly because of the unusual character of the organization created. Most of the companies which travelled overland drew up certain rules to apply during the journey, and sometimes these rules were printed; in a majority of cases, however, the companies did not formally organize until a day or two after they had set out on their journey.[27] Where this was the

24. Aisquith had previously been Postmaster of Charlestown, *Spirit of Jefferson*, Dec. 25, 1849.

25. *Spirit of Jefferson*, Feb. 4, 1849.

26. *Spirit of Jefferson*, Feb. 20, 1849. This Constitution is printed in full in Appendix A.

27. For general information on the practice of making regulations and selecting officers after the journey had begun, see Irene D. Paden, *The Wake of the Prairie Schooner* (New York, 1943), p. 39, and Elizabeth Page, *Wagons West, a Story of the Oregon Trail* (New York, 1930), p. 117. Also, a number of diaries or letters of travellers of the season of '49 illustrate this custom. Immediately below are listed the names of such writers with the dates of their diary entries or letters. In the bibliography the reader will find a full list of all Forty-niners whose diaries or letters are cited, with full bibliographical information in the case of printed items, and with corresponding information for manuscript items. Some diarists who record the practice of organizing or electing officers after leaving the States are Backus, May 28; Brown, June 10; Caldwell, May 27; Delano, p. 21; Johnston, May 5; McCall, May 12; Pleasants, p. 21; Swain, May 22; Tiffany, May 10, 11; Wistar, May 21.

practice, their agreements were either unwritten, or were recorded in manuscript form. The survival of such manuscripts was, of course, precarious, and even where they have been preserved they have seldom received attention in historical accounts of the Gold Rush.[28] Consequently, much less is known about the organization of the groups which went to California than about the journeys themselves.

Enough data are available, however, to suggest that the organization adopted by the Charlestown Company was a distinctive one, in which precedents from diverse sources were united. In essence, the constitution established two organizations, a business co-partnership and a military company; and to the economic and military functions which were indicated, it added a governmental function as well.

The military provisions in this Constitution were its least distinctive part, for nearly all overland parties adopted some form of military organization. The Charlestown Company did this by providing that there should be a first, a second, and a third Commander. These officers, who were alternatively known as the Captain and the first and second Lieutenants were to have "entire and complete control" of the company in any emergency of defense or attack in which military action seemed indicated, and the two Lieutenants were to "assist the Captain according to their . . . ranks." Apart from emergencies, the first Commander was also to arrange for the posting of the guard "when invested with command on the route," as he was likely to be in regions where Indians were a potential danger, and where no law was operative. Furthermore, a Quartermaster was designated to "superintend the Commissary, . . . provide . . . the necessary food for the Company, and discharge . . . duties usually pertaining to his office."

For these military arrangements, the organizers of the Charlestown Company had ample precedent in the previous experience of

28. For companies which travelled by the South Pass route in 1849, I know of but two constitutions which have found their way into print. These are the constitution and by-laws of the California Association (ten men of Monroe County, Mich.) in Owen C. Coy, *The Great Trek* (Los Angeles, 1931), pp. 98–103; and the constitution and by-laws of the Green and Jersey County Company, in Page, *Wagons West*, pp. 336–341. Johnston, May 5, mentions that, when his company organized formally, officers were elected, and a committee was appointed to draw up "articles for our government. They, however, never found time to act." Bruff, May 12, belonged to a company which certainly had a constitution, for all members were sworn to uphold it.

overland travellers, and ample reason in the logic of the circumstances. From the earliest days of organized travel on the Plains, that is from the opening of trade over the Santa Fé Trail in the 1820's, it had been the custom of the participants in that trade to gather at the Council Grove, soon after leaving Missouri, to elect a captain and lieutenants.[29] The authority of these officers was wholly without basis in law, and was imperfect enough in fact, but the Captain was usually recognized as the person to select the camp site, to direct the order of travel, and to organize the watch. This arrangement was so natural, and perhaps even inevitable, for travel on the plains, that when migrants began to move toward Oregon, and later toward California, they borrowed the practice. They did this the more readily because of the fact that Independence, Missouri, was the rendezvous for their journey, and there they received advice from the Santa Fé traders who had always swarmed in the town and used it as their headquarters.[30] Consequently, when John Bidwell went with the first overland wagon train to California in 1841, his company, as a matter of course, selected a captain,[31] and it appears that every company for more than twenty years thereafter must have followed this example. The danger of Indians or of lawless whites, the necessity of maintaining some formation in travelling and of regularizing the guard duty, all combined to make the military arrangement universal.[32] Moreover, in the case of the Charlestown Company, the logic of the situation was supplemented by the personal experience of the members, for at least six of them are known to have been officers in the Mexican War,[33] and it is not

29. Josiah Gregg, *Commerce of the Prairies, or the Journal of a Santa Fe Trader* (New York, 1845), pp. 38–39, 44–46.

30. "This town is full of men who have been to Santa Fe . . . repeatedly." John A. Johnson, Independence, Mo., Apl. 1, 1849, to his wife, in [John McCoy], *Pioneering on the Plains* (Kaukauna, Wis., 1924).

31. Rockwell D. Hunt, *John Bidwell, Prince of California Pioneers* (Caldwell, Idaho, 1942), pp. 40–41.

32. All overland diaries abound in references to company organization. The specifically military character of these companies is shown in Brown, June 10; Bruff, July 9; B. C. Clark, May 10; Delano, May 15, June 29; De Wolf, May 20; Foster, May 16; Hackney, May 29; Johnston, May 5; Kelly, p. 34; Long, Apr. 4, June 1; Lyne, May 4, 22; McCall, May 12; Page, letter, May 13; Pleasants, p. 21; Sedgley, May 14; Swain, letter, May 6; Tiffany, May 11, 30; Wistar, May 18, 21.

33. In addition to the service of Geiger and Bryarly, discussed above, the following members of the Charlestown Company had served as second lieutenants in the Virginia Volunteer Regiment: Robert H. Keeling, John W. Gallaher, Thomas Moore, and Lawrence B. Washington. William H. Robarts,

unlikely that twice as many more had been soldiers in the ranks. In these circumstances the military element was almost strong enough to make the Gold Rush appear as a final campaign in the war to appropriate the Far West, and the maintenance of the military organization takes on an added fitness. In adopting the military pattern, therefore, the Charlestown promoters were simply conforming to the universal practice, and their action was unusual only in that they chose their officers before leaving Virginia, instead of waiting until they reached the edge of the prairie.

The military arrangement, then, was commonplace. But in a separate sphere, the Constitution set up a business organization— a co-partnership, of a much more unusual character. This part of the Constitution provided for other officers, namely a President, a Secretary, and a Treasurer, and it specified that these officers, together with the military officers, should constitute a Board of Directors. This Board was to exercise "supreme regulation and government of the Company." It was to determine when the President should act as chief administrative officer, and when the first Commander should act—that is, it was to alternate civil with military control, as the circumstances seemed to require. Moreover, it was to decide virtually all disputed questions.

The fact that each member had paid $300 into the company treasury indicated, of course, a business organization, and it was natural that such an organization should have a Board of Directors and be defined as "a joint co-partnership." But the astonishing aspect of the Constitution lay in its provisions for the association to continue for the duration of the stay in California, for it to return to the States in a body, and for the wealth taken at the diggings to be pooled and subsequently divided on a share basis. These purposes were indicated by constitutional requirements that the association should continue at least until April 1, 1850—in other words, until more than half a year after they expected to reach California—and that until that time, members must pay over

Mexican War Veterans, a complete Roster of the Regular and Volunteer Troops in the War between the United States and Mexico . . . (Washington, 1887), p. 79. There is an opportunity for very interesting research on the question of the extent to which the Gold Rush was a movement of demobilized war veterans. Johnston, May 5, observed that two veterans of the Doniphan regiment joined his company, and commented: "By these accretions . . . we have been gradually forming a reunion of many who belonged to an arm of the service which acquired unusual distinction during the late war."

"all the minerals, gold, silver, piatina, or other valuable[s] of whatever character which may be gathered . . . into the hands of the Treasurer, to go into the joint funds of the Company." Further, it was also provided that the Company might reorganize and continue after April 1, 1850, and plainly this was the expectation, for another article provided that, "should the company return in a body, as is contemplated," the division of funds should be made after the return. To this end, still another article provided for the possibility of having their gold carried by the Directors and Treasurer to the mint at Philadelphia to be coined. Finally, "The general fund of the Company, embracing all that may have been acquired by the entire membership, shall be equally divided among the members." [34]

In other words, the Charlestown Company planned to set up a thoroughly collectivist organization which was almost wholly at odds with the individualist tradition of the West. Individual initiative alone could stimulate men to undertake the journey, but collective security loomed large in their preparations. The desire to obtain personal fortune impelled all of the gold-seekers, but here was a group in which each member renounced, beforehand, his chance to acquire wealth for himself alone by his own endeavor. The decision to make the journey, itself indicated an independence of spirit that was restive under ordinary controls, and yet the men who made this decision bound themselves voluntarily to obey the orders of the Directors and to labor for the association after they reached the diggings. This meant, in effect, that the individual had renounced his freedom of action, and could not recover it except by sacrificing his equity in the company. Plainly, individualism and collectivism here met in paradoxical combination and upon this paradox, the Charlestown Company, in due time, was broken.

Until the Gold Rush as a whole is studied more carefully, with less of an eye to the merely picturesque, it will be impossible to say to what extent collectivist ideas modified the individualism of the emigration in general. Certainly it is known that, in thousands of cases, little individualistic groups of four to six men equipped themselves personally, bought their own provisions, and proceeded with their own teams and their own wagons to the Missouri river towns, where they organized companies bound by ties which were

---

34. Pertinent sections of the Constitution are Article I, Section 1; Art. II; Art. VIII; Art. XIII, Sec. 8; Art. XIV; Art. XV.

casually made and as casually broken. For such men, the association with messmates in their own wagon, or with other wagons in a company, was purely a temporary expedient, based upon the necessities of overland travel, and not upon any acceptance of collectivist ideas. But at the same time, there were a number of factors which prompted some individuals to seek more binding and more lasting association. Most emigrants were oppressed at times by a sense of the fearful remoteness of the gold regions. At such a distance, loneliness seemed doubly terrible, and men welcomed a plan to maintain a kind of brotherhood with old neighbors. It was very much the same basis on which volunteer military companies were organized. Moreover, it seemed likely that, in a land as lawless as California was reputed to be, group protection would be necessary; or that, in the techniques of mining, group labor would be required. These factors undoubtedly caused many Forty-niners, like the Charlestown group, to form associations which they imagined would endure until their return from California. The actual conditions, of course, operated to shatter, rather than to perpetuate, these associations, but they seem to have played a far more important part in the dynamics of the Gold Rush than is commonly recognized.

The prevalence of the collectivist form of organization is strikingly illustrated in Octavius T. Howe's searching study of one hundred and twenty-four companies which went from Massachusetts to California in 1849.[35] Of these, one hundred and two went by sea, and they seem uniformly to have adopted the co-partnership or the joint-stock form, with provision for a common treasury and an equal sharing of profits, and with requirements that the members work exclusively for the company. Some of these companies purchased their own ships and planned to engage in trade.[36]

In land travel, compulsions toward group action were less strong. Emigrants by land did not need heavy capitalization for the purchase of a ship, nor did they find the coherence of the group reinforced by the confines of a vessel. Instead, the more efficient travellers chafed at the delays of the laggards and were constantly tempted to break away from the group. Moreover, large parties often

---

35. Octavius Thorndike Howe, *Argonauts of '49. History and Adventures of the Emigrant Companies from Massachusetts, 1849–1850* (Cambridge, 1923), pp. 171, 187–213.

36. *Ibid.*, pp. 4–7.

found that forage was too thinly distributed to support their concentrated numbers, and they were therefore forced to scatter.[37] Consequently, the co-partnership type of organization seems to have succeeded far better at sea than by land. In this connection, it is pertinent to note that the Charlestown Company was not exclusively an overland company, for it sent large stores of supplies to California by the water route. However, many companies that moved exclusively by land were organized with a common treasury and business officers, on a co-partnership basis similar to that of the Charlestown Company,[38] though the available information does not show whether others went as far as the Charlestown Company in planning to require all members to work for the association while in California.

Although the Charlestown group was more highly organized than most companies in its military and business structure, it lacked complete development in a third field in which organization might have been expected—that is in the field of government, or, more simply, the enforcement of law and order. Since very early times,

---

37. *Ibid.*, pp. 175–176. For illustrations of companies which dissolved because of these motives, see below pp. 38–39.

38. Other diarists of the '49 season on the South Pass route, who describe such arrangements include: Brown, pp. 133–137, who combined with five other men, each paying $186.66 and assenting to a written constitution; Bruff, p. xlvii, who was Captain of the Washington City and California Mining Association, a joint-stock company with a capital of $11,000; S. B. F. Clark, p. 7, who forfeited a $95 fee by resigning from the Pittsburgh Company; Dundass, May 8, whose company, the Steubenville Company, was a joint-stock organization; Long, Apr. 4, June 5–8, who speaks of the election of civil officers including a President, Vice-President, Secretary, Book-keeper, and Committee on Finance, and who later describes a financial dissolution of the company; Johnson, May 10, who speaks of the treasury funds of his company; Sedgley, who, with 51 companions, formed the Sagamore and California Mining and Trading Company, of Lynn, Mass., whose members wore uniform dress; Swain, letter May 6, diary, Aug. 24, Sept. 7, 16, who paid $125 to join the Wolverine Company of Michigan, and subsequently served on a committee to scrutinize the report of the company's Board of Directors; and Webster, pp. 19–21, who paid $300 to join the Granite State and California Mining Company, organized at Boston, with constitution, by-laws, joint stock organization, and arrangements to travel with the similarly organized Mount Washington Company. The Constitution of the California Association given in Coy, *The Great Trek*, pp. 98–100, resembled the Charlestown Company's Constitution in requiring that each member of the association should work under the direction of the majority, pay his acquisitions to the financial officer, and participate, on a share basis, in the total earnings. The California Associates, moreover, borrowed their funds, and assigned a one-fourth interest in the enterprise to their creditor, who did not go with them to California.

travellers who had passed the limits of any existing jurisdiction, which usually meant those on the high seas, had followed the practice of forming an association for order and self-government during their voyage.[39] Their rule was known as the "sea-law" and it perhaps formed a precedent for early American acts of self-government, such as the Mayflower Compact. In the later course of American history, the constant recurrence of situations where authority was lacking stimulated the Americans to develop great facility in improvising government. This was true from the earliest frontier settlements of the Old West to the mid-nineteenth century mining camps of California, where, as Bayard Taylor observed, "When a new placer or gulch was discovered, the first thing done was to elect officers." [40] The practice, so clearly embodying the democratic principle, later seemed to Frederick J. Turner one of the most significant aspects of the frontier experience, and much attention has been given by historians to various manifestations of pioneer self-government.[41] Little of this attention has been directed upon the overland companies, yet they were faced with the problem of spending an entire season in a region which knew no law, and they were prolific of constitutions, elections, laws for the regulation of the group, and procedures for enforcement. West of Missouri and Iowa lay a region unorganized and unpatrolled. Basically, travellers over this land expanse, like the sea-voyagers of an earlier time, were beyond any existing jurisdiction; there was even less law upon the trackless prairie than upon the trackless ocean; and a

---

39. "It was apparently the custom, I know not how widely practiced, for passengers, not the seamen, to form among themselves and for themselves an association for order and self-government during the duration of their voyage. This, seemingly, was an old and established method whereby those not immediately subject to the skipper's discipline looked after their own affairs." This was the old "sea law." Andrew C. McLaughlin, *Foundations of American Constitutionalism* (New York, 1932), pp. 21–25.

40. Bayard Taylor, *El Dorado* (New York, 1850), p. 101. Taylor continued, "The capacity of a people for self-government was never so triumphantly illustrated."

41. "This power of the . . . pioneers to join together for a common end without the intervention of governmental institutions was one of their marked characteristics." Turner, *The Frontier in American History* (New York, 1920), pp. 343–344. Turner cites as examples the squatters' associations, the mining camp codes, the vigilantes, the cattle raisers' associations. He goes on to speak of this pioneer "power of spontaneous association," and to say, "They yielded to the principle of government by agreement." He does not mention the overland companies.

"plains-law" was as badly needed as a "sea-law" had ever been.[42] To care for this need, many of the Gold Rush companies drew up appropriate regulations and even miniature governments. Alonzo Delano describes one extreme example of this: a company which set out equipped with "a constitution and by-laws, a president and vice-president, a legislature, three judges and court of appeals, nine sergeants as well as other officers"; but this "travelling republic" broke down because the members of the "legislature," who were exempt from onerous camp duties, refused to entertain a constitutional amendment which would have abolished their privilege.[43] Simpler arrangements, however, were more characteristic. For instance, the Green and Jersey County Company had only a few officers, but its by-laws provided for jury trial for those who were accused of violating either the specific regulations or "the laws of order, right, and justice, which are evident to all men." [44]

42. It may be pertinent to compare the earlier seaman's phrase, that there were "no Sundays off soundings," with the later plainsman's statement that there was "no Sunday west of Junction City and no God west of Salina."

43. Delano, June 17. Two written company constitutions are cited in note 28, above. Specific mention of sets of regulations, presumably written, appears in Brown, p. 133; Delano, p. 21, June 29; Hackney, May 9; Kelly, p. 34; McCall, May 12; Pleasants, p. 21; Tiffany, May 10; Webster, p. 17; Wistar, May 21. Also, it seems valid to assume that the joint-stock organizations mentioned in note 38 must necessarily have had written constitutions.

44. Text of these by-laws in Page, *Wagons West*, pp. 338–339. Edwin Bryant, journeying to California in 1846, wrote on May 26, "a public meeting [of the company] is being held in the area of the corral. There is much speaking and voting upon questions appertaining to the enforcement of by-laws, and regulations heretofore adopted, but rarely enforced. We are a pure democracy. All laws are proposed directly to a general assembly, and are enacted or rejected by a majority. The court or arbitrators, appointed to decide disputes between parties, and to punish offenders against the peace and order of the company, does not appear to have much authority. The party condemned is certain to take an appeal to an assembly of the whole, and he is nearly certain of an acquittal, whatever may have been his transgressions." Bryant, *What I Saw in California* (New York, 1848), pp. 60–62, 68.

It is probably true that in most companies, the enforcement of rules was lax. Bruff, July 9, however, relates that when, in his company, a guard sergeant struck a man, the company was convened as a court martial, and proceeded to punish the offender by depriving him of his office, and imposing extra guard duty.

Jesse Applegate, on the Oregon Trail in 1843, described the government in his company by a council. "The council was a high court in the most exalted sense. It was a senate composed of the ablest and most respected fathers of the emigration. It exercised both legislative and judicial powers. . . . It first took the state of the little commonwealth into consideration; revised or repealed rules

The Constitution of the Charlestown Company lacked full development in this sphere. It made no provision for the punishment of serious offenses such as theft or acts of violence, and it did not provide for a method or procedure, such as trial by jury, even in the case of offenses which it sought to penalize. But in spite of these deficiencies, it contained definite provisions for the maintenance of order. Certain practices, including Sabbath-breaking, gambling, intoxication, or failure to perform the duties required by the Company, were made the subject of penalty. These penalties, varying with the offense and with the number of times it had been repeated, ranged from a fine in the amount of the value of a day's labor to expulsion from the Company. The Constitution did not specify whether fines should be levied by the Board of Directors or by the Company as a whole, but it did require that expulsion should be only by vote of a majority of the Company members.[45] Imperfect as this arrangement was in detail, it clearly embodied the principle that the group might enforce these regulations upon the members. Insofar as it did this, it imparted a governmental capacity to the Charlestown organization, quite distinct from its military and economic functions. Taken collectively, these three phases of organization gave to the company a cohesive strength surpassing that of most overland parties.

WITH funds subscribed, officers elected, and organization complete, the Charlestown Company members were in position to turn to the actual preparations for their long journey. This necessitated much planning, and also much learning, for California had burst upon the consciousness of most Americans as a new planet, and every preparation for the journey, from the overall selection of a route to the smallest detail of equipment, bristled with questions to which answers must be attempted. In general, information for these an-

---

defective or obsolete, and enacted such others as the exigencies seemed to require. The commonwealth being cared for, it next resolved itself into a court, to hear and settle private disputes and grievances. The offender and aggrieved appeared before it, witnesses were examined, and the parties were heard by themselves and sometimes by counsel. The judges thus being made fully acquainted with the case, and being in no way influenced or cramped by technicalities, decided all cases according to their merits.'' *A Day with the Cow Column*, edited by Joseph Schafer (Chicago, 1934), p. 14–15.

45. See Constitution of the Charlestown Company, articles XVI and XVII.

swers was scant, and its paucity led the emigrants of '49 to make some monumental mistakes. Even so, however, the gold-seekers benefited by the fact that an overland trail to California had been worked out, and information relating to this trail and to methods of travel had reached many of the Forty-niners in published form.

As late as twenty-two years before, no white man, so far as the record shows, had ever travelled overland to California, and when Jedediah Smith did it in 1826–27, he went by a route so difficult as to prevent its ever becoming an artery of travel.[46] For more than a decade thereafter, Americans scarcely conceived of California as being contiguous by land, but regarded it as a remote region beyond the seas—eight thousand miles the other side of Cape Horn. In 1841, however, the barrier of isolation was broken by the development of a deviation from the Oregon Trail. This most famous of transcontinental routes had first been discovered by Robert Stuart on a trip eastward from Astoria in 1812–13,[47] and after being known for years to the fur traders, it began to secure a wider recognition when Jason Lee, Samuel Parker, Marcus Whitman, and other missionaries traversed it in the late 1830s. John Bidwell, an Ohioan living in Missouri, was one of the many who knew of this route and he joined a group who were determined to attempt a divergent trail which would lead into California. Accordingly, Bidwell's party left the Missouri in 1841, travelling in the company of Father de Smet and the great scout, ''Broken Hand,'' or Thomas Fitzpatrick. At Soda Springs, in what is now southeastern Idaho, the main party continued on the path to Oregon, while Bidwell and his group veered off into unknown country. Without quite knowing how they did it, or by what route, these trail-blazers at last struggled into the San Joaquin Valley, and thus became the first American settlers to

46. For Smith's trips to California, see Harrison Clifford Dale, ed., *The Ashley-Smith Explorations and the Discovery of a Central Route to the Pacific, 1822–1829* (Cleveland, 1918), and Maurice S. Sullivan, ed., *The Travels of Jedediah Smith* (Santa Ana, 1934).

47. Stuart's manuscript account of this important journey is in the Coe Collection. It has been edited by Philip Ashton Rollins, and published under the title *The Discovery of the Oregon Trail. Robert Stuart's Narrative of his Overland Trip Eastward from Astoria in 1812–13* (New York, 1935). For the general history of the Oregon Trail, see James Christy Bell, *Opening a Highway to the Pacific, 1838–1846* in *Columbia University Studies in History, Economics, and Public Law*, XCVI (New York, 1921), and W. J. Ghent, *The Road to Oregon, a Chronicle of the Great Emigrant Trail* (New York, 1929).

go overland to California. Every year thereafter parties bound for California were to be found in the stream of travel that flowed toward Oregon.[48]

Though the trail had been broken, knowledge of it was largely confined to the inarticulate scouts of the West, and it remained for information of the new route to reach the public. Bidwell himself had prepared in 1842 a condensation of his journal of the first passage into California, but this account manifested extreme vagueness for that part of the journey where precision was most needed—that is, after leaving the Oregon Trail. Other guides for the Oregon Trail left the potential migrant to California to shift for himself over the most difficult part of his journey.

The first useful and widely circulated account of the journey to California was John C. Frémont's account of his explorations thither in 1843–44. This report, published in 1845, was full, accurate, and vividly written. It enjoyed a heavy circulation, and was widely used by emigrants. However, it had certain defects as a guide: Frémont's wanderings far and wide befitted an explorer, but were no pattern for an ordinary traveller; he had not traversed the Humboldt, which was a vital segment in the California Trail; and his narrative of such dramatic adventure as the crossing of the Sierra in mid-winter was better adapted to provide thrills for the reader than to avoid them for the traveller. Despite these deficiencies, however, Frémont did as much as any writer to make Americans conscious of the Far West, and many of the Forty-niners relied upon him as a guide. Geiger and Bryarly were among the diarists who referred to his writings.[49]

In the same year in which Frémont was published, there also ap-

48. Bidwell's journal of this trip was published in Liberty or Weston, Mo., in 1842, but the only known copy, in the Bancroft Library, has no title page. This pamphlet, with an introduction by Herbert I. Priestley, was reprinted as *A Journey to California, with observations about the Country, Climate, and route to this Country* (San Francisco, 1937). A later narrative, ''The First Emigrant Train to California,'' was first published in the *Century Magazine* (1890) and later as part of *Echoes of the Past* (Chico, Cal., 1906).

49. Frémont's narrative was entitled *Report of the Exploring Expedition to the Rocky Mountains in the Year 1842, and to Oregon and North California in the Years 1843–'44* (Washington, 1845). Geiger and Bryarly's familiarity with Frémont is shown by the entry on August 11. Other diarists of '49 who refer to his book are: Delano, June 29, July 6, 13, 30; Doyle, June 4; Hale, Aug. 10; Johnston, p. 13; Kelly, p. 295; McCall, Aug. 10, 16; Sedgley, June 12, 31; Swain, June 28, 29, 30; Webster, Aug. 1, 16.

peared *The Emigrants' Guide to Oregon and California*, by Lansford W. Hastings, an Oregon pioneer. Hastings had not personally traversed the California Trail, however, and his account suffered accordingly. A detailed, accurate itinerary of the road to California was still lacking, therefore, until 1848. In that year, the need was met by Edwin Bryant's *What I Saw in California*.[50] This compendious account gave more than two hundred pages to a day-by-day record of a journey which Bryant had made over the Oregon and California Trails in 1846. This was explicit, complete, and reliable; its only appreciable defect was that Bryant travelled with pack animals after leaving Fort Laramie, and his experience was, therefore, not always pertinent for wagon trains. However, his book probably played a greater part than any other single work in guiding the epic emigration of 1849. Geiger and Bryarly, who allude to four different books, refer to Bryant more frequently than to any other.[51]

Two more guides were to appear in time to serve the Forty-niners. One of these, the so-called *Mormon Guidebook* of William Clayton, carried the traveller only as far as Great Salt Lake but was, nevertheless, widely used.[52] The other was *The Emigrants' Guide to California*, by Joseph E. Ware.[53] Ware's was the first guide-book proper for the California Trail. Where Bryant and Frémont were lengthy and distended by narrative, Ware was concise, beginning with a few paragraphs of pointed general instructions, and continuing with a succinct and specific itinerary of the journey. An appendix on methods of detecting gold, and on other routes concluded this

---

50. New York, 1848.

51. Geiger and Bryarly refer to Bryant on May 31, June 7, July 11, Aug. 11, 21. Other Forty-niners whose diaries show that they had used Bryant are: Badman, June 20; S. B. F. Clark, June 6; Delano, June 29, Aug. 3; Johnston, p. 13; Kelly, p. 130; Long, May 9; McCall, Aug. 24; Hackney, May 18; Searls, May 19, 26; Tiffany, June 1; Webster, Aug. 16. It is notable that, of the thirty diaries analyzed, eleven contain references to Bryant, nine to Frémont, five to the Mormon Guide, three to Ware, and one to Samuel Parker's *Journal of an Exploring Tour Beyond the Rocky Mountains* (Ithaca, 1838). There are also several allusions to ''guide-books,'' not further identified.

52. W[illiam] Clayton, *The Latter-Day Saints' Emigrants' Guide* (St. Louis, 1848). Geiger and Bryarly refer to this on June 30. Other diarists who allude to it are: Badman, July 7; B. C. Clark, July 27, ''the Mormon guide by which we travel''; Long, June 19; McCall, June 20; and Orvis (see Introduction to Manuscript, by Edward Eberstadt).

53. St. Louis, 1849. For the present study I have used the reprint (Princeton, 1932) edited with excellent notes and introduction by John Caughey.

volume, which, next to Frémont and Bryant, provided the marching orders for the army of Forty-niners.[54]

Of course no company was content to rely upon the printed page;
wherever possible, some man familiar with the route was employed
as a guide. The Charlestown Company, in due time, secured such
a guide, and profited greatly thereby, but it is suggestive of the in-
telligence with which the Charlestown project was managed that
the writings of Frémont, Bryant, Clayton, and Ware were all utilized, and were familiar to the diarists of the expedition.

To what extent these writings influenced the Charlestown group
in the selection of their route of travel, it would be impossible to
say. A number of routes were available, as Ware remarked in his
guide, and each of the ones he mentioned attracted a large number
of emigrants. Oldest of all was the all-sea journey around Cape
Horn. This voyage took as long as the trip overland and was more
expensive; it appealed chiefly to the New Englanders with their
strong sea-going tradition.[55] A variant of this was the so-called
Panama route, which, as the name implies, involved water transit
to and from Panama, and a land passage across the Isthmus. This
route, at its best, took far less time than any other, but in the absence of a railroad, the journey across Panama was difficult, and
the traveller was sometimes forced to wait for accommodations both
in crossing the Isthmus and in departing from the Pacific shore.
Such delay was rendered ominous by the heavy incidence of diseases,
and the Panama route in time acquired a reputation as the most
dangerous way to California.[56] A third route was suggested by the

54. Geiger and Bryarly refer to Ware on July 19. Other diarists do so as
follows: Brown, July 18; B. C. Clark, June 23, July 18, 20, 23; and Hale,
July 6.
55. Howe, *Argonauts of '49*, is by far the best account of the route around
South America, even though it deals only with emigrants from Massachusetts.
Howe states (p. 172) that he studied the records of 124 companies, of which 6
went by the South Pass, 9 by Panama, 2 through Mexico by Vera Cruz, 7
through Texas and Northern Mexico, and 102 around South America. There is
a discrepancy of 2 in the total, but Howe's record is very full, and the proportions are clear. He estimates that not less than 4,567 people went from Massachusetts to California via Cape Horn. The quickest voyage was 145 days and the
longest was 267 days, while the average length was 168 days. The total cost of
a trip by this route, Howe estimates, was $500.
56. An excellent treatment of the journey via the Isthmus is to be found
in John Haskell Kemble, *The Panama Route*, in *University of California Publications in History*, Vol. 29 (Berkeley, 1943), especially chapters II, VI, and
VII. This treatment shows (p. 254) that some 6,489 passengers went to California via the Isthmus in 1849. An uninterrupted journey from New York to
San Francisco might be completed in as short a time as 33 days (p. 148), but it

experience of the Mexican War: this was by water to Vera Cruz and across Mexico to some such Pacific port as Mazatlan; this route was not extensively used, but it appealed to the veterans of General Scott's campaign.[57] A fourth general area of travel, containing an intricate series of routes, was the region now known as the Southwest, including northern Mexico. This section had received attention during the Mexican War, and many Americans were familiar with the success of Philip St. George Cooke and Stephen W. Kearny in opening trails from New Mexico along the Gila River into California.[58] Moreover, the warm weather permitted an earlier start on the journey than was possible in more northern climes. All these advantages were eagerly publicized by frontier towns of Texas, Arkansas, and Missouri, which hoped to prosper as terminals. As a result, a network of trails appeared. The southernmost, starting at the lower tip of Texas, traversed Mexican territory almost all the way, ending at the port of Mazatlan. Variant routes lay across southern Texas and northwestern Mexico, or all the way across Texas and thence via the Gila. Still further north, travellers from Arkansas might follow the Canadian River, and those from Missouri might take the Santa Fé Trail; in both cases, the route led to Santa Fé, from which point most of the traffic moved to the Gila.[59]

frequently developed that passengers during the Gold Rush could not secure passage on the Pacific side, and were stranded indefinitely, often paying high speculative prices for their passage. The advertised prices for this journey were $100 to $150, New York to Chagres; across the Isthmus, $35 or more; and from Panama to San Francisco, $150 to $300 (pp. 37–38, 54–55, 169–173) but travellers stranded on the Isthmus had additional costs, while speculation drove prices up so high that a steerage space, Panama to San Francisco, at times cost $1,000.

57. Little information is available on this Mexican route. A good account of two companies which went via Vera Cruz appears in Howe, *Argonauts of '49*, pp. 27–31, 37. Hastings, *Emigrants' Guide*, pp. 138–141, describes this route very unfavorably, and estimates the time at 36 days, the cost at $500.

58. Kearny, in command of the Army of the West, and Cooke, in command of the Mormon Battalion, both traversed the Gila River Route in 1846–47. The record of their marches was given to the public in detail in a report by Maj. William H. Emory, called *Notes of a Military Reconnaissance from Fort Leavenworth in Missouri to San Diego in California, including part of the Arkansas, del Norte, and Gila Rivers . . . made in 1846–7 with the advanced guard of the "Army of the West"* (House Executive Doc. 41, 30th Cong., 1st sess., Washington, 1848). The similar Senate Executive Doc. 7 is inferior in that it gives only an abridgement of Cooke's report, which is given more fully in the House Document.

59. The definitive treatment of the Southwestern trails is Ralph P. Bieber, ed., *Southern Trails to California in 1849*, in *Southwest Historical Series*, Vol. V (Glendale, Cal., 1937). Bieber estimates (p. 62) that 9,000 Forty-niners went to the gold mines by way of these trails. Proponents of the southern route claimed

Each of these four routes—Cape Horn, Panama, Mexico, the Southwest—had its devotees, and between them, the four probably carried a little more than half of the great migration which flowed toward California in 1849.[60] But far the best known, the least expensive, the most fully tested, and the most accessible route was that which utilized the Oregon Trail along the Platte, past Fort Laramie, across the South Pass, and then, going either by way of Fort Hall or of Great Salt Lake, converged again to follow the Humboldt, cross the Humboldt Desert, and then push up the valley of the Truckee, or the Carson, over the Sierra Nevada, and into the valley of the Sacramento. This route, which was essentially that of Bidwell, Bryant, and Frémont, was the classic Oregon and California Trail. As the main artery of travel it carried about twenty-five thousand people into California in 1849 alone. It appealed to landlubberly and provincial Americans, because it involved no sea journey, and no contact with foreigners, with their unfamiliar language, food, money, and religion. It appealed to a nation of small farmers because it was inexpensive, and they could use their own wagons, their own draft animals, and their own skill in handling this equipment. Even for those, like the Charlestown group, who planned to purchase their wagons and animals, it appealed as a familiar way of doing things. As they fondly imagined it, the journey would take but two months during the pleasantest part of the year[61]—a kind of protracted excursion during which they could hunt buffalo, meet the Indians of the Plains, view the Independence Rock, and share in all the other experiences which Frémont and Bryant had described with such infectious enthusiasm. As early as January, the Charlestown gold-seekers were committed to the California Trail.[62]

that it could be traversed in 60 days, and that the distance was only 1,287 miles (*ibid.*, p. 137), whereas the northern route was reckoned at 2,291 miles (Bryant, *What I Saw*, p. 248).

60. In the absence of reliable statistical information, recent scholars have been content to quote, without necessarily endorsing, Bancroft's estimate that about 16,000 emigrants from foreign countries and 23,000 from the United States used the sea routes by Cape Horn or Panama, while 9,000 came by central or northern Mexico, 8,000 by New Mexico, and 25,000 by way of the South Pass. Bancroft, *Hist. of Cal.*, VI, 159.

61. *Spirit of Jefferson*, Jan. 16, estimated the time at sixty days. This was arrant optimism, perhaps of a promotional nature, for Bryant had taken four months on the journey.

62. *Spirit of Jefferson*, Jan. 16, indicated the selection of a route via Fort Laramie.

A journey across the continent in 1849 was controlled by extremely rigid physical necessities. The maximum number of men who could travel together was limited by the insufficiency at many places of forage for large numbers of animals; the minimum number was governed by the necessity for division of labor in certain functions such as standing guard over the animals at night. The possibility of early departure was reduced by the fact that forage did not appear on the prairies in sufficient quantity to feed the animals until May; the necessity of a prompt arrival was increased by the fact that snows blocked the passes in the Sierras as early as October. The route of travel was determined by the inexorable fact that the animals must find forage and water daily—that is, at intervals of twenty miles or less—or they would quickly lose vitality and leave the emigrants without motive power. Only on the Humboldt Desert did the emigrants attempt to move more than forty miles without forage and water, and where they did this, the animals were driven to the utmost limits of their endurance. Had the Humboldt Desert been ten miles broader, probably only a small fraction of the emigrants would have lived to reach its western side. As for the volume of supplies to be carried, if it sank below a sufficient minimum, the traveller might be faced with starvation before he reached California; if it rose above a frugal maximum, it constituted a dangerous burden upon the animals, for every pound of baggage had to be hauled thousands of miles through mud holes and heavy sand, across rivers, and up steep declivities. Since overloading penalized itself by retarding the rate of speed, and light loading made a rapid journey imperative, the margin of safety between the volume of goods carried and the volume needed was always narrow.

As a consequence of all these factors, every detail required careful planning. Baggage must be reduced to essential items; perishable goods must be excluded; and articles admitted only if they possessed a high degree of usefulness in proportion to their bulk. Animals must be selected for their stamina, and for their capacity to convert a minimum of forage into a maximum of horsepower. All this must be done with an eye to economy, for most emigrants expected the journey to cost less than $100.[63]

---

63. The problem of costs was vital to most emigrants, and great stress was laid upon the inexpensiveness of the South Pass route. Hastings, *Emigrants' Guide*, p. 142, said, "the expense is much less, by this route. . . . As nothing is required upon this route but such teams and provisions as the farmer must necessarily have at home, it may be truly said that it costs him nothing but his

The organizers of the Charlestown Company showed a sound appreciation of some of these factors, from the beginning. In their first plan, they limited the size of the company to sixty men, though they later permitted increases, first to seventy, and then to seventy-five.[64] Moreover, they sought to assure themselves of the physical fitness of this personnel by requiring each man to submit to a physical examination.[65] A further evidence of sound planning was the adoption of a fifty-pound limit upon the personal belongings of each member. This limitation was, in fact, even more rigorous than it appears, for the company also decided to specify the clothing which each member must carry, and to include these required articles within the fifty pounds. The items of clothing, wisely chosen, included eight shirts, one pair of drawers, four undershirts, two pairs of trousers, one vest, one coat, one overcoat, two pairs of boots or shoes, eight pairs of wool socks, and four coarse towels.[66] In addition to these items, the company planned to furnish hats, gloves, blankets, combs, and soap for the members. For the protection of the men and their clothing in wet weather or at stream crossings, the company also planned, very appropriately, to provide a rubber knapsack, a "gum overcoat," and an oilcloth cap, "with cape," for each

time; for he can expend no money, as he travels entirely among . . . Indians, who know nothing of money or its value.'' Ware, *Emigrants' Guide*, p. 1, described the overland route as ''the cheapest and best,'' estimated that the expenses by all routes except the overland would exceed $300, and proceeded (p. 7) to estimate costs per person, overland, as low as $55.19. For costs to emigrants who joined joint stock companies, see note 38, above. For costs via other routes see notes 55, 56, and 57 above.

64. The decision of the organizers to accept no more than 60 applicants is reported in the *Spirit of Jefferson*, Jan. 30. The increases to 70 and 75 are shown in *ibid.*, Feb. 13 and Mar. 6. Ware, *Emigrants' Guide*, p. 4, said, ''Your travelling parties should not be too large, not more than fifty men.''

65. Edward Washington McIlhany, a member of the Charlestown Company, wrote, nearly fifty years afterwards, his *Recollections of a '49er* (Kansas City, 1908), in which he devoted about twenty-six pages to the overland journey. On page 10 he speaks of the physical examination of forty of the members, for the company wanted ''strong, able-bodied men who could endure the hardships of such an adventure.'' The Mount Washington Mining Company also required a physical examination. R. C. Shaw, *Across the Plains in '49* (Farmland, Ind., 1896), pp. 18–20.

66. *Spirit of Jefferson*, Jan. 30. Randolph B. Marcy later wrote what was perhaps the soundest of all guides, *The Prairie Traveler, a Handbook for Overland Expeditions* (New York, 1859), and in it he listed what he regarded as essential clothing (p. 39). This list included 2 flannel overshirts, 2 woollen undershirts, 2 pairs thick cotton drawers, 4 pairs woolen socks, 2 pairs cotton socks, 4 colored silk handkerchiefs, 2 pairs stout shoes (one pair boots instead of shoes for horsemen), 3 towels, 1 broad brimmed, soft felt hat.

man.[67] Such apparel could be worn against the rain by day, or placed between the blankets and the wet ground at night, and it later did good service.

In addition to his clothing, or indeed almost as part of it, each man was expected to bear arms, both for securing game, and for protection against Indians. This precaution, the Charlestown Company certainly did not overlook, for it planned to provide "one pair revolving pistols ($20 pair)" for each member, and it adopted a motion on February 10 to purchase thirty rifles and forty double-barrelled shot-guns—one such weapon for every man. A committee purchased these arms in Baltimore, and the Virginia Company became, like most of the overland parties, a kind of roving armory. As a final and quite unnecessary measure of security, a small cannon—a six pounder—was also procured, and this weapon was lugged all the way to California, despite the chilling statement in Ware's guide that, "some companies foolishly talk of taking small cannon along." [68]

During February and early March other preparations went forward. The first installment of membership payments fell due on February 10, and at that time, the President, the Treasurer, and the Quartermaster were appointed a committee for the purchase of supplies. The first business of this committee was to go to Baltimore, where $7000 worth of provisions were purchased to be shipped by sea around Cape Horn for the use of the company after its arrival in California.[69] This plan was based, of course, on the mistaken belief that the company would continue to operate as a unit after it reached the diggings, but despite this error, it was a far better arrangement than attempting to carry a year's provisions overland, as Ware had recommended, and as many emigrants sought

67. *Spirit of Jefferson*, Jan 16, 30; McIlhany, *Recollections*, p. 11.

68. *Spirit of Jefferson*, Jan. 16, Feb. 13, speaks of both shot guns and rifles; McIlhany, *Recollections*, p. 15, speaks of 80 shotguns, no rifles. Marcy, *Prairie Traveler*, p. 41, said, "Every man who goes into the Indian Country should be armed with a rifle and revolver, and he should never, either in camp or out of it, lose sight of them." Ware, *Emigrants' Guide*, p. 6, specified, "For arms you want a good rifle and a pair of long pistols." The history of the Charlestown Company's cannon is shown in the Geiger–Bryarly diary and in McIlhany, *Recollections*, pp. 23–24, 34.

69. *Spirit of Jefferson*, Jan. 30, Feb. 13; McIlhany, *Recollections*, p. 15. McIlhany later remembered the amount spent in the East as $10,000, but the Company's plans called for the spending of $7,000 in the East, $10,000 in the outfitting towns, and the holding of $1,000 as a reserve.

to do.[70] Meanwhile, an iron works near Charlestown was engaged in making two large sheet-iron wagon beds, which could be, and later were, used as boats for transporting equipment across unfordable rivers.[71] Here was another evidence of able planning.

For the most important equipment of all, however—the wagons, draft animals, and provisions with which they would make the journey—it was decided not to make the purchases in the East, where problems and expenses of transportation to the setting-out place would be involved, but to send men ahead to procure these items in Missouri. The river towns such as Independence and St. Joseph were marts for such equipment, and the guide books recommended that the outfits be bought there.[72] Accordingly, separate committees on the purchase of mules and of wagons were appointed, and these committees were sent west in advance of the company, the mule committee being instructed to leave on March 6, and the wagon committee on March 13, while the company itself did not set out until March 27.[73] Whether the committee on supplies was also to leave in advance was not specified.

At an earlier time, the company had planned to travel with only one wagon for every fifteen men, and to supplement this outfit with a large number of riding animals,[74] so that, essentially, the company would travel in the saddle, while the provisions would be hauled in wagons. The principal defect of such a plan lay in the fact that the food alone for fifteen men, according to Ware's estimate, should weigh 8175 pounds, while the maximum load which a team could effectively haul over a long distance, again according to Ware, was

70. Ware, *Emigrants' Guide*, pp. 6–8.

71. *Spirit of Jefferson*, Mar. 6, noted a vote of thanks by the Company to John E. Penman of the Taylor Iron Works, no doubt for the construction of these boats. For account of the boats and their use, see McIlhany, *Recollections*, p. 16, and below, p. 133. Johnston, Apr. 24, mentioned meeting a company from Cincinnati which had had iron wagon beds made for use in crossing streams, but he subsequently (May 2) observed that these ''boats'' did not work.

72. ''Westport, Independence, and St. Joseph have facilities peculiar in themselves, for the outfitting of the Emigrant—every requisite for comfort or luxury on the road can be obtained at either of these places on nearly as low terms as at St. Louis.'' Ware, *Emigrants' Guide*, p. 3. Also, see Bryant, *What I Saw*, p. 14.

73. *Spirit of Jefferson*, Mar. 6, tells of appointment of committees, Mar. 3. The committee to buy mules consisted of Cockrell, Engle, Gallagher, and Moore, who was later made team master. The committee to buy wagons consisted of Keeling (Captain), McCurdy, Seevers (Quartermaster), and Slagle.

74. *Spirit of Jefferson*, Jan. 16.

about 2500 pounds.[75] When the weight of clothing, weapons, casks, and other equipment is taken into account, it is clear that one team and wagon would scarcely carry the supplies for five men, much less for fifteen. Evidently the Charlestown leaders recognized this, for they altered their original plan drastically, and purchased sixteen wagons, or about one for every five members.[76] By the time of this purchase, the great volume of traffic of the '49 season was beginning to cause a rise in prices, and many emigrants regretted that they had not bought their supplies further east. The mule committee of the Charlestown Company shared in this experience, for when its members reached St. Louis (Geiger was travelling with them), prices for mules were "very high." At Lexington, five days later, they were "most exorbitant"—$70 to $100 apiece.[77] Despite these difficulties, however, one member of the committee bought 30 mules at Lexington and another bought 60 nearby. Other purchases included a number of horses and enough additional mules to raise the total mule herd to over 100.[78] Thus, there were approximately six mules available as a team for each wagon, with a small surplus of riding animals.

The only remaining preparation was the securing of foodstuffs and equipment for the journey. Exactly what rations were purchased, and in what amounts, it is not recorded, but various diary entries show that the Quartermaster's office carried large quantities of flour and bacon, and also a supply of coffee, rice, beans, peaches, sugar, salt, and molasses. In addition, some pickles—included on account of their value as an anti-scorbutic—and a barrel of

75. Ware, *Emigrants' Guide*, p. 6, listed foodstuffs of a total weight of 545 pounds which were recommended for each man. Limitation of wagon load to 2500 pounds is proposed on p. 5. Marcy, *Prairie Traveler*, pp. 27, 36, later recommended a smaller quantity of food, but also a lower limit on weight carried.

76. McIlhany, *Recollections*, p. 16; below, p. 76.

77. Below, pp. 227–228. The diary of Philip Badman shows that, by May 4, mule prices had risen to $110. Soon the outfitting towns acquired an unsavory reputation for their high prices. An emigrant of 1850, Eleazer Ingalls, wrote from St. Joseph "every little thing costs three or four times as much here as at home. The markets are filled with broken down horses jockeyed up for the occasion, and unbroken mules which they assure you are as handy as sheep." Quoted in Lorenzo Sawyer, *Way Sketches*, edited by Edward Eberstadt (New York, 1926), p. 17.

78. Stock acquisitions shown below, pp. 76, 228, and in McIlhany, *Recollections*, p. 16.

whiskey found their way into the commissary.[79] If this list of foodstuffs be compared with the list recommended by Ware, a high degree of correspondence will be noted, and an approximate idea may be reached as to the quantities of each food carried. Ware suggested that each person would need, on the trip, a barrel of flour, 150 to 180 pounds of bacon, 25 pounds of coffee, 40 pounds of sugar, 25 pounds of rice, 60 pounds of peas or beans, 30 or 40 pounds of dried peaches, molasses, vinegar, and a keg of clear beef suet as a substitute for butter, which could not be carried because it would go rancid. Captain Marcy was later to offer a far more frugal list— 150 pounds of flour, 25 of bacon with fresh beef driven on the hoof, 15 pounds of coffee, 25 of sugar, and a little baking powder (saleratus as it was then called), and salt and pepper. In 1849, however, this wise minimum had not been suggested, and the emigrants cheerfully loaded their wagons with the assorted groceries suggested by Ware.[80]

In addition to rations, it was also necessary to carry an important minimum of equipment. The Charlestown Company anticipated many needs by providing cooking utensils, sun goggles, casks, canteens, rope, a fishnet, fishhooks, and scythes with which to cut hay for the animals when a grassless stretch was expected.[81] Few companies, apparently, were so well equipped.

When everything was assembled, it was found that the loads ranged between 2500 and 3000 pounds per wagon. Ware said that no one should attempt to leave with more than 2500 pounds, but the Charlestown loads were not far above this limit. Everyone else was overloading, and the members could not anticipate that Captain Marcy, with riper experience, would later set 2000 pounds as a maximum load, nor that they themselves would come to regard 1800 pounds as a proper limit.[82] It seemed to the advance com-

79. For specific references to these commodities in the diary, see index. McIlhany, *Recollections*, pp. 19, 24, especially mentions the whiskey and the pickles. ''Sunday was our day for cooking beans and eating pickles. We never ate pickles except on Sunday.''

80. Ware, *Emigrants' Guide*, p. 6; Marcy, *Prairie Traveler*, p. 36. Foster, in a letter of May 9 from Council Bluffs, observed that his party had secured 300 pounds of provisions per man, which was as much as was considered advisable. This, it will be noted, was less than Ware suggested, and even at this amount, Foster and his companions were later obliged to throw away part of their load.

81. For specific references, see index, under Equipment.

82. Ware, *Emigrants' Guide*, p. 5; Marcy, *Prairie Traveler*, p. 27. A letter on June 11, at Chimney Rock, from one of the company (probably J. Harrison Kelly, since he was the regular correspondent), in the *Spirit of Jefferson*, Aug.

mittee that everything was shipshape, and that all that remained was to proceed to St. Joseph and to await the arrival of the main body of the company, when the breaking-in of the mules could be undertaken.

St. Joseph, or St. Joe as it was more appropriately called, was one of the principal competing towns which had sprung up along the Missouri to challenge the supremacy of Independence as an out-fitting place for the West. The original importance of Independence had arisen from the fact that it was located at that point on the Missouri which was nearest to Santa Fé, and it was therefore the logical terminus for the Santa Fé trade. When the Oregon Trail came into use, and travel moved by the valley of Platte, Independence, because of its earlier leadership, became a setting-out place for this new travel also, but there were many points, farther up the Missouri, which were nearer to the Platte. These points—Westport, St. Joe, Council Bluffs, and others—soon began to claim a share of the westbound traffic. St. Joe was two days farther up the river and fully 70 miles farther west, and in the season of '49, this crude, straggling, hectic, river town ranked second only to Independence as a port for the voyagers over the prairie. Here the Charlestown Company had fixed its rendezvous.

While mules and wagons were being purchased, the main body of the company had gathered at Charlestown for their departure on March 27. Some came from the adjoining counties of Berkeley, Clarke, Loudoun, and Frederick, but most of this group of about seventy men were residents of the home county of Jefferson. In general, they were farmers or mechanics who had grown up thereabouts, and were widely known. Their number was sufficient to cause the entire community to suffer by their absence,[83] and individually, many friends and relatives dreaded their departure upon so long and so dangerous a journey. Among the men themselves, probably few, except those who had been in the Mexican War, had ever been far from home before. They too, must have dreaded the parting, and the scene of leave-taking was an affecting one. As one youthful member later recalled ''there were hundreds of our friends to bid us good-bye,'' including ''fathers, mothers, brothers, sisters, wives, sweethearts, and even old family darkies—all with tears in their

21, said that their wagon loads had been from 2500 to 3000 pounds, and should not have been more than 1800 pounds.

83. ''A little family like ours can scarcely afford so large an inroad upon its members.'' *Spirit of Jefferson,* Jan. 30.

eyes.'' This same young man received a Bible and a hymn book as parting gifts from his mother and father. ''We were sad at the thought that perhaps we might never see our loved ones again.'' [84]

The bustle of departure, no doubt, prevented any protracted indulgence in sentiment, and the young Virginians soon set out on the first leg of their long journey. Less than ten miles from Charlestown, the Baltimore and Ohio Railroad ran through Harper's Ferry, and this railway carried them their first day's travel to Cumberland, Maryland. From this point, the historic Cumberland Pike led to the Ohio River, and the second day found the company rolling westward across the Alleghenies in nine chartered stage coaches. One stage driver, exhilarated by many toddies which he procured for 6 3/4¢ each, alarmed them by his furious driving around mountain curves. But no damage was done, and after traversing one hundred miles, they slept that night by the Ohio. On the third day, still another means of transport, the river boat, came into play as they boarded the steamship *Niagara,* bound for Cincinnati. On deck, they found another emigrant company, and from that time until they reached the diggings they moved in the main stream of the Gold Rush. There was a band on board, and at night, as they floated down the Ohio and the Mississippi, the Negro deck hands ''sang old plantation songs.'' The record does not say so, but probably there was homesickness in the crowd.[85]

After a change of boats at Cincinnati, they continued down the Ohio and the Mississippi to St. Louis, where they remained for three days. The enticements of this gaudy river town must have seemed alluring to many of the unsophisticated young men from Charlestown, and it is likely that others did as Geiger had done when he went through St. Louis with the mule-purchasing committee—''took several cocktails and had some fun.'' But on April 10, the party

84. McIlhany, *Recollections*, p. 11. On the place of residence and previous occupation of the members, *ibid.*, pp. 10, 15, and *Spirit of Jefferson*, Jan. 16.

85. McIlhany, *Recollections*, pp. 11–15; C. H. Ambler, ''West Virginia Forty-niners,'' in *West Virginia History*, III (1941), 59–75. McIlhany stated that the party left on Mar. 3, but this was clearly a mistake of memory, for the *Spirit of Jefferson*, Mar. 6, showed that the company had not left at that time, but had voted to leave on Mar. 27. Professor Ambler states that the company went to Pittsburgh, rather than over the Cumberland Pike, but McIlhany's description of this part of the journey is so logical and so circumstantial that it invites credence. One of the advance committees did go by way of Pittsburgh, and it is perhaps to this that Ambler refers. McIlhany says that the company boarded a steamboat at ''Brownsville,'' probably meaning Moundsville, near Wheeling.

were again in motion, this time by river boat up the Missouri, and on this stage of their journey, the festive spirit of the trip was suddenly stilled by the abrupt presence of death. On the second day out of the St. Louis, one of the members of the company, by name Thomas Washington, fell victim to the great scourge of the emigration of 1849—that is, to the Asiatic cholera. This disease, having first appeared at the port of New Orleans, had moved by river boat up the Mississippi, and was already beginning to make fearful inroads upon the emigrants in the outfitting towns. Under circumstances where people were crowded together with inadequate sanitation and impure drinking water, cholera spread furiously, and inflicted heavy mortalities upon travellers who could not receive suitable treatment, and whose vitality had, in many cases, been lowered by the conditions of travel. Furthermore, very little was understood about either the cause or the prevention of the malady, but its course was fearfully well known. It might appear in the morning, and kill before noon. The death of Thomas Washington, on board the river boat *Embassy* was almost this sudden, for he was first taken ill one day, and died at ten o'clock the next morning.

Regardless of ceremony, cholera could not remain aboard overnight, and before sundown, the *Embassy* had drawn up near the shore at a point where a cluster of trees shaded a grassy slope. Here Washington's sobered companions dug a grave, and the passengers all went ashore, to stand with bared heads, while someone read the Episcopal burial service. Alonzo Delano was one of the solemn group who stood about the grave, and he wrote what must have passed through the minds of all, ''How little can we foresee our own destiny! Instead of turning up the golden sands of the Sacramento, the spade of the adventurer was first used to bury the remains of a companion.'' [86]

On April 19, with a new gravity, and with a dawning realization

---

86. Delano, *Across the Plains*, p. 15, does not mention Washington's name, but describes the death and burial of a ''young gentleman belonging to a company from Virginia,'' and states that he was on the steamboat *Embassy*, which reached St. Joseph April 19. Brown also travelled on the *Embassy*, and obviously on the same passage, for he reached Independence, April 17. He describes the death on April 10, of ''one young man of the Virginia Company''—evidently the same death described by Delano. The Hoffman diary, in Ambler, ''West Virginia Forty-niners,'' shows that the Charlestown Company arrived at St. Joseph on April 19 (same day as Delano), and McIlhany, *Recollections*, p. 17, states that Washington died of cholera on the trip up the Missouri. Evidently, Washington and the ''young man of the Virginia Company'' were identical.

of what gold-seeking could sometimes mean, the company reached St. Joseph, where the advance committees were waiting, and there, all together, they encamped for the first time.[87]

Until the Spring grass should grow up in sufficient abundance to provide forage for their animals, there was nothing to do save loiter in St. Joseph—and break mules. This activity went far to relieve the monotony, for a Missouri mule was a formidable adversary, and the business of taming him was a task that evoked complaint from many emigrants. One diarist of another company described his experience with, "thirty wild, unbroken, two year old mules, the best to be had, but of whom only five or six had ever felt a collar. We all fell at once to work on these *ferae naturae* and had a high old time breaking them to harness. . . . They were lassoed, thrown, harnessed, and dragged into place by sheer and simple force, to which only were they in the least amenable. . . . We gradually, and with much tribulation reduced our mules to a condition that might be called hostile subjection, that is to say where the subject, while in the main yielding to force and necessity, maintains a noble and gallant spirit of subdued revolt, always watchful and ready to seize every opportunity for liberty, if possible—if not, for vengeance." After three days of this, the same diarist was encouraged to note that "the mules are perceptibly tamer, and it is now possible to go within a stone's throw of them without open war; and they even seem to be taking in the notion that it is easier to give a good pull all together than to jump over each others backs and kick and bite at everything within reach." [88]

The record of the Virginia Company is more laconic, but no less telling. Nearly a month was spent in breaking the mules, and almost daily, a runaway team would jeopardize one of the wagons. Two of the men who were thrown in these contests of will narrowly escaped being crushed beneath the wagon wheels. Others took "flights off ground and lofty tumblings" and even the Captain of the company was not spared. After the animals were partially subjugated, the decision was made to cross the Missouri, and complete the process of mule-training on the western bank. Accordingly, the company took

87. Ambler, "West Virginia Forty-niners." Ware, *Emigrants' Guide*, p. 4, said, "Your time for starting from home should be arranged so as to be on the frontier by the 20th April."

88. Wistar, pp. 44, 51. See also Kelly, p. 45; McCall, p. 5; and Webster, pp. 35–37.

a ferry at Savanna Landing, and pushing through the bottom lands, pitched camp on bluffs which marked the edge of the prairie.[89]

Before leaving St. Joseph, the Company made one very fortunate arrangement. Some of the members had met a certain Frank Smith, who had been over the Oregon Trail as early as 1845, and who had thus learned the art of successful travel overland. He had never traversed the California Trail from the point where it left the road to Oregon, but his knowledge of the craft of emigrant travel applied even in unfamiliar country. Also, he seems to have possessed excellent all-round judgment and superior qualities of leadership. The Charlestown Company secured the services of this talented frontiersman as a guide, and it later elected him a member, with full financial rights in the Company. Much of the success of the journey resulted from his leadership.[90]

In the season of 1849, warm weather came unusually late, and the growth of grass on the prairie was retarded by at least two weeks.[91] Thousands of emigrants, with outfits ready, impatiently awaited the appearance of this forage,[92] but not until the second week in May

---

89. McIlhany, *Recollections*, p. 16; letter, May 25, in *Spirit of Jefferson*, June 19; below p. 76.

90. McIlhany, p. 18; letter of J. Harrison Kelly, Sep. 29, in *Spirit of Jefferson*, Dec. 11; diary of Benjamin Hoffman, July 19, in Ambler, "West Virginia Forty-niners." For diary references to Smith, see index.

91. Johnson, letter, Independence, Apl. 22, "the day of departure has been deferred in consequence of cold weather. . . . It was a little hard for me to make up my mind to wait patiently 15 or 20 days longer than we expected."

92. An excellent statement of the problem of fixing the time of departure is given in Johnson, letter, Apl. 22: "But it is not enough to have good mule teams. They must have a sufficiency of grass (new grass) to live on and perform the day's journey, and if, in our anxiety to get under way, we start one week too soon, our mules will fall away in the week more than can be regained in four weeks afterward on good grass, and they very often get so sore as to require rest for a week or two in which time they will be passed by those who start one week or even two weeks later. . . . Now it is natural and safe to divide these emigrating parties into three classes so far as regards the supply of grass. 1st. The first, who leave just in time to get enough, none others having gone before, and they not being so numerous as to require large quantities of grass. 2nd, those who rush after . . . in greater number, and who being thrown so close upon the heels of the first will for a time at least see their animals suffering and falling away for the want of sufficient sustenance. And 3rd, those who do not start until there is plenty of grass which will probably be in 6 or 8 or 10 days after the second class leave. . . . How narrow must appear to any the chance of hitting the precise point of time when the grass is barely sufficient and before the masses shall begin to crowd in."

For cases of parties which set out too soon, incurred losses, and were forced to turn back because of lack of grass, see Johnson, letter, Apr. 29.

did it materialize. As it did so, the emigrant wagons began to roll out,[93] and on May 12, the Charlestown Company left the encampment which they had made on the bluffs about seven miles west of the Missouri. After only eight miles of travel, they went into camp and laid over the rest of that day and the next day which was Sunday. At that time they branded their mules with the initials of the Charlestown, Virginia, Mining Company. Then on May 14, they started the true overland routine, travelling from eight o'clock until sundown, despite a driving rain which lasted for several hours. As they pitched camp that night, almost every wet and weary man in the company must have realized that the great trek had begun in earnest, and that he could not expect to sleep in a bed, eat at a table, or find shelter under a roof again until he reached California, two thousand miles away.

WHILE the company still lay in its encampment on the west bank of the Missouri, Vincent Geiger began to keep a daily journal to record the trip. He continued it faithfully for forty-four days, until the company had left the North Platte. Then, on June 23, apparently having wearied of it, he turned it over to his friend, Wakeman Bryarly.[94] Bryarly kept it even more fully than Geiger had done, making daily entries for the next sixty-nine days, or until they had reached the diggings near Sacramento. This joint diary of the two emigrants is the substance of the present volume. It tells the story of the journey with completeness, authenticity, and vigor, and it renders any supplementary narration here superfluous. The only further purpose which an introduction can serve is to suggest

---

93. Nearly all accounts show that the emigration moved pretty much in unison, but a more precise idea of the time of setting out may be gained by comparing the record of the various diarists of '49. On Apr. 16, Kelly left Independence (p. 50) and on Apr. 23 and Apr. 28, Long and Johnston, respectively, left from the same place, but both of these had arranged to be accompanied for two or three weeks by wagons carrying feed. By the time feed was exhausted, the grass would be up, and in this way they would get in advance of the general migration, and thus enjoy, for the rest of the journey, the first use of forage along the way. McCall, May 1, and Page, letters, Apr. 24, May 8, refer to this practice.

The median date of departure among the diarists included in this study was May 12, and it would appear that those who started early moved slowly, awaiting grass, for Hackney wrote, May 6, "we intend to keep on a few miles each day till the grass is grown enough for the cattle to go ahead on." For a full schedule of departure dates, see the table in Appendix D.

94. The exact point at which the authorship changed is shown by the change of handwriting in the manuscript.

certain conclusions on the experience of the Charlestown organization, and to show something of the later lives of the two men whom circumstances had brought into propinquity as fellow travellers and fellow diarists on the California Trail.

One hundred and ten days after their departure, the Charlestown emigrants reached the end of their journey at the diggings above Sacramento. Four members of the company had died in transit, but more than seventy of them had successfully met what one called "the perils and hardships of that terrible journey across the continent." [95] Only five mules and one horse had been left behind, either dead, exhausted, or lost. Most remarkable of all achievements, however, was the fact that the company's organization had held together through all the stresses and strains of the march, and while other companies were disintegrating, dividing, and reforming, only to divide again, the Virginia Company remained a successful and reasonably co-operative unit. With understandable pride, a member wrote from California, "it is a matter of note that ours was the largest company that ever crossed the plains, although many, when they started, were fully as large, but by reason of the difficulties of the trip, were induced to separate." [96]

This claim of uniqueness for the Charlestown organization appears to be justified, for the records of other large overland companies invariably show the triumph of disruptive forces. Alonzo Delano commented that, "On leaving the Missouri, nearly every train was an organized company," but that, "on reaching the South Pass . . . the great majority had either divided or broken up entirely, making independent and helter-skelter marches towards California." At Fort Kearney, Captain Bonneville told J. Goldsborough Bruff that he had had "an excellent opportunity of observing joint stock companies," and that he had seen several, which, in spite of their sworn constitutions, had "dissolved, fought, damned everything, & divided their property." Similarly, Israel Hale, while on the overland journey, wrote, "hardly a day passes that a train does not split or a division take place." A month later Hale wrote again of a nearby train: "There is laying a few rods above us a joint stock company from Ohio. They have fell out and divided and fell out again and agreed to leave it to the Yankees.

95. Diary of Benjamin Hoffman, Sep. 1, in Ambler, "West Virginia Forty-niners," in *West. Va. Hist.*, III, 75.
96. Letter of J. Harrison Kelly, Sep. 29, in *Spirit of Jefferson*, Dec 11.

. . . Who the Yankees are, I do not know, but I have seen enough on this trip to satisfy me that a co-partnership or stock company will not do. The reason is: men do not think alike.'' [97]

In detail, the record fully substantiates this generalization. Hale himself started out with a company of twenty wagons, but the number was reduced by withdrawals to sixteen, then to eleven, later to eight, and finally to six. A smaller company, of which G. Backus was a member, began with seven wagons, was reduced to five, and by July, three of these were abandoned, as their owners decided to shift the provisions to the backs of pack animals and push ahead of their companions. David De Wolf became a member of a company of sixty men, whom he described in June as being ''like a band of brothers,'' but when they reached the Humboldt Desert, only eight of the original twenty-one wagons still travelled as a unit. William Swain joined a company which enjoyed the cohesive bond of a $125 membership fee, but despite this equity, nine of the members abandoned their share in the joint property of the company, in order that they might travel with pack animals, and thus reach California more quickly. Similarly, the companies in which Philip Badman, T. G. Caldwell, Samuel Dundass, L'Hommedieu Long, James Lyne, Simon Doyle, Alexander Love, John Evans Brown, Ansel J. McCall, W. J. Pleasants, and Joseph Sedgley travelled, all experienced at least one major split.[98]

These divisions did not always result from personal dissension or antagonism. Often they arose from a dispassionate recognition of the fact that the mobility of a small group is naturally greater than that of a large one, and especially that the difficulty of finding adequate forage increased directly in proportion to the size of the company. A company with thirty animals might advantageously

---

97. Delano, June 29; Bruff, in Read and Gaines, eds., *Gold Rush*, I, lxi; Hale, July 9, Aug. 14. In a letter of May 23, Johnson wrote: ''The only thing counted foolish here is to be caught in a large train of 50 to 100 men; from 15 to 30 men are counted all-sufficient and most companies have split all up into small parties. Some are going with one wagon and 4 and 5 men. There are scores of parties of 8 to 10 men.'' Cf. the lines from the Gold Rush song, ''Seeing the Elephant'':

''So we split up and I made a break
With one old mule from Great Salt Lake.''

98. Hale, May 23, July 9, Aug. 8; Backus, May 28, June 16, July 6; De Wolf, letter, June 17, diary, Oct. 1; Swain, May 5, Sep. 7; Badman, July 13; Caldwell, May 30; Dundass, May 8; Long, June 5–8, 20; Lyne, June 30; Doyle, July 7; Love, Aug. 13, 14; Brown, June 22; McCall, June 2, 9, July 15, 27; Pleasants, p. 57; Sedgley, June 24, July 10.

camp on a forage ground whose limitations would force a larger company to push on in search of more abundant grass. It was this factor, according to Alonzo Delano, which caused his company of fifty men to divide into two sections, and the same reason was given by Bennett C. Clark for a schism in the company of which he was captain. Similarly, the company to which W. J. Pleasants belonged travelled in complete harmony, but at the crossing of the North Platte, he wrote, "we conclude to divide our party into three divisions or separate trains, not because of any ill feeling or misunderstanding among us, but for the simple reason that we have now reached a section of country where stock feed is becoming scarcer all the time . . . and the smaller the number of cattle, the farther the feed will go." Another Forty-niner, Isaac J. Wistar, travelled for two months with a party of seventy-six men, and apparently they were entirely congenial, but the difficulty of finding grass, and the fact that some had lightened their loads more than others and were therefore under the necessity of reaching California more quickly, at last compelled them, against their wishes, to separate. Samuel F. McCoy, P. C. Tiffany, Samuel R. Dundass, and John F. Lewis also belonged to parties which separated more promptly and more willingly, because of their belief in the greater efficiency of small units and their resentment of "the bondage which a large company necessarily inflicted upon us." [99]

In a few cases, there were companies which surmounted the forces of disruption. For instance, William Kelly formed a party of seventeen men from the British Isles, and eight "Yankees," and this group, adopting a uniform dress, made the trip as a unit. Another triumph of cohesion was that of the Green and Jersey County Company, from Illinois; this party experienced a schism, in which it lost its captain only four days after being organized, but fifty-two members were left, and they remained banded together until they reached California. A third durable organization was that of the twenty-nine men who formed the Granite State and California Trading and Mining Company, but even this organization "would have been dissolved before it reached California had it not been for the beef cattle. . . . They were their principle [*sic*] dependence for food, and it was not practical to divide them among

---

99. Delano, June 13; B. C. Clark, June 13; Pleasants, p. 57; Wistar, July 29; McCoy, June 11, 12, July 18; Tiffany, May 30; Dundass, May 8; Lewis, May 28, June 4, July 2. The quotation is from Lewis, July 2.

small squads.'' Still another lasting organization was that of the
Washington City and California Mining Association, which owed
much to the firm control of its captain, J. Goldsborough Bruff.[100]

Despite these exceptions, the process of disruption prevailed so
generally that the cohesion of the Charlestown Company stands
out as a notable exception, and one which cannot be explained
merely in terms of a superior *esprit de corps*. In fact, the performance of the Charlestown Company could not have been achieved
without very specific success in dealing with the problems of the
journey and avoiding the pitfalls which wrecked other organizations. It is essential, then, in understanding the Charlestown Company in particular, or the Gold Rush in general, to inquire as to
what were the factors in that success.

Since draught animals were the motive power of the journey, a
proper selection and a proper use of beasts of burden was as important to that era as the development of effective truck and tank
models is to a modern army. The significance of this factor was
universally recognized, and it precipitated a vigorous and unend-
ing dispute as to the relative merits of oxen and mules. Horses, by
general agreement, could be used as saddle animals, but lacked the
stamina for drawing wagons or carrying pack-loads over so long
a distance under such adverse conditions of forage and water.[101]
For the heavy work, it was a choice of mules or oxen.

In certain respects, oxen possessed an indisputable advantage.
Nowhere was this advantage so clear as in the fact that they were
more easily handled, and less subject to loss through straying or
being driven off by thieves. The docility of oxen, and their slowness
meant that most emigrants could manage them without difficulty,
and that a man on horseback could easily overtake them if they
wandered away. With mules, it was another story, for they were
difficult to break, and often intractable even when broken. If they
got loose at night they might disappear over the horizon before
their absence was detected, and even when they were found, it was

---

100. For the account of the cohesion of these units, see Kelly, *passim;* Page,
letter, July 2, and Hackney, *passim;* Webster, Oct. 19; Bruff, *passim.*

101. Marcy, *Prairie Traveler,* does not even discuss the possibility of using
horses as draught animals; Hastings, *Emigrants' Guide,* p. 145, says, ''For the
harness, mules are preferable to horses . . . but oxen are considered preferable
to either.'' Nevertheless, some parties attempted to use horses in this way; *e.g.,*
see Brown, Aug. 16.

no easy task to catch them.[102] One company made it a practice to leave picket ropes on the mules as a means of recapturing them whenever they were turned loose, for no one in the party knew how to use the lasso in roping them.[103] A man on foot, attempting to catch a loose mule on the open prairie, faced no mean problem, and it was a truism that animals which gained their freedom during the first few days of the journey would go all the way back to the Missouri before they could be recovered.[104] When this danger had passed, a new one replaced it: that Indians might drive the animals away by stealth, and in two or three hours' time, escape to such a distance that they could not be overtaken.[105]

Further, some persons claimed that, on a long journey, the stamina of the oxen compensated for their slowness,[106] and that they could actually reach a distant destination as promptly as the faster moving mules.[107] According to this argument, they could endure more labor on less forage, and it was an undenied fact that they could subsist on vegetation which would not sustain a mule. In a case of acute food shortage, also, oxen could be slaughtered and eaten,[108] whereas mule meat was taboo; a final point, which rendered oxen more attractive, even though it did not prove them superior, was their price, for a team of eight oxen cost about $200,

102. On the relative ease in managing oxen, see Marcy, *Prairie Traveler*, p. 28; Hastings, *Emigrants' Guide*, p. 145; McCall, p. 7; Johnson, letter, Mar. 23.

103. Kelly, p. 104.

104. This happened to the mules of the Granite State and California Mining Co., Webster, May 30. Also, see Wistar, p. 52.

105. Marcy, *Prairie Traveler*, p. 28; Hastings, *Emigrants' Guide*, p. 145; Swain, letter, May 6; Johnson, letter, Mar. 23.

106. On the greater stamina of oxen, see Hastings, *Emigrants' Guide*, p. 145; McCall, p. 7; Marcy, *Prairie Traveler*, p. 28. Marcy conceded the superiority of mules in only one respect: they would bear the heat better. Hastings did not admit even that.

107. "When the march is to extend 1,500 or 2,000 miles, . . . I believe young oxen will endure better than mules; they will, if properly managed, keep in better condition, and perform the journey in an equally brief space of time." Marcy, *Prairie Traveler*, p. 28. For other claims of equal speed over long distances, see McCall, pp. 7, 53; Webster, June 8; Swain, letter, May 6; and especially, Johnston, July 16. At that date, Johnston's party, with mules, were along the Humboldt, several hundred miles in advance of the bulk of the migration. They were astounded, therefore, to overtake an ox-train which had remained ahead of them up to this time.

108. Marcy, *Prairie Traveler*, p. 28; Hastings, *Emigrants' Guide*, p. 145; Paden, *Wake of the Prairie Schooner*, p. 15.

whereas six mules cost approximately $600.[109] The majority of emigrants were responsive to one or another of these considerations, and as a result, the bulk of them travelled by ox-team.

To the mule enthusiasts, however, there seemed something wrong with an argument which claimed an animal's slowness as his principal merit, and which was addressed more to the owner's fear of his own mismanagement than to his desire for an animal of maximum capacity. It was an inescapable fact that mules could travel faster than oxen, and if they could do that, they ought to reach their destination sooner.[110] At least, so reasoned those who knew they could afford to buy mules, and believed they could contrive to manage them. These partisans of the mule were clearly in the minority, but they maintained a spirited argument, and much of their experience on the journey suggests that, when properly handled, the mule may actually have been more suited to the task.[111]

109. Marcy, *Prairie Traveler*, p. 28. On lower cost of oxen, see also McCall, p. 7.

110. Marcy, *Prairie Traveler*, p. 27; Johnson, letters, Mar. 23, Apl. 22.

111. Marcy, *Prairie Traveler*, p. 28, and Hastings, *Emigrants' Guide*, p. 145, both stated that oxen were preferable. Swain, letter, May 3, and McCall, July 18, also declared that the best opinion was in favor of oxen. However, Paden, *Wake of the Prairie Schooner*, p. 15, concludes from the historical viewpoint that mules were more successful.

The factors influencing one man's decision are vividly shown in two letters of Johnson. In the first, Mar. 23, he defended his intention to use oxen: "they are much better liked here than mules . . . for several reasons, the principal of which are that there is not so much danger of oxen running away and the Indians will not steal them as they care nothing for an ox but they will steal a mule wherever they can catch him. Oxen will probably require some fifteen days more on the road, but what is that compared with the safety of an ox-team? . . . Oxen will perform the journey but nearly all the American mules in Missouri are three years old and under and are not regarded as safe for the journey; and many of the Spanish mules (the only other kind, being such as are got from Mexico in the Santa Fe trade) are broken down with previous hard service, and hence are not fit for such a trip."

By Apr. 22, he had changed his mind: "Here, as everywhere else, men talk and advise as their interest may happen to lead them and every other man you meet in Independence has either oxen or either mules to sell . . . and they that have neither have the interest of some friend to promote who has them to sell. So you will see that it was no easy matter for us to determine, in less than a week, after the most diligent inquiry, which, all things considered, were the best, oxen or mules. We have decided in favor of mules. After all that can be said in favor of oxen, only one thing can be said in favor of the ox—and that it is not so liable to run away or be stolen by the Indians, while the mules will perform the journey a little quicker, will subsist on less, endure warm weather better, and go longer without water, while a little increase of watchfulness will guard against Indian stampedes."

The Charlestown Company, of course, had decided in favor of mules, and its subsequent success proved that efficient management was all that was needed in order to utilize mule power with complete effectiveness.

Whether oxen or mules were chosen, the handling of the animals was as vital as any part of the craft of overland travel, and neglect or ignorance in this department were far the most productive causes of disaster. Experienced plainsmen knew that the welfare of the animals was vital to the safety of the emigrants, and therefore more important than their comfort. As one traveller expressed it, "our lives depend on the lives of our animals"; another remarked that his company often camped without wood, though this meant there could be little cooking, if an adequate supply of forage and water were available: "our practice is first to look for a good place for the cattle, and then think of our own convenience." [112] But while the soundness of these policies was generally recognized, human nature often shirked applying them. Everyone knew, for instance, that animals which were driven too hard during the first stages of the journey were likely to suffer total exhaustion later, thus imposing a delay of days for the sake of a gain of a few hours. Nevertheless, the temptation was great to push ahead as rapidly as possible; and most emigrants succumbed to it.[113] Again, it was pretty generally understood that animals which were in harness most of the day, ought to be allowed full opportunities for forage in the early morning, and late afternoon, and even at night. Marcy stated that "unless allowed to graze at night they will fall away rapidly." One of the Forty-niners declared, "the reason we have travelled so fast and so successfully is, that we have rarely tied our cattle down at night, but have guarded them as they were eating or laying down—thus they had all the grass and rest they wished & were ready

112. Johnson, letter, Apr. 22; Page, letter, May 13. Johnston, Apr. 21, remarked that his company's guide, Jim Stewart, "cared more for mules than for men, and considered it his first duty to look out for them; the men, he always said, could take care of themselves."

113. Marcy, *Prairie Traveler*, p. 44, warned, "The great error into which inexperienced travelers are liable to fall, and which probably occasions more suffering and disaster than anything else, lies in overworking their cattle at the commencement of the journey. To obviate this, short and easy drives should be made until the teams become habituated to their work, and gradually inured to this particular method of traveling. If animals are overloaded and overworked when they first start out into the prairies . . . they soon fall away, and give out before reaching the end of the journey." Also, see Johnson, letter, Apr. 22.

for an early start." [114] But few travellers were so diligent. Some kept the animals on tether the greater part of the time, thus restricting their forage; others left them freer, but without adequate guard, so that they were exposed to theft.

In addition to the dangers of loss through theft or of weakening the animals by over-driving or depriving them of sufficient forage, there was an additional hazard—that of permitting them to drink alkali water, which was especially in evidence in the vicinity of the South Pass and in the valley of the Humboldt.[115] This draught was fatal to many of the animals that drank it, and ruinous to the vitality of those that survived. But it could be avoided only by a degree of vigilance which was often lacking.

The failure of the emigrants in general to meet these difficulties is vividly attested by the heavy animal mortalities which, save for the cholera among the human population, became the most painful aspect of the overland journey. There was scarcely a diarist who failed to note the profusion in which the bodies of mules and oxen littered the trail. On the Humboldt Desert, the stench and the spectacle were as hideous as anything that most of the travellers had ever experienced. At the outset, of course, there were few records of such losses, and along the valley of the Platte the number of dead animals remained negligible, but at Fort Laramie the losses became appreciable, and near Independence Rock, they were disastrous. Some travelers attributed these losses to overdriving; others, to the effects of alkali water; one even surmised that heavy exertions in a rarefied atmosphere were responsible. But all agreed in constantly noting, day after day, "many dead cattle," "more or less stock lying dead every day," "large numbers of horses and mules," and the like.[116] These notations reached a fearful climax on the Hum-

114. Marcy, *Prairie Traveler*, p. 92; Page, letter, June 13.
115. Marcy, *Prairie Traveler*, pp. 124–125, Also, see below, pp. 113–114, 116.
116. Delano, June 28, suggested the rarefied air as a cause of cattle losses. He had previously (May 31) noted the prevalence of overdriving: "Many cattle were becoming lame and many showed evidence of being hard driven. In the great desire to get ahead, and the foolish rivalry of passing other teams, no rest was given to the cattle." Diary entries which note the presence of dead cattle and attribute their death to overdriving or to insufficient forage include De Wolf, July 22; Foster, June 30; Hale, July 7; McCoy, July 17, Aug. 7; Orvis, June 17; Searls, July 10. Those which speak of the bad condition of the animals due to these factors include Doyle, June 25; Tiffany, May 29; Long, July 20–Aug. 2.

Those which note dead animals and attribute death to alkali water include: De Wolf, July 22; Hale, June 25, July 7; Dundass, June 26; Foster, June 30;

boldt or Black Rock Deserts, where weakened animals faced a fierce test to which great numbers succumbed. One traveller counted 500 dead animals at the Humboldt, another spoke of hundreds, and others, doubtless, preferred not to count in the midst of a scene that reminded one of them of Dante's *Inferno*.[117]

Another source of heavy loss of cattle was the ineffectiveness of safeguards against Indian depredations. Most companies started out with a rigid system of night guards, which were maintained inflexibly in a region where the Indian menace was slight. But, by the time they reached the South Pass, the original companies had disintegrated into parties so small that there were not enough members to maintain a guard in rotation, and even when the number sufficed, the precaution had been relaxed. In these circumstances, the emigrants approached the Humboldt Valley, which was inhabited by as diligent and skillful a tribe of cattle thieves as the continent could produce, namely the Utes, whom the emigrants called Diggers, without discriminating between these marauders and the Shoshokees to whom the term more properly belonged. The Indians promptly inaugurated the practice of approaching the camps at night by stealth, putting an arrow into the guard if there happened to be one, and driving off the mules or cattle. Early arrivals on the Humboldt at the end of July noted that "there had been much stock stolen by the Indians." Soon, theft became chronic; one diarist said, "they are stealing oxen and horses every night"; another wrote, "cattle are stolen almost every day." Individual losses included five oxen, eight oxen, ten oxen, fifteen oxen, three oxen and four horses, one horse and three mules, four horses, and so forth. One company relaxed its guard for the second night since leaving Missouri, and lost thirty-five head of cattle. Another party, calling itself the Helltown Greasers, lost "a lot of cattle," and learned that it enjoyed no more immunity than companies with more genteel names. No real relief from this thieving occurred until the territory of the marauders had been passed, but, "for five hundred miles they were excessively troublesome."[118]

Badman, July 5, 6, 7; Doyle, July 1; Orvis, June 23; Searls, July 10; Sedgley, July 9; Swain, July 17; Webster, July 22; and Hackney, June 23, 24, 26, 27.

Other diarists who note presence of dead cattle without indicating cause of death include: Lewis, June 25, 26; Caldwell, July 5; S. B. F. Clark, July 2; Brown, July 10; Bruff, July 23.

117. For animal deaths on the Humboldt Desert, see below, pp. 189, 192.

118. For the distinction between Utes and Diggers, see Paden, *Wake of the*

In the light of the varied hazards which were common to all, and the heavy losses which other companies experienced, the success of the Charlestown Company with its animals is remarkable. Near the beginning of the journey, the boggy condition of the trail necessitated exertions which almost exhausted the mules, and later there were stretches where the sparseness of grass or the necessity of a long drive to water placed the teams under a severe strain. But the company made it a practice to rest for a day after any such extraordinary effort.[119] This gave the animals opportunity to recuperate. Moreover, it was a cardinal rule of the company to stop at midday for a period of rest known as a "nooning." This spared the mules from labor during the hottest part of the day, and gave them opportunity to graze. If the departure at morning had been early, the nooning might last for as long as six or seven hours; it frequently lasted for four hours, and apparently it was very rarely omitted, for the diary of Geiger and Bryarly specifically relates the circumstances of the nooning for forty-seven days of the journey, and it contains only twice a statement that the nooning was omitted. This practice of halting for a long mid-day rest undoubtedly became a major factor in maintaining the stamina of the teams.[120]

Another practice, perhaps as important as the nooning, was that of herding, rather than picketing the animals at night. That is, a guard stood watch over the beasts to keep them together, but they were not tethered nor confined within a corral of wagons. This

Prairie Schooner, pp. 379–380. The five quoted phrases are, respectively, B. C. Clark, July 30, Hackney, Aug. 9, Hale, Aug. 12, Hale, Aug. 16, and Delano, Aug. 6. Accounts of specific thefts appear in Badman, Aug 17, Sep. 4, 8; Brown, Aug. 15; Backus, July 28; Delano, Aug. 6, 7; De Wolf, Sep. 17; Doyle, Aug. 20; Foster, Aug. 18; Johnston, July 16; Lewis, Aug. 11; Love, July 28; Hale, Aug. 16; Hackney, Aug. 6, 7, 8, 9; Sedgley, Aug. 10, Sep. 4; Swain, Aug. 28; Tiffany, Aug. 8–9 (on the Carson River).

119. On May 13, June 2, 17, July 1, 4, 17, 23, 30, Aug. 5, 9, 10, 18, 23, and 27, the company remained in camp all or part of the day. Most of these layovers were for the purpose of resting the animals after a hard drive or in anticipation of one.

120. The nooning lasted 8 hours on Aug. 2; 7 on Aug. 1; 6 on July 16; 5 on June 3, 7, July 6; 4 on June 24, 25, 26, 27, 28, 29, July 7, 24, 29, Aug. 6, 7. Usually, the length of time is not stated. On Aug. 22, it is stated that the company did not rest at mid-day.

Marcy, *Prairie Traveler*, p. 45, said: "In traveling with ox teams in the summer season, great benefit will be derived from making early marches; starting with the dawn, and making a 'nooning' during the heat of the day, as oxen suffer much from the heat of the sun in midsummer. These noon halts should, if possible, be so arranged as to be near grass and water, where the animals can improve their time in grazing."

meant that they were not limited to the grass which lay within the radius of a tether rope, and accordingly, they were more free to forage at night. The value of this night feeding was very important for the animals. Captain Marcy was later to note that diverse methods prevailed—"some will picket their animals continually in camp, while others will herd them day and night"—and while he did not attempt to prescribe any one method as essential, he did insist that if picket ropes were used, they should be long enough: "under no circumstances, unless the Indians are known to be near and an attack is to be expected, should they [the animals] be tied up to a picket line where they can get no grass." [121] Ware and Hastings seemed to approve the use of picket ropes of sufficient length, but in the areas of sparse vegetation the surest way to avoid too short a rope was to use none at all. Another traveler, Henry Page, recognized this when he wrote, "When we stop early enough for the cattle to fill themselves before night, we larriet (tie with long ropes to stakes) them 'till just at daylight when they are turned loose till we are ready to start—If we are late in stoping, we herd the cattle out all night." But what Page's company did in unusual circumstances, the Charlestown Company did regularly. This is shown by references in the diary to the fact that, where forage was sparse, mules scattered during the night, or that one of them, at morning, was found to have bogged down in a nearby mire, or on an evening before an early start was intended, "we were ordered by our Captain to piquette our mules . . . instead of herding them as usual." [122]

Under a regime where the animals remained unconfined, the dangers of straying, of exposure to alkali water, and of Indian depredations were greatly enhanced, but these risks were successfully averted. Probably luck favored the Virginians, but much of their immunity to misfortune must have resulted from the maintenance of a vigilant night guard. Other companies, of course, had intended to maintain such a guard, but whereas many of them failed to adhere to their original resolution,[123] it appears that the

---

121. Marcy, *Prairie Traveler*, pp. 91–92.

122. Ware, *Emigrants' Guide*, p. 12; Hastings, *Emigrants' Guide*, p. 148 (However, Hastings, p. 145, also spoke of the advantage of oxen, that they were not "necessarily tied or otherwise confined, but are permitted to range about uncontrolled, both by day and night"); Page, letter, May 13; below, entries for Aug. 7, 19, 24, 27.

123. Long, July 21 (along the Humboldt), wrote: "People in Cincinnati would be astonished at the *nonchalance* with which we three laid down to sleep at nights in the center of a tribe of hostile Indians without a guard and with

Charlestown Company held to the practice constantly. As a result, no animals were lost by theft or straying, even when the journey lay through the valley of the Humboldt, where companies in the vicinity of the Charlestown Company were losing stock to the Diggers night after night. In explanation of the immunity of his own group, Bryarly wrote simply: "We were prudent enough to be cautious and careful, and lost not one [animal]." [124]

These practices of the Charlestown group—the resting of their animals after excessive exertion, the habit of "nooning" during the hottest part of the day, the system of herding to permit grazing at night, and the maintenance of an effective guard—resulted in a minimum of losses and a maximum conservation of the animals' vitality. Not until the company had reached the Green River, more than a thousand miles from Missouri, did they lose their first mule, by the accident of drowning. After that, one exhausted horse had to be left behind, and it also proved necessary to leave two mules, which became bogged in a mire, and were successfully removed, but in such exhausted condition that they could not travel. Finally, two more mules and a pony were lost by straying when the company was distant only five days' journey from the diggings. But no animal died of alkali poisoning; not one was stolen by the Diggers; and when the Company reached the supreme obstacle of the journey, the Humboldt Desert, where beasts of burden died like flies, the crossing was accomplished without the loss of a single animal. [125]

Another factor, as important as the care of the animals, was the reduction of the loads which the animals must draw. At the out-

---

no living white man within miles around. What a difference between now and when we first started on the trip. Then the whole company was on guard every night when there was no real danger. Now when there is, not one guard is stationed, though we carry our arms close bye." Hale, July 26, said, "Some few days since, our company came to the conclusion that they would dispense with the cattle guard." McCall, Aug 15, asserted, "I find that many emigrants keep no guard at night and turn out their cattle and horses without an attendant. So far as I have been able to ascertain, it is only such that have met with losses." Despite McCall's statement, there are instances where marauding Indians killed or wounded the guard. See Wistar, July 30, Aug. 3.

124. McIlhany, p. 22, speaks of a guard being posted every night; diary, Aug. 8, shows that guard was maintained at that time. Quotation is from diary, Aug. 2.

125. For the losses described, see diary entries, July 3, 27, 29, Aug. 7, 25. For crossing of the Desert without loss, Aug 13. A statement by McIlhany, p. 33, that not a single mule or horse was lost, throughout the journey, is clearly an error.

fitting towns, as has already been shown, the emigrants of 1849 al-most universally made the mistake of over-loading. Most of them were painfully inexperienced, and they not only started out with greater quantities of foodstuffs than it was practicable to carry, but attempted to transport heavy mining equipment or valued personal effects such as feather beds, stoves, and other articles of furniture. A. J. McCall disgustedly wrote, "they laid in an over-supply of bacon, flour, and beans, and in addition thereto, every conceivable jimcrack and useless article that the wildest fancy could devise or human ingenuity invent—goldometers, gold washers, pins and needles, brooms and brushes, ox shoes and horse shoes, lasts and leather, glass beads and hawksbells, jumping jacks and jewsharps, rings and bracelets, pocket mirrors and pocket-books, calico vests and *boiled shirts*. A full inventory would occupy pages and furnish an assortment for a variety store. It was said that they would be handy some time and enable them to drive a profitable trade with the unsophisticated Indians." [126]

Ultimately, of course, this vast surplus was thrown overboard, with the result that for hundreds of miles, the trail was littered with articles of value. Traveller after traveller recorded his astonish-ment at the abundance of this jetsam and at the magnitude of the waste, and at the same time, almost every one told of his own com-pany's adding to the accretion. Yet, while everyone deplored the loss of goods, few perceived the most tragic aspect of it—namely, that most of the excess was hauled for hundreds of miles, constantly retarding the journey and weakening the teams, before the penny-wise emigrants could bring themselves to face the inevitable. The waste of energy of mules and oxen, rather than the waste of goods, was the significant loss.[127]

A few companies had the foresight to recognize their error and to abandon part of their property promptly. Accordingly, a few goods were to be found even along the Blue River near the outset of the journey.[128] At Fort Kearney, Isaac Wistar's company began a

126. McCall, p. 5.

127. Foster, letter, June 23, said, "Hundreds of teams start with twice as much as they can carry and, after wearing out their teams in hauling useless trash, throw it away. We started with a light load and have thrown out some of that." Johnston, May 29, at Fort Laramie, said, "It were wise not to bring goods this great distance, only to be obliged to part with them."

128. Hale, May 15; Long, May 16; Tiffany, May 11. Johnston, Apr. 29, tells of his party discarding "a fair sized library . . . two pigs of lead . . . and half a keg of nails" on the first day after leaving Independence.

reduction of load, and between there and Fort Laramie, the companies of Bennett Clark and Alonzo Delano also discarded much of their surplus.[129] But it was not until most emigrants had reached Fort Laramie, 560 miles along the way, that they began to lighten their loads. Here the stockpile of derelict goods assumed spectacular proportions. "Not less than 30,000 lbs. bacon," said one emigrant; "the destruction of property is immense," said another; boxes, trunks, tools, wagons, bacon, dried beef, salt, hard bread, gold washers, spades, shovels, and a scythe and snath were among the items noted by a third.[130] Yet even beyond Laramie, the teams struggled on with far more than they could ever haul to California. At Independence Rock, therefore, Philip Badman recorded, "our trane has threw away today what cost more than 500 $ at home. I think this is the gratest cite I ever see clothing of all kinds threw away without reserve." Six days past Laramie, Simon Doyle's company cast an unexplained surplus weight of 300 pounds of lead into a cannon. An attempt to fire a salute with this ordnance failed when the weapon burst, but at least Doyle was enabled to note, "In this manner we lightened up considerable." At about the same point, George Carlton of the Granite State Company, also "lightened up considerable," but in a less overt matter. His company had placed him in charge of a heavy gold filter, which he packed on muleback for fifty-four days. As the mule began to fail, he proposed to abandon the filter, but could not secure the consent of the company. On July 20, however, he took matters into his own hands and surreptitiously left the utensil in a thicket.[131]

But still, men and animals struggled on with outlandish cargo. Geiger and Bryarly noted a turning machine worth over $600, and a steam engine and coining machine worth between $2,000 and $3,000 which some resolute visionary had hauled through as far as

129. Wistar, May 30; B. C. Clark, June 1, 4; Delano, June 3.

130. The items cited are from Lyne, June 30; Hale, June 15; and Tiffany, June 6, 7. For other comments on the quantities of goods left behind at Fort Laramie, see Backus, June 15; Brown, June 29; Bruff, July 12; Doyle, June 19; Foster, June 16; Johnston, May 29; Long, June 8; Love, June 7, 9; Orvis, June 18; Sedgley, July 1; Swain, July 6; Webster, July 9, 11; and Wistar, June 15, 17.

131. Badman, July 9; Doyle, June 25; Webster, June 18, July 20, referring to Carlton. Also see Bruff, July 17; Dundass, July 3; McCoy, Aug. 7; Pleasants, p. 81; Searls, July 11, 12, 13; Swain, July 16; and De Wolf, Aug. 27, Sep. 14, and Oct. 3. De Wolf's party carried a gold washer, shovels, and picks until Sep. 14, and a cook stove and a number of trunks until Oct. 3.

the Humboldt Desert before he learned that it was hopeless. Even within a few days of Lassen's Ranch at the end of their journey, many travellers gave up, and left large quantities of goods, "the owner calculating to return for it, which was never done." Several small law libraries, male and female apparel, kitchen utensils, tools, and other lost hopes were among the abandoned goods. "No articles of a full and complete outfit but what could be picked up here, beside many nonsentiel & useless ones that was hawled here to be thrown away, breaking down the teams and causing distress and suffering beyond description." [132]

The Charlestown Company, of course, did not escape the error of overloading. In fact, members later expressed keen regret for their mistake. Nor did it immediately recognize the blunder and correct it. But it did rectify the mistake far more promptly than most companies. Where the majority did not act until they reached Fort Laramie, 560 miles from Missouri, the Charlestown group began to throw away certain articles such as horseshoes, boxes, and lard when they were only eight days out, and at Fort Kearney, 265 miles from the setting out point, they drastically reduced their entire load. A supply of picks was abandoned, some goods were sold, and the supplies of flour and bacon were reduced to one hundred pounds of the former and fifty pounds of the latter per man. This was twenty-five pounds less weight than Captain Marcy later proposed to allot to flour and bacon, and it indicates that the overloading was largely corrected thus early in the trip. Other goods were thrown away about two weeks later, but from the time the company left Fort Kearney, the wagons ran with relative ease and, consequently, with greater rapidity.[133]

This relative advantage in speed shows up clearly when the travel schedule of the Charlestown Company is compared with that of other companies which were travelling along the overland trail during the same season. In the present study, such comparison has been made with thirty other companies for which detailed records are available.[134] Of these, seventeen set out on the journey at intervals of from four weeks to two days ahead of the Charlestown Company. That is, the Charlestown group was eighteenth in the order

132. Diary entry for Aug. 12; Doyle, Oct. 5.
133. Diary entries for May 20, 27, 28, 29, June 16.
134. For a detailed tabulation of the travel schedules of all diarists included in this analysis, see Appendix D.

of leaving. From St. Joseph, Independence, Westport, and other points along the Missouri, the roads converged upon Fort Kearney, on the Platte. The Charlestown travellers made this journey in exactly two weeks, whereas other travellers required an average of nearly twenty days to reach this fort. From Kearney, up the valley of the Platte, the trail led to Fort Laramie. This leg of the journey was completed by the Charlestown group in seventeen days. The average of others was again between nineteen and twenty days; and only three companies out of the thirty covered the span more rapidly than did the Charlestown Company. By this time, the Virginians had advanced from eighteenth to ninth in order of travel. From Laramie the route lay along the North Platte and the Sweetwater until it crossed the Continental Divide at the South Pass. On this span, more than anywhere else, the Overland Trail was a single road rather than a series of roads. Here, the Charlestown Company was in transit for fifteen days. One other company made it in twelve, one in thirteen, and three in fourteen, but twenty-two required more than fifteen days. At this point, seven companies were still ahead; one arrived on the same day; but twenty-two were in the wake. Of the entire group of thirty, only three, the companies of Isaac Foster, William G. Johnston, and Andrew Orvis, had made the trip from the Missouri to the Continental Divide in a shorter interval of time. The journey of Orvis from Council Bluffs with pack mules had consumed only thirty-two days; that of Foster from Council Bluffs had taken forty-three; that of Johnston from Independence had also taken forty-three. The Charlestown Company from St. Joseph had required forty-six; all others had lasted more than fifty.

After the crossing of the South Pass, the trails diverged, offering alternative routes by way of Great Salt Lake, Fort Hall, and Hudspeth's Cut-off. After merging once more along the upper Humboldt, they again split, affording entry into California by way of the Carson River, the Truckee River, or Lassen's Cut-off, as it was deceptively called. Because of these variations in the route, and because diarists in the Great Basin could not usually state their position as explicitly as they could at Fort Kearney, Fort Laramie, or the South Pass, a comparison of time tables for the latter part of the journey presents difficulties. Finally, the problem is rendered no easier by the fact that travellers differed in what they regarded as the end of their journey. To some, it was Lassen's Ranch, Johnson's Ranch, Weaverville, or Sacramento. To others, it was the first place where they found supplies being sold or the streams being panned for gold. Allowing for these variables, however, the continued superiority of the Charlestown Company in rate of travel is clear. A number of companies which had started earlier reached the diggings during the first half of August, and two, the companies of William Kelly and William Johnston, arrived before the end of July. But where most of these early arrivals required about 114 days, the Charlestown Company, starting later, arrived at Johnson's Ranch on September 1, which meant that they had completed the journey in 110 days. Andrew Orvis, travelling alone after reaching Salt Lake City, using a pack animal rather than a wagon, and running completely out of provisions along the way, had reached California in the remarkable time of 77 days; William Kelly's company, and Sterling B. F. Clark, both using pack animals, from Fort Laramie, had made the entire trip in 101 days and 107 days, respectively. But the only party with wagons which made better time than the Charlestown Company, was that of William Johnston, whose company made the entire trip in ninety-one days. With these exceptions, none of the companies included in this comparison made the trip across two thousand miles of prairie, desert, and mountains as rapidly as the Charlestown Company. In the company itself, the belief prevailed that they had passed no less than three thousand wagons of other emigrants along the way.[135]

Throughout the record of the Charlestown Company, there runs the same characteristic superiority of performance, resulting from an equally characteristic soundness of policy. This policy is reflected in the care of the animals, in the reduction of cargo, and also in the choice of route, and it produced significant consequences in the maintenance of the organization and the attainment of a relatively quick and easy journey with light casualties and a minimum of deterioration. Anyone seeking an explanation of the sound judgment consistently shown must reckon with the fact that it could not have derived entirely from the original officers, for, no matter how talented they may have been, they possessed no experience of the technique of overland travel except what a few of them may have learned in the Mexican War. The key to the Company's success, therefore, must lie elsewhere, and in all probability it is to be found in the leadership of the guide, Frank Smith, upon whom Bryarly and Geiger made many admiring comments. This seasoned plains-

135. Letter of E. M. Aisquith, Aug. 21, in *Spirit of Jefferson*, Nov. 20.

man had traversed the Oregon Trail at least as early as 1845, and had apparently made other trips into the Far West, though he had never followed the California Trail. His experience, therefore, as well as his personality, must have won the confidence of the Virginians when they met him in St. Joe, for they soon arranged for him to travel with them as their guide. After less than two weeks of travel, his leadership had succeeded so well that he was unanimously elected to full membership in the Company and the previously elected Captain, Robert Keeling, resigned and placed entire control in Smith's hands. Thereafter, the new captain exercised his leadership with exemplary skill: his early reveille daily held the Company to a schedule of efficient travel; his choice of river crossings and his advance selections of camp sites greatly facilitated the journey; his bridging of a slough and his decision to dismantle one wagon in order to mend several others showed experienced craftsmanship; and his ready response to an apparent danger from Indians was but one example of his energy and resoluteness. When the inevitable hardships of the journey brought complaints against his leadership, he promptly met the disaffection by refusing to continue as Captain, whereupon the full realization of his value brought a prompt restoration of his ascendancy. Probably the success of the Charlestown Company was more the work of Frank Smith than of any other single person.[136]

WHILE the record of the Charlestown Company was in many respects distinctive, it was also, in some other ways, characteristic of the usual experience of the Forty-niners. This representative aspect of the company's history is especially evident in its elaborate preparations for certain hazards which did not materialize, and its losses from other hazards which were not foreseen.

The great unforeseen danger of the '49 emigration was the cholera

136. For Smith's previous experience in the West in 1845 and 1846, see diary entries June 10, 16, July 11; for his membership in the company, May 26; for some of his exploits as leader of the Charlestown Company, June 1, 4, 5, 20, 26, July 3, 5, 7, 17, Aug. 1, 15, 17. Also see McIlhany, *Recollections*, p. 18, and Hoffman diary, July 19, in Ambler, "West Virginia Forty-niners." Hoffman states that Smith had never been over the California Trail. A letter of J. Harrison Kelly, Sep. 29, in the *Spirit of Jefferson*, Dec. 11, said, "One great bond of strength consisted in having for our guide and captain (S. F. Smith) a man of the most indomitable energy and perseverance united with a bland and courteous character." See Johnston, Apr. 21, on the importance of an experienced and able guide.

epidemic of that year. Where the emigrant ordinarily thought of going out to meet the risks of Indian savagery and untamed nature —dangers which would increase as he penetrated deeper into the region of mountain and desert—the fact was that the major danger came from the river towns of the South. The heaviest mortalities swept the ranks of the emigrants while they were crowded together on the river boats of the Missouri, or in the outfitting towns. When the emigrant set out for the wilderness he was both reducing his risk and carrying his principal danger with him.

Altogether, estimates indicate that five thousand Forty-niners died of cholera, either before setting out or somewhere along the trail.[137] The incidence of death from this cause declined steadily as the emigration pushed west, and after it passed Fort Laramie there were scarcely any victims. But before reaching that point, few companies escaped without losing one or more of their members. Fourteen of the diarists whose records were used in this study told of losses in their own parties which they ascribed specifically to cholera, and several others spoke of deaths which may well have resulted from the same malady. William Swain's party lost four members in two weeks; W. J. Pleasants' company experienced equally heavy mortalities; and Niles Searls travelled with a group which suffered six deaths in three weeks.[138] These mortalities were not nearly so heavy as some others of which diarists heard, or which were called to their attention by the pitiful and hasty graves which abounded fearsomely along some parts of the trail. Relatively, the Charlestown Company escaped with lighter losses than most, but when Thomas Washington died on board a river boat ascending the Missouri,[139] it was characteristic of the common experience that this, the company's first fatality, resulted from cholera.

Other forms of illness, of which diarrhea was perhaps most notable, were also prevalent in the emigrant ranks, and amid cir-

137. Bancroft, *Hist. of Cal.*, VI, 149; Georgia Willis Read, "Diseases, Drugs, and Doctors on the Oregon-California Trail in the Gold Rush Years," in *Missouri Historical Review*, XXXVIII (1944), 260–276.

138. Diarists note the death of members of their own party by cholera as follows: Badman, July 21; Brown, May 26; Bruff, July 8; Delano, p. 17; De Wolf, May 2; Hale, May 10; Lewis, May 19; Love, Apr. 17; Lyne, June 2; Pleasants, pp. 30–45; Royce, p. 15; Searls, May 16, 17, 30, June 2, 4; Swain, May 14, 15, 19, 28; Tiffany, Apr. 22; Webster, June 2, 3. Other mortalities, perhaps ascribable to cholera are noted by B. C. Clark, July 3; Hackney, May 11; and Wistar, July 26.

139. See above, p. 33.

cumstances where exposure was chronic and care of the sick could not be adequate, they were sometimes fatal. Also, some fatalities resulted from tuberculosis, but these can hardly be counted as part of the loss of life caused by the journey, for many persons who were already victims of the disease undertook the journey as a desperate remedy for a desperate illness, and it is possible that the journey cured more sufferers than it killed. Again the experience of the Charlestown Company is pertinent, for it sustained its fifth and final death when Newton Tavener succumbed to tuberculosis on September 7, one week after the Company arrived at Johnson's Ranch. An earlier death, also resulting from illness, was that of Joseph C. Young, who perished of typhoid fever on May 22.[140]

Losses of this character were to be expected, but another of the unforeseen dangers was that of drowning. To an Easterner, the risk of drowning on the arid plains or amid mountain peaks must indeed have seemed negligible, but in fact, the necessity of crossing numerous large streams, many of them with swift current and quicksand bottom created a major hazard. The lack of bridges and ferries and the necessity of effecting a crossing for wagons or for frightened and unruly animals enhanced the risk, with the result that one of the tragedies most frequently described by the diarists is that of someone being drowned.

The first major river crossing was that of the South Platte, a wide but shallow crossing at which there seem to have been almost no losses. But along the North Platte, one young man was drowned near Chimney Rock,[141] and at the crossing of the North Platte, the loss was appalling. On June 20, at this point, Geiger told of the drowning of a young man of another party while the Charlestown Company itself was crossing. He added that seven men had been thus drowned within a week. It is interesting to compare the journal of Joseph Hackney at the same place on the same day, for he wrote that five men had been drowned in a day, four by the upsetting of a raft. Only a few days earlier, another diarist had mentioned the drowning of four people, also at the North Platte,[142]

140. On the death of Tavener, see letters of B. F. Washington, Sep. 9, and J. Harrison Kelly, Sep. 29, in *Spirit of Jefferson*, Nov. 20 and Dec. 11, respectively; also McIlhany, *Recollections*, p. 33. On the death of Young, these same letters, and also a letter of May 25, in *Spirit of Jefferson*, June 19; diary entry, below, May 22.

141. Badman, June 22.

142. Long, June 14.

and there were others, some days later, who similarly reported a number of persons—perhaps the same ones—as having lost their lives in the river.[143]

After the North Platte, there was no other dangerous crossing until the emigrants moved down from the South Pass to the crossing of Green River. Here, in June, it was said that men drowned at the rate of one a day, and at the same place in August, David De Wolf's discovery of a drowned man showed that casualties continued even though a ferry had been put into operation.[144] The Truckee was also a dangerous stream, and both Bryarly and other travellers made note of fresh graves which testified to its treachery.[145]

By an irony, the Virginians negotiated all these difficult crossings successfully, but lost one of their number, a young man named Taliaferro Milton, at a minor, and relatively easy crossing, that of Thomas' Fork of Bear River. The circumstances of his loss, fully recounted by Bryarly,[146] need no comment here, but it is again significant that one of the hazards which cost the Charlestown Company a life was also outstanding as a general cause for losses throughout the emigration.

Bacteria, unsound dietary, exhaustion, exposure, lack of skill in the water were deadly perils but prosaic ones, and it is abundantly clear that, in the preparation of safeguards, they went unheeded, while attention focussed upon the absorbing and romantic menace of Indian hostility. Frémont, Ware, Hastings and other writers had warned of the danger of Indians[147] and even if they had not, any American automatically identified the wilderness with Indians and Indians with danger. Some of the Western tribes were, of course, aggressive and treacherous, and weapons of defense were quite genuinely essential to the emigrants. But fear of the Indians far

---

143. Orvis, June 21; McCall, June 25; Dundass, June 25. Foster, June 24, spoke of 24 deaths, mostly from drowning, that had occurred at the North Platte crossing. Kelly, pp. 175–176, also tells of a drowning in the North Platte. Wistar, June 16, Doyle, June 17, and Sedgley, July 1, had told of previous drownings near Fort Laramie, where the confluence of the Laramie River and the North Platte necessitated a crossing of the Laramie.

144. Hixson, June 21; De Wolf, Aug. 7.

145. Diary entry, Aug. 17; Backus, Aug. 19.

146. Diary entry, July 9.

147. Frémont, *Report of the Exploring Expedition to the Rocky Mountains in the Year 1842* . . . , p. 15; Ware, *Emigrants' Guide*, pp. 13, 15, 33; Hastings, *Emigrants' Guide*, pp. 58–60, 67–68.

exceeded the actual danger from them, and rumors of wholesale
Indian slaughter outnumbered authentic incidents of Indian
violence at least ten to one.[148] As a consequence, most parties of
emigrants carried with them an enormous armament. Perhaps there
was never, at any other time, so great a number of firearms per
capita among a civilian population, as was to be found on the
overland trail. In William Kelly's party, for instance, every man
was provided with a revolver, as well as with a bowie knife and a
broadsword. Mounted men carried, in addition, holster pistols and
rifles. Other rifles were placed in the wagons, suspended from loops
in order to be readily accessible. Finally, the company carried
single and double-barrelled shot guns.[149] Apparently, this represented a more varied arsenal than most companies maintained, but
the probability is that very few ventured to set out with less than
the minimum of one rifle and one pistol per man, which the guide
books recommended.

As a result, the emigrants, many of whom were inexperienced in
the use of firearms, were constantly surrounded with dangerous
weapons, which they sometimes used recklessly. Geiger notes, that,
on the river boat which took him down the Ohio, he encountered
about thirty gold-seekers from Maine, who were ''exceedingly
verdant—always shooting guns, pistols, etc.'' William Kelly similarly declared that the passengers on the boat in which he ascended
the Missouri kept up ''an unintermitting fusilade'' and he regarded
it as a miracle that no serious accident resulted.[150]

148. Johnson, May 10, wrote, ''We cannot rely with any certainty upon the
truth of anything we hear as having transpired 5 miles ahead. . . . We hear all
kinds of bug-bear stories about Indian depredations but when we come a little
closer to the scene of action we can hear nothing of it.'' McCall, May 21,
entered in his diary this statement: ''We constantly hear reports of outrages
committed by Indians some little distance ahead, but when we reach the locality,
it is news there. A day or two ago, we found a note conspicuously posted by the
wayside, purporting to have been placed there by a Mr. Fowler, stating that
twenty miles from this point the evening before his train was attacked by
Pawnees and his cattle stampeded and driven off. This created some little alarm
among the timid but I am satisfied it is all a hoax.'' Johnston, June 3, learned
that a notice had been posted, stating that his party had been attacked by
Indians, though there had actually been no trouble with them. It is a notable
fact that a number of diarists tell of expected Indian attacks or of reported
Indian violence (Badman, May 29, June 16; Hale, June 2; McCoy, June 6;
De Wolf, June 13, 17; B. C. Clark, July 23) but only one (Wistar, July 30, Aug.
3) relates instances of which he personally was a witness. He tells of three men
killed by the Diggers along the Humboldt.

149. Kelly, p. 44.

150. Below, p. 226; Kelly, p. 39.

If this was a miracle, however, it was not a lasting one, for emigrants all along the trail fell victim to accidental shootings inflicted by their own guns or by those of their companions. Most of the diarists mention at least one such accident of which they learned because it happened in a nearby company, or because they passed the grave of a victim, and no less than nine of them record shootings which befell members of their own company, or even themselves. These gunshot accidents began to occur in the river towns, and one of the Argonauts wrote from Independence that, ''a good many accidents have occurred by the careless use of firearms. One man was killed and two or three others have been wounded; two or three others were shot at a purpose in affrays, wounded but not killed.'' [151] In this writer's own company, one of the men, five months later, dropped his gun on a rock while he was standing guard. It was discharged, wounding him so severely that he died on the following day.[152]

As the emigration moved from the rendezvous towns, the shootings continued. On the third day of his journey, Andrew Orvis accidentally discharged a revolver which lodged its bullet in his hip. A month later, he had recovered, but noted that others were victim to the same misfortune: ''a man was shot in the knee by the accidental discharge of a rifle. Thare has been several kiled and wounded on the road in the same way.'' [153] Near the outset of the journey, William Kelly reported that one John Coulter shot himself fatally while taking a gun from a wagon at the crossing of the Blue River. A member of Dundass' company was also killed by the accidental discharge of a gun which he was unloading near this same place, and the same area was the scene of an accident in which one of William Johnston's company shot himself through the hand.[154] Later emigrants in that region spoke of passing the grave of a victim of accidental gunfire; this was perhaps the grave of one of these, perhaps that of some other victim.[155] Also in the valley of the Blue, Ansel J. McCall witnessed an episode in which the

151. Johnson, Apr. 29. Doyle, Apr. 18, tells of a member of the Keokuk Company shooting himself, and Love, April 18, tells of the member of a ''Dutch Company'' being accidentally shot.
152. McCoy (of Johnson's Company), Sep. 29, 30.
153. Orvis, May 29, June 28.
154. Kelly, p. 76; Dundass, May 22; Johnston, May 11.
155. Long, May 9; Backus, May 22; Lyne, June 5. Johnston, May 8, found a notice telling of the death of a man who, in taking a gun from a wagon, shot and killed himself. This may well have been the same man described by Kelly.

company's physician put a bullet through his hand when pulling a rifle out of the guard tent. "I confess," McCall wrote, "to more fear from careless handling of fire-arms than from any external foe." [156]

This fear had ample justification, and others soon came to realize that more of the Forty-niners would be killed by their own weapons than by the enemy against whom these weapons were intended as a protection. John Evans Brown was brought to this realization when a member of his company, pulling a coat from under a gun, set off the weapon and shot a companion through the knee. He wrote, "I felt persuaded that more danger is to be apprehended from the carelessness of arms among fellow emigrants than from the hostile Indian." [157] At Fort Kearney, Joseph Sedgley reported four emigrants under treatment for gunshot wounds. Between Fort Kearney and the South Pass, the toll continued to mount: in one company, a young boy playfully stalked a guard, in Indian fashion, and the guard, entirely convinced by the deception, inflicted a severe bullet wound; in another, a gun exploded in the hands of its owner; in a company from Pittsburgh, a grazing horse drew its halter across a gun lying on the ground, discharged the piece, and dangerously wounded a nearby man; in another, the moving of a wagon cover caught the cock of a gun within the wagon, shooting and instantly killing a passer-by; in another, "a man was shot by foolishly holding a trunk cover for another man to shoot at." At the North Platte, three deaths resulted when one man was "shot accidentally and two intentionally." [158]

Beyond the Green River, it was Alonzo Delano's opinion that accidental shootings diminished somewhat in number, but the record shows that they remained a factor of substantial danger. Along Goose Creek, a blacksmith shot himself in the foot, and died of the lockjaw which ensued; near Fort Hall, a man shot himself while dismounting from a mule; along the Humboldt, a member of Isaac J. Wistar's company seized a gun by its muzzle to draw it from a wagon for use against the Diggers, but it shot him through his

156. McCall, May 26. Swain, June 10, tells of a member of the Plymouth Company shooting himself through the knee. This accident, like McCall's, occurred a few days before reaching Ft. Kearney.

157. Brown, June 26.

158. In sequence corresponding to that of the statements, references are: Sedgley, June 13; Delano, June 4; Backus, June 8; Delano, June 28; Hackney, June 21; Sedgley, July 2; Foster, June 24.

heart.[159] The marksmanship of hostile Indians was seldom this deadly.

While gunshot accidents were a cause of almost daily casualties along the trail, the Charlestown Company completed four-fifths of its journey without any injury from this source. It was true that Doctor Bryarly once discharged his pistol accidentally, singeing B. F. Washington's hair and putting a bullet through James Cunningham's "pantaloons," [160] but all gunshot injury had been avoided until the Company reached the Sink of the Humboldt. There, a young member named James Davidson was shot and killed. The circumstances of this desert tragedy are fully set forth in the diary,[161] but it is significant to note here that the experience of the Charlestown Company reflected the experience of overland emigrants as a group, in this loss, as well as in others. One death by cholera, one by drowning, one by accidental gunfire, none by the hostility of the Indians—these losses were characteristic; they were indicative of the principal dangers that the journey held for every traveller, and the two deaths resulting from typhoid and tuberculosis were suggestive of the further fact that every Forty-niner who set out faced fierce demands upon his physical vitality—heavier demands than some of the emigrants could meet.

AFTER their arrival at Johnson's Ranch on September 1, the Charlestown emigrants pitched camp. For the next two weeks they remained there, more or less inactive, for there were a number of factors which prevented an immediate rush to the diggings: for one thing, the mules desperately needed a period of rest in which to consume the abundant forage that had so long been denied them; for another, Newton Tavener was dying, and there may have been a reluctance to abandon him—he died on September 7; most of all, the members faced the dilemma that they could not separate because they collectively owned $10,000 worth of provisions which they soon learned had arrived safely in San Francisco via Cape Horn, and they could not remain united because the technique of gold washing did not admit of the employment of so large a number of men on a single claim.

159. Delano, July 22; McCall, Aug. 8; B. C. Clark, July 14; Wistar, Aug. 6. Wistar later (Aug. 25) put a bullet through his own hat, but without injury.
160. Diary entry, June 6; letter of J. Harrison Kelly, June 11, in *Spirit of Jefferson*, Aug. 21.
161. Diary entry, Aug. 8.

They found a solution of their dilemma when the Quartermaster, Nat Seevers, whose wealth is unexplained, offered to buy the entire stock of goods which were being held in San Francisco. Even in the presence of this offer, however, many of the members desired to maintain the company organization, and on September 13, a motion to dissolve was defeated by a vote of 41 to 32, and a committee was appointed to draft a new constitution. On the day following, however, the advocates of separation had gained strength, and on a second vote, by a majority of 50 to 19, it was resolved, "that the co-partnership existing between the members of the Charlestown Virginia Mining Company be dissolved." The company had existed and had given collective organization to a body of emigrants for exactly seven months and three days.[162]

Once the principle of dissolution was accepted, it was accepted completely. As the members left the camp at Johnson's Ranch, they went out in messes of five or, at the most, ten men. Some went alone, with packs on their backs and without even a work animal. Even the groups of eight or nine did not cohere for very long. Scattered to every point of the compass, they dispersed to meet fates as varied as the directions they took. Five of the party had already died; at least two survived until half a century after Marshall's discovery of the yellow metal in Sutter's millrace. One of the Charlestown party died the first winter in California; another, a homesick boy, started on the return trip overland the following season and died en route. Others ran the gamut of activities, and attained widely varying degrees of success and failure. At first, nearly all went to the diggings, where the fortunate made as much as $200 in two days, and the others averaged less than one dollar a day for periods of two weeks at a time. Later, they resorted to varied occupations such as raising melons, operating pack trains, serving in the state legislature. Some ended destitute, while one secured the most lucrative office in California, the Collectorship of the Port of San Francisco.[163] With all the diverse ends which they went to meet, how-

162. On the Quartermaster buying the provisions, see McIlhany, *Recollections*, p. 34, which gives other details also. For accounts of the dissolution, see letters: unsigned, Sep. 9; from T. C. M[oore ?], Sep. 16; of John T. Humphries, Sep. 17; and of J. Harrison Kelly, Sep. 29, in *Spirit of Jefferson*, Nov. 20, Dec. 11, 18.

163. McIlhany, *Recollections*, p. 35 *et passim;* letters in the *Spirit of Jefferson*, Nov. 20, 27, Dec. 11, 18, 25; and the Hoffman Diary, in Ambler, "West

ever, probably none were bound for places more remote or experiences more unforeseen than those which awaited Bryarly and Geiger.

The determining condition for the future of both men lay in the fact that, as Southerners, they were associated with an exceedingly active and aggressive faction within the Democratic Party in California. This faction was the Southern wing, known somewhat mockingly as the "Chivalry," to distinguish it from the "Tammany" or Northern element, and it combined the hot temper of the South with the recklessness of the West. It also manifested the traditional Southern talent in matters political. The result was that it enjoyed during the decade of the fifties, an almost unbroken political ascendancy, constantly punctuated by duelling and gunplay. The leader of this faction was William M. Gwin, originally of Tennessee and Mississippi, who represented California in the United States Senate for all but two years from 1850 to 1861, and who stood very close to President Buchanan. Gwin's position assured the Chivalry of access to the Federal patronage, and, at the same time, their powerful state organization enabled them to dominate the government at Sacramento, except during a two-year interlude of Know-Nothing

Virginia Forty-niners," all give information on the subsequent activities of the Charlestown members.

During the period when they worked at the diggings it is known that one mess of ten members consisted of Aisquith, Burwell, Boley, Barley, Fagan, Harrison, Mackaran, Marmaduke, Murphy, and Seevers. It was in this group that Harrison and Fagan made $200 in two days. Another mess of nine had Edward McIlhany as one of the members and, apparently Charles Thomas and the three brothers Charles, George, and James Cunningham. T. P. Hardesty, with two other men, went to wash gold on Deer Creek. Another group went north to Pit River, where they were attacked by Indians and where J. Goldsborough Bruff encountered them (Bruff, Oct. 5). J. T. Humphries and four others went to the dry diggings, where, as they expressed it, "you never get your feet wet or your pockets full." Benjamin F. Washington and Dr. Bryarly made plans to go to the diggings in a party formed by one, Long, who had not been a member of the Charlestown Company, but whether they did this is not known (letter of Washington, in *Spirit of Jefferson*, Nov. 20).

James McCurdy died the first winter in California, and young Enos Daugherty died on the trip East the following spring. James Cunningham died in the fall of 1850. William Rissler and Edward McIlhany both survived when McIlhany wrote his *Recollections* shortly before 1908. Edward Hooper became a melon farmer; Charles Thomas became a member of the California state legislature; Benjamin F. Washington became Collector of the Port of San Francisco; Edward McIlhany for a time operated a pack train, but he sold it to Noble T. Herbert, Robert Blakemore, and Charles and George Cunningham. Herbert later operated the pack train alone.

control. Throughout this time one of Gwin's principal supporters
was Benjamin F. Washington, who as former President of the
Charlestown Company was a personal friend of Bryarly and Geiger.

Fortunately for Bryarly, the political contest only involved him
indirectly. Primarily, he seems to have been concerned with a re-
sumption of the practice of medicine, and, either at this time or
later, with the acquisition of mining properties which ultimately
attained considerable value.[164] But it is clear that he enjoyed cordial
relations with the Chivalry, for in April, 1851, the state legislature
elected him visiting physician to the state hospital at Sacramento.
At almost the same time, Governor McDougall appointed him
Surgeon-General of the militia of California, and in the same year,
he was also chosen as a delegate to represent California at the
Crystal Palace Exhibition in London, though there is no evidence
as to whether he actually attended the exhibition.[165] Two years
later, John Bigler had succeeded to the governorship and the appointments of the McDougall administration had expired, but
again Bryarly was favored. Bigler appointed him a visiting physician to the State Marine Hospital at San Francisco, Surgeon of the
Second Brigade, First Division, California Militia, and, later, Second Inspector of the Seventh Military District with the rank of
Colonel. Bigler also named him as delegate to represent California
at the New York City Industrial Exhibition in 1853.[166] At about
this time, it appears that Bryarly had settled in San Francisco and
become a member of the Society of California Pioneers.[167]

Positions of rank in the California militia no doubt looked more
military on paper than they did in reality, and they apparently
failed to satisfy Bryarly's zest for campaigning. But even before
this second group of appointments expired, the opportunity of distant adventure again appeared, as the Pacific Mail brought news of

164. Letter of William B. Marye to the editor, Jan. 15, 1944.

165. Documents preserved by Bryarly's niece, Miss Victoria Gittings, at
"Roslyn," Baltimore County, Maryland, include communications to Bryarly
from: the clerk of the Assembly, Apr. 17, 1851, notice of state hospital appointment; Governor John McDougall, Apr. 13, 1851, appointment as Surgeon
general; and —, 1851, appointment as delegate to London Industrial Exhibition.

166. All of these appointments are shown by documents signed by Bigler and
now in the possession of the Gittings family. Dates of appointments in the
sequence listed in the text, are July 1, Mar. 18, Oct. 7, and June —, 1853.

167. Frank Soule, John Gibon, James Nisbet, The Annals of San Francisco
. . . (New York, 1855), p. 824.

another war. The principal antagonists this time were Great Britain and Russia, and the military arena was the Crimean Peninsula. Neither the parties nor the issues appeared to be such as would concern a San Francisco physician, but sympathy for Russia ran very strong in America and especially on the West Coast. Senator Gwin and Beverly C. Sanders, a prominent merchant of San Francisco, were spokesmen of this sympathy, and Gwin even supported a plan to authorize privateers to operate from Pacific ports against British shipping.[168] Although nothing came of this astonishing proposal, it is indicative of the temper of opinion among Bryarly's associates. Apparently, his feelings became aroused, and the combined force of his sympathy for the Russian cause and his temperamental fondness for adventure brought him to the decision to seek service in the Russian Army.

It cannot be said, however, that he was precipitate in his haste. He remained in San Francisco, apparently as late as June, 1855, at which time Major-General John E. Wool gave him a very warm farewell letter of commendation, which was probably intended to be shown to the Russian authorities.[169] Then, instead of going direct to Europe, he returned to Maryland.

During his visit in Maryland, Bryarly was married. It must have been soon after his return that he either met for the first time, or renewed an earlier acquaintance with, Miss Mary Sterett Gittings, daughter of a Maryland physician and gentleman farmer, David Sterett Gittings, whom he had probably known in his earlier life. There ensued a courtship—necessarily a brief one—and on September 5, 1855, Bryarly and Miss Gittings were married at Grace Church in Baltimore. After the marriage, it is said that the bridal couple repaired to Barnum's Hotel, in the same city, where their friends honored them with a callithumpian serenade.[170]

Weddings are not unusual among warriors on the eve of their

---

168. Frank A. Golder, ''Russian-American Relations During the Crimean War,'' in *American Historical Review*, XXXI (1926), 470.

169. John E. Wool, Major General, from Headquarters, Pacific Division, San Francisco, to Bryarly, June 1, 1855. Original in possession of the Gittings family.

170. Information on David Sterett Gittings, 1797–1887, M.D., University of Maryland, and Edinburgh University, from William B. Marye, his grandson, in letter, Jan. 23, 1944. The issuance of the marriage license, Sep. 5, 1855, is shown in the records of the clerk of the Circuit Court of Baltimore County, at Towson, Md. The marriage itself was recorded in the Baltimore *American and Commercial Daily Advertiser*, Sep. 14, 1855.

departure for the wars, and apparently, Bryarly's wedding was of this sort, for he was in England before the end of the year, and there Ambassador James Buchanan made him a bearer of dispatches to Prussia. By that time, the armistice was only two months away, and Bryarly was destined to miss the main action even more completely than he had in the Mexican War—which was perhaps fortunate for one who had chosen the losing side. However, the needs of the wounded lasted for many months longer than the war itself, and were no doubt as great within the Russian lines as Florence Nightingale found them among the British. At any event, Bryarly was commissioned at St. Petersburg as a Surgeon with the rank of Major. He served at Odessa, Simperopol, Kichenev, and Ismael, and continued in this service until July, 1856, about five months after the termination of the war. At that time he received his *congé* and returned to the United States.[171]

The veteran of two wars, and an overland journey was, by this time, thirty-six and, one might have supposed, ready to settle at last to the quiet amenities of country life in Maryland. But Bryarly's adventures were not yet ended. He returned with his bride to California, and when that Big Bonanza, the Comstock Lode, brought Virginia City into gaudy life, Bryarly went to live, at least for a time, in that classic mining town.[172]

During this phase of his life, the Civil War had begun. For Bryarly, it must have presented something of a dilemma. His antecedents and his connections identified him with the landowning class in Maryland; his associations had been with the "Chivalry" in California. But, on the other hand, his native state did not secede,

171. The following documents relating to Bryarly's Russian experience are all in possession of the Gittings family: letters to his wife; a letter of Buchanan, Dec. 24, 1855, declaring Bryarly to be the bearer of dispatches to the American legation in Berlin, and bespeaking courtesy for him; and especially, a letter, undated, of Bryarly to Baron Edward de Stockel, Russian Minister to the United States, giving a resumé of his service record in the Russian Army. See also the frontispiece, showing Bryarly in the Russian uniform. The original daguerreotype, also in the possession of the Gittings family, bears on its back, in both French and Russian, the name of the maker, "C. Dauthenday, Rue grandes ecuries, Maison Koschansky, . . . S. Petersbourg."

172. Bryarly's return to the West is shown by a letter of his wife's, from San Francisco, June 19, 1861, and by a photograph of Bryarly made by "Hedger and Noe, photographers, Virginia [City], Nevada," both in possession of the Gittings family. Also by the fact that the obituary notices of Bryarly in the Baltimore papers requested that California and Nevada papers reproduce the notice.

and as for himself, he had scarcely more than visited in the South for the fourteen years prior to the outbreak of the war. So far as the record shows, he remained in the West throughout the conflict. But, at the end, his birthplace claimed him. He returned to Maryland and, while there, was stricken with pneumonia which resulted in his death at his father-in-law's home, ''Roslyn,'' on March 13, 1869.[173] His wife survived him, but he left no children.

In his forty-eight years, Bryarly had accumulated a moderate fortune, enjoyed a successful medical career, and cultivated the bearing of a member of the Maryland gentry.[174] Moreover, he had lived life to the full. As a volunteer on the plains of Mexico, as a Forty-niner on the California Trail, as a soldier of fortune in the Crimea, and as a resident of Virginia City at its heyday, he had experienced more than his share of the excitement which the world offered to men of his generation.

Meanwhile, life had dealt more harshly with Vincent Geiger, primarily because he had been drawn steadily deeper into the bitter factional fight which was the extension into California of the political and military conflict between North and South. As a Virginian, Geiger had promptly associated himself with the ''Chivalry'' Democrats, of whom his friend Washington was a leader. Where Bryarly had remained an individualist, enjoying cordial relations with this group, Geiger became a staunch political henchman.

For a time he operated as a trader living in Sacramento and as a lawyer in Shasta City,[175] but his first partisan activity came at the time when the state legislature first met at Sacramento in 1852. The new seat of government already had a Democratic newspaper in the *Placer Times and Transcript*, operated by George K. Fitch, but some of the ''Chivalry'' must either have doubted Fitch's orthodoxy or

173. Obituaries in Baltimore *American and Commercial Advertiser* and Baltimore *Sun*, Mar. 15, 1869; tombstone in Greenmount Cemetery, Baltimore. Mr. Marye has kindly checked these sources for me.

174. Letter of D. Sterett Gittings to the editor, Feb. 15, 1944.

175. The *Sacramento City Directory*, 1851, lists Geiger as a trader, with residence at the Missouri Hotel. For this and other reference to California newspapers and directories I am indebted to Miss Mabel E. Gillis of the California State Library.

W. P. Dangerfield & V. E. Geiger, attorneys at law, Shasta City, Shasta County, Cal., were advertised in the Sacramento *Placer Times and Transcript*, Sep. 24, 1851, as quoted in Mae Hélène Bacon Boggs, *My Playhouse was a Concord Coach* (Oakland, 1942), p. 100. Also see account of a trial in which Geiger was counsel, p. 112.

coveted his potential monopoly of state printing, for a rival printing establishment was organized under the name of V. E. Geiger
and Company. From this press, a new daily, the *Democratic State
Journal* began to appear in February, 1852, with Geiger and B. F.
Washington as co-editors.[176]

The new paper appeared in time to welcome the new legislature,
to support the Democratic candidates for Governor and President—
and to bid for the lucrative state-printing contracts. Fitch, of the
Placer Times, of course resented the competition of his new rival,
and a bitter contest resulted. Feelings ran high and personalities
were exchanged, in the course of which the *Times* spoke of Geiger
as a "spunger." This touched off a scene in which the two editors
came to blows in the hall of the State House.[177] Here Geiger gave
evidence of the quick and violent temper that was later to ruin him,
but this particular episode was patched up. Democrats in general
were resolved not to lose the support of either of the two papers, and
consequently, a settlement was brought about, whereby the *State
Journal* paid the *Placer Times* the sum of $3,000 to remove to San
Francisco.[178] The bargain was apparently sealed by the association
of Fitch and Geiger and the award to them jointly of contracts for
the state printing.[179]

However, Geiger did not long enjoy this lucrative position. In
November, 1852, a fire destroyed the offices of the *State Journal,*[180]
and in the following February, Geiger and Fitch assigned their
printing contracts to a third party.[181] About this time, Washington
left to join the staff of the *Placer Times,* and a new co-editor replaced him. In the following summer, the *State Journal* was sold to
the owners of another paper, the *Californian,* for $15,000, but it
is unlikely that this sum was free of debt, or that Geiger received
much of it.[182] After scarcely more than a year, his newspaper career

---

176. [Edward C. Kemble], *A History of California Newspapers* . . . edited
with an introduction by Douglas C. McMurtrie (New York, 1927; originally
written in 1858), p. 154; John Denton Carter, "George Kenyon Fitch, Pioneer
California Journalist" in *California Historical Society Quarterly,* XX (1941),
334.

177. Carter, in *Cal. Hist. Soc. Quart.,* XX, 334.

178. *Ibid.* p. 334; [Kemble], *Hist. of Cal. Newspapers,* p. 154, names $6000 as
the amount paid to Fitch.

179. Theodore H. Hittell, *History of California* (San Francisco, 1898), IV,
162.

180. [Kemble], *Hist. of Cal. Newspapers,* p. 154.

181. Hittell, *Hist. of Cal.,* IV, 162.

182. [Kemble], *Hist. of Cal. Newspapers,* p. 155.

was unsuccessfully ended, though he continued to operate a printing office in Sacramento.[183]

Meanwhile, he had participated regularly in party councils. The State Democratic Conventions of 1854 and 1855 both placed him on the State Committee, though the latter convention nominated another candidate over him for the office of state printer. Again in 1857, he was placed on the State Committee and became its chairman.[184] It was a propitious time for a member of the "Chivalry" group, for, in that year James Buchanan became President, and the Southern faction found the entire Federal patronage opened to them. B. F. Washington received the prize appointment as Collector of the Port of San Francisco, and Geiger, upon the recommendation of Washington, was named Indian Agent and assigned to the Nome Lackee Reservation at a salary of $3,000 a year.[185] The Nome Lackee Reservation was situated in Tehama County in northern California, and Geiger therefore moved his residence to the little town of Red Bluff, in that county. He continued to live there during the next six years, and during Buchanan's Presidency he retained his post at the Reservation[186] and continued active in party affairs.

183. The Sacramento City Directory, 1856, lists Geiger as a printer, unmarried, with rooms in the Tehama Building, at Front and J. Streets. For 1857–1858, he is listed with address the Orleans Hotel.

184. Winfield J. Davis, *History of the Political Conventions in California, 1849–1892* (Sacramento, 1893), pp. 31, 42, 77, 79, 88.

185. Records of the office of the Secretary of the Interior and of the office of Indian Affairs, in the National Archives; *Register of Officers and Agents, Civil, Military, and Naval in the Service of the United States on the thirtieth September, 1859,* p. 95.

186. Previously, Geiger had been employed as Special Indian Agent and assistant to Thomas I. Henley, Superintendent of Indian Affairs for California. At that time, he had served from Sep. 1 to Dec. 31, 1855. During Buchanan's administration, he was commissioned as Indian Agent for California on Apr. 11, 1857, and reappointed Mar. 3, 1858. Instructions for the termination of his service were contained in a letter of the Commissioner of Indian Affairs to the Superintending Agent of the Northern Indian District of California, July 30, 1860. This letter explained that the discharge of Geiger and other agents was ordered in pursuance of the repeal of the law under which they had been appointed. (Records of the Office of the Secretary of the Interior and of the Office of Indian Affairs, in the National Archives). However, he must not have been removed at all promptly for he was still at the Nome Lackee Reservation on June 10, 1861 (*Report of the Commissioner of Indian Affairs accompanying the Annual Report of the Secretary of the Interior for the Year 1861* [Washington, 1861], p. 147). For Geiger's reports as Indian Agent, see the *Reports of the Commissioner of Indian Affairs for 1857* (pp. 392–393), *1858* (pp. 288–290), and *1859* (pp. 438–441). For further material on Geiger as agent, or on the Nome Lackee Reservation, or both, see San Francisco *Alta*

In 1858, he was superseded as Democratic State Chairman, but he remained a State Committeeman for another year. An effort to win the nomination for a seat in Congress failed in 1859, but in 1860 he was named to run as a presidential elector on the Breckinridge ticket.[187]

That was his last success. Breckinridge failed to carry California,[188] and, worse by far for Geiger, the election of Lincoln destroyed any prospect of his continuing to hold Federal office. His most hated political adversaries, the "Black" Republicans, were now in power, and within a few months, the bitter hostility of the sections had reached its culmination in the Civil War.

Following these reverses, Geiger's ruin began to approach with the inevitability of Greek tragedy. Once before, when he and Fitch came to blows in the State House, a violent streak in his nature had cropped out. It is not likely that this quality had been inhibited subsequently, for Geiger lived in violent times among violent men. The "Chivalry" maintained their hair-trigger honor with hair-trigger arms, and the formal duel flourished. Oftentimes, impulsive spirits waived the formality and resorted to impromptu gunplay. In fact, chronic violence characterized this "dark period" of "moral, political, and financial night," as Bancroft has called it, and all factions were quick to resort to weapons. The most famous of these episodes was the duel in which Judge Terry of the California Supreme Court killed Senator David Broderick in 1859, but there were many others. Broderick himself, although lamented as a martyr, had previously assaulted a newspaper reporter, fought a duel with Caleb B. Smith, and promoted a duel between City Alderman John Cotter of San Francisco and John Nugent, editor of the San Francisco *Herald*.[189] George Pen Johnston, clerk of the United States Circuit Court, had killed State Senator William Ferguson with a pistol at six paces in 1858; Assemblyman Daniel Showalter had killed the *pro tempore* speaker of the Assembly, Charles W. Piercy, with a rifle at forty paces in 1861; Senator Gwin himself

---

California, May 28, 1858; Red Bluff *Beacon*, Apr. 3 and Oct. 23, 1862 (citations furnished by Cal. State Library); and Alban Hoopes, *Indian Affairs and their Administration with Special Reference to the Far West, 1849–1860* (Philadelphia, 1932), pp. 57–58. The records of the Office of Indian Affairs, in the National Archives, contain seven routine letters by Geiger.

187. Davis, *Hist. of Political Conventions*, pp. 88, 104, 111, 112, 123.
188. *Ibid.*, p. 127.
189. Bancroft, *Hist. of Cal.*, VI, 661; Hittell, *Hist. of Cal.*, IV, 143, 220–221.

had fought a duel with Joseph W. McCorkle.[190] Amid these circumstances, Geiger had certainly not been an aloof or disapproving spectator, for his friend Benjamin F. Washington had wounded Charles A. Washburn of the *Alta California* in a duel with rifles in 1854,[191] and Geiger himself had acted as second to Secretary of State James W. Denver in a duel in which his principal killed Edward Gilbert, ex-Congressman and editor of the *Alta*.[192]

While the leaders of the State had set the pattern of killing according to the code, less prominent persons gave themselves to less genteel homicide. The extent of this practice defies enumeration, but Bancroft accepted the estimate that 4,200 murders were committed in California in the years 1849 to 1854 inclusive, and that 1,200 murders in San Francisco were punished by one conviction.[193]

Even before war broke out, frontier violence, superimposed upon sectional hatred, had produced almost blood lust. With the beginning of hostilities in 1861, bitterness became even more intense, and may even have reached its apogee in California, because there men could not find, on the battlefield, a catharsis for their hatred, as they could in the East. Great numbers of Confederate sympathizers enrolled as Knights of the Golden Circle, and for a time they waited hopefully for an invasion which Senator Gwin was expected to lead northward from Sonora to unite California with the Confederacy.[194] But the invasion did not come, a separate Pacific republic did not materialize, and almost from the beginning, events went against the Southern faction. In March, 1861, the legislature, by a vote of 40 to 32, passed a resolution declaring secession to be treasonable. In October, Leland Stanford, running on the Republican ticket, was elected Governor of California, and a decade of Democratic control came to an end; at the same time, Senator Gwin was arrested in Panama and held for a time in prison. Soon, the

190. Bancroft, *Hist. of Cal.*, VI, 729; Hittell, *Hist. of Cal.*, IV, 221, 246–247, 279; Franklin Tuthill, *The History of California* (San Francisco, 1866), pp. 569–570.

191. Oscar T. Shuck, *History of the Bench and Bar of California* (Los Angeles, 1901), p. 412; Hittell, *Hist. of Cal.*, IV, 221. Washington was also said to have shot and killed John Maloney, leader of riots by the Squatters in Sacramento. *Ibid.*, III, 675.

192. *History of Sacramento County* (Thompson and West, pub., 1880), p. 213; Bancroft, *Hist. of Cal.*, VI, 687.

193. Bancroft, *Hist. of Cal.*, VII, 215, 191–219.

194. Benjamin Franklin Gilbert, ''The Confederate Minority in California,'' in *California Historical Society Quarterly*, XX (1941), 154–170.

only consolations for the Chivalry were the periodic reports of Confederate victories on the Virginia battlefront. Stonewall Jackson, in 1862, conducted some of his most brilliant operations only a short distance north of Geiger's boyhood home. Geiger, meanwhile, in Tehama County, California, could find release for his frustration and bitterness only by service to the Democratic Party. He served again as a member of the Democratic State Committee in 1861 and 1862, and he addressed the Democrats of Red Bluff in August, 1862.[195] On July 1, 1863, the Red Bluff *Beacon* reported his activity in another Democratic Convention. But on that very day, Lee's army faced Meade's south of Gettysburg, while Grant and starvation closed in upon Vicksburg. After that, there was no more news of Confederate victories to console Southern sympathizers in California, and they must have found that the gibes of the Unionists stung as never before.

Three months later, in October, 1863, the Red Bluff *Beacon* recorded, under the heading "A Dreadful Affair," the dénouement for one of the Chivalry. This account, with its circumspect allusion to "two groups of men" and with its anatomical particularity, typifies early Western journalism and therefore partakes of the quality of the violent Western episode which it describes. The crucial event in the life of Geiger should stand, therefore, in the language in which a pioneer editor stated it:

It is our painful duty to record a dreadful affray which occurred in front of the Magnolia Saloon last Wednesday night, a little after ten o'clock, between Vincent E. Geiger and Capt. A. S. Wells, of Shasta county. Both parties were seated on the pavement near the entrance of the saloon, talking. There were two groups of men seated there, Capt. Wells sitting with one group and Mr. Geiger with the other. The latter made some remark concerning Rosecrans' army, and the former replied to it. The remark was repeated, and Mr. Geiger staggered toward where Capt. Wells was sitting, and either slapped him or hit him with his fist. A scuffle ensued between the parties, and Capt. Wells held Mr. Geiger's head under his arm, hitting him repeatedly in the face. It is supposed that it was at this time Mr. G. drew his knife and stabbed Capt. Wells in the right breast about one inch below the nipple. They were still scuffling when they were separated. It was not known that the unfortunate man had been cut until he went into the saloon and was leaning upon the counter. Blood was noticed about that time, and he was taken by the arm by Mr. Riley

---

195. Davis, *History of Political Conventions*, pp. 173, 191; Red Bluff *Beacon*, Sep. 12, 1861, and Aug. 9, 1862.

and Mr. ——, in order to be put in bed at the Luna House. After walking out on the pavement he suddenly fell from loss of blood. He was removed as soon as something could be got to place under him, back into the saloon, and from there into the adjoining building, formerly used by Pierce, Church & Co. as a store. He is in a very critical condition, with scarcely any probability of recovery. Mr. Geiger disappeared about five minutes after the cutting took place, and has not been heard of since. At the time the affray took place Mr. Geiger was badly intoxicated. Capt. Wells had also been drinking freely, but was not intoxicated. The wounded man was a peaceable, kind-hearted and law-abiding man, and a good citizen and neighbor.

P.S.—Since writing the above we learn that Captain Wells died at half past 2 o'clock yesterday afternoon. His funeral will take place today at 4 o'clock, under the direction of the Red Bluff Lodge of Odd Fellows. That body will meet at their hall at 3 o'clock precisely.[196]

Where did Geiger disappear to "about five minutes after the cutting took place"? This the record has not disclosed, and probably it never will. But California was a poor locality in which to stand trial in 1863 for killing a Unionist. Therefore, six years of Geiger's life must be left blank. But in 1869, the year of Bryarly's death and also the year when the transcontinental railroad ended an epoch in the history of the West, the record was resumed—and terminated. On October 15, 1869, the United States Consul at Valparaiso, Chile, sent a dispatch to the State Department from his remote diplomatic outpost. In it, he reported, with no word of comment, that Vincent E. Geiger had died at Valparaiso on September 6.[197]

---

196. Red Bluff *Beacon*, Oct. 17, 1863. Another account of the killing appeared in the Red Bluff *Independent*, Oct. 16, and was copied by the Sacramento *Union*, Oct. 19. This second account is less detailed than the first, and, for the most part, is consistent with it. It adds that "a warrant was issued by Justice Gage on the night of the attempted homicide, for the arrest of Geiger, but up to the present time little has been effected toward his arrest." The Sacramento *Union*, Oct. 20, reported Wells' death, and noted that Geiger was said to have been praising General Bragg when his quarrel with Wells began.

197. Report of John C. Caldwell, U. S. Consul at Valparaiso to the Department of State, Oct. 15, 1869, in the National Archives. On Dec. 8, following, the Department of State requested the Stockton (Cal.) *Independent* to publish notice of Geiger's death—letter in National Archives. The Sacramento *Union*, Dec. 18, 1869, reported the death, and commented that, "Geiger, some years ago killed a man at Red Bluff, and has since been a fugitive from justice."

JOURNAL
OF THE ROUTE OF THE CHARLESTOWN, VIRGINIA, MINING COMPANY FROM ST. JOSEPH, MISSOURI, TO CALIFORNIA— FRANK SMITH AS GUIDE

I ST. JOSEPH TO FORT KEARNEY

IN setting out on their overland journey, the Forty-niners did not blaze a new trail, distinctly their own. Instead they followed the route originally established by the Oregon pioneers of a few years earlier, and known to history as the Oregon Trail. Not until they reached what is now the state of Idaho did most of them strike off on a diverging road to California.

To understand the route followed by the Oregon Trail, it is necessary to understand that the point of departure was determined by an historical development—namely the growth of Independence, Missouri, as an outfitting post for the Santa Fé trade, for which it was perfectly located—while the roadway itself was determined by a geographical factor—namely the manner in which the affluents of the Platte extended to the very foot of the South Pass. The point of departure, therefore was not located at the mouth of the Platte, as it logically might have been. To meet this discrepancy, two adjustments were made: first, outfitting towns, such as Westport and St. Joseph, developed further up the Missouri, and therefore nearer the Platte; second, a trail was established which crossed over from the valley of the Kansas, traversed some minor watersheds, and finally reached the south bank of the Platte.

The Charlestown Company, leaving from St. Joe, followed a route which led due west along the ridges as far as possible, avoiding any important watershed until, after nearly a hundred miles, it struck the valley of the Big Blue, a tributary of the Kansas, flowing southward from what is now southeastern Nebraska. A few miles beyond this crossing, the St. Joe road met and entered the road from Independence, which was the Oregon Trail proper. After a few miles more, the road reached the Little Blue, a tributary of the Big Blue, flowing southeastwardly. This stream offered an ideal transit toward the valley of the Platte, for its headwaters were within an easy day's march of the larger stream, and emigrants could go from one to the other without suffering from lack of water. Further, the northwestwardly direction up the valley was economical of distance. Therefore, the trail followed the Little Blue across what is now the Kansas-Nebraska line, and then, crossing a ridge, descended to the Platte, whose watercourse it would follow longer than any other stream. Near the point where they reached the river, emigrants found a military post, Fort Kearney, which afforded protection from the Plains Indians. Their arrival there, after 275 miles of travel, meant that they had completed the "shaking down" process, and were, to some degree, adapted to the regimen of the trail.

For the Charlestown Company, this first stage of the journey took nineteen days (May 10–May 28).

Thursday, May 10th, 1849.[1]

LEFT our encampment on the west bank of the Missouri River opposite St. Joseph's and with seven of our wagons encamped about 7 miles from the river at a place called the Bluffs.

Friday, May 11th.

The remainder of our wagons & mules got into camp today, together with a lot brought from below by John Moore, Jr. & [Frank] Smith.[2]

Saturday, May 12th.

Left encampment at the Bluffs with our 16 wagons and travelled over the raising ground of the pararie about 8

---

1. The diary from this date until June 23, except for part of June 5, was written by Geiger; thereafter, it was kept by Bryarly. Prior to the departure of the company from St. Joseph, Geiger had kept a brief daily record of his trip west from Virginia, during which trip he was travelling in advance of the main body of the company. This preliminary diary is given in full in Appendix C.

2. The complete roster of members of the Charlestown Company is given in Appendix B. All persons mentioned in the text are also listed in the index, and wherever additional information is available by means of cross reference, it is indicated there. Footnotes of cross reference are therefore omitted.

miles and encamped at a spring called by us "Branding Spring," from the fact that on the next day we branded our mules with the initials V. C. [Virginia Company]. I neglected to mention that on our way from the last camp several of our men took "flights of [f] ground and lofty tumblings" off mules' backs. Capt. Keeling took a "high fall" from an old white mule, and a man by the name of Miller was thrown "Hell, west & crooked."[3]   [*Distance, 8 miles.*

Sunday, May 13th.

At camp. Remained there over day & branded our mules.

Monday, May 14th.

Left camp at about 8 o'clock A.M. The rain fell in torrents & continued for several hours. At about 4 o'clock we came to Spider Creek, a very small stream but an excessively bad crossing. In the forks of a tree on the bank of this stream, about 30 feet high, there is a coffin containing the bones, beads &c. of an old Indian Chief who died about 4 years ago. He was of the Iowa tribe. I got a bead from the box.[4] One of the wagons broke down—the axle tree. Reached camp at sundown, at a small spring.
       [*Distance from the last camp, about 9 miles.*

Tuesday, May 15th.

Laid up today until about 11 o'clock A.M. to repair the wagon that was broke[n] on yesterday. The country continues to be beautiful. Grass, water, & wood plenty. Passed

3. A number of diarists speak of injuries resulting from men being thrown by mules or horses: Badman, May 9; Hale, June 1; Johnston, Apr. 17, 27; Lewis, May 14; Long, June 11; McCoy, June 22; Searls, May 9; Sedgley, Apr. 24, 25, 26. For discussion and other references, see above, p. 34.

4. The placing of the dead on scaffolds or in trees was a form of "burial" practiced by the Sioux, Chippewa, Arapaho, and other Indians, from Wisconsin westward, and it appears to have been motivated by the desire to protect the dead from the ravages of wild animals. See H. C. Yarrow, *Introduction to the Study of Mortuary Customs among the North American Indians* (Washington, 1880). Many diarists commented, with amazement, upon this practice. See S. B. F. Clark, May 9; Foster, June 15; Johnston, May 21; Kelly, p. 130; McCall, June 10; Pleasants, p. 62; Searls, June 18, 19; Swain, June 27; Tiffany, May 3, 31; Wistar, June 18.

several emigrant camps & met a number on their way back. Crossed Wolf Creek[5] & had to pull our teams out with ropes. Visited several Indian lodges belonging to the Iowas & met a Chief of that tribe who was one of the noblest looking men I ever saw. The *Sacs* presented a bill for wood which was paid.[6] Some were painted greene &c. They presented a wretched appearance.[7] Saw but one good looking squaw. Encamped for the night near the Indian Station. A farm is here cultivated &c. under charge of Col. Vaguhn, at Government expense.[8] I have been very sick for two days. Diaheria prevails alarmingly in camp.

I learn from B. F. Washington, Esq., who visited the mission, that he witnessed an examination of a school of about 40 young Indians at the station. They sung many very pretty songs & gave indications of great advancement. He was also shown a *wolf skin* taken near the station, which was as large as that of a common sized buffalo skin. It was used as a cloak. Everything about the farm & house looked well. The schoolhouse is of brick & about 70 feet long, with a stone foundation. Mr. D. Cockrell came across an Indian grave the first day's drive from the Bluffs, in which the Indian

5. Wolf Creek, a tributary of the Missouri, was crossed by the trail from St. Joseph in what is now Doniphan County, Kan.

6. Since the emigrants were using wood from land which had been set apart for the Sacs, the Indian agent for this tribe had given them a paper which requested emigrants to make a small present for the use of the wood. Journal of Major Osborne Cross, May 22, 1849, in Raymond W. Settle, ed., *The March of the Mounted Riflemen* (Glendale, Cal., 1940), pp. 40–41.

7. The Sauks or Sacs were a tribe of Algonquian stock, originally living in the Michigan area. Later uniting with the Fox Indians, they were driven westward from successive points by the advancing whites. After their defeat under Black Hawk, they retired to Iowa, and thence into Kansas. The Iowas were a tribe of Siouian stock. After being pushed west from the Illinois region, they had, in 1824, ceded all their land in Missouri, and in 1836 they were assigned to the Great Nemaha Agency in northeastern Kansas.

8. Col. Alfred J. Vaughan was Indian sub-agent for the Great Nemaha Reservation of Iowa, and Sauk and Fox Indians. This reservation was situated on the emigrant road some twenty-six miles northwest of St. Joseph, and had been established in 1837. In connection with the reservation, the Presbyterian Board of Foreign Missions had established a mission and school in 1837, and this was the school which Washington visited. See Vaughan's report in the *Annual Report of the Commissioner for Indian Affairs* for 1849, pp. 1081–1085. Also see Pryor Plank, ''The Iowa, Sac and Fox Mission and its Missionaries . . .'' in Kansas State Historical Society, *Transactions*, X (1908), 312–325.

was placed in a sitting posture covered with his blanket &
decked with the fantastic ornaments he wore whilst living.

Today we helped to pull out an ox-team. The emigrants
were very grateful & *treated* liber[al]ly with their whiskey.

[*Distance, about 8 miles.*]

Wednesday, May 16th.

Got off about 7 o'clock A.M. & pursued the ridge & rolling
country, the grass good. Passed several detachments of
Government troops & wagons on their way to California &
Oregon. The guide of the Government train, a Mr. Hendrick,
was shot by an Indian the day before—severely but not
dangerously wounded. Continued to catch up and pass emigrants. Got to camp about 4 o'clock P.M. Scarce of wood &
water.

An Iowa Chief, some squaws & two boys visited our camp.
The Chief had seven *wifes, much* children. The boys shot
well with bow & arrow. Our mess fed them, for which they
seemed little thankful.

About 9 o'clock at night we were visited by a perfect
shower of *bugs*. The air was filled with them & they fell like
hail on our tents. The mules became frightened & the men
were compelled to go out & hold them to prevent their escape.
It appeared to me that there were millions of them. About
12 o'clock they settled on the ground & tents & everything
was black with them. The next morning we had to shake them
off our blankets. The bugs were about the size of a June-bug,
of a dark brown color & rather redish on the belly. They appeared to be perfectly harmless.[9]

[*Distance, about 15 miles.*]

Thursday, May 17th.

Made pretty early start this morning. Continued to
wind around the ridges. Had some very hard pulls. Passed
several graves where emigrants had been buried in the last

9. McIlhany, *Recollections*, p. 22, also speaks of the mules being stampeded
by "thousands and millions of bugs, covering the ground entirely." From the
description it would appear that the insects were some form of May beetles.
Searls, June 4, noted, "tormented by clouds of beetles."

few days. Great deal of clothing, boxes &c., lying on the road side. From every camp we hear of sickness. Camped about 5 o'clock P.M. Wood & water scarce. Grass good.

[*Distance, not stated.*

Friday, May 18th.

Rather late leaving camp and were detained some time by the sticking of several of our teams near the camp. Had a very good road. Came to Chickawau Creek about 2 o'clock P.M. A beautiful stream of clear water. The crossing is very difficult. We had to let the wagons down by ropes. Large trees are on the bank of the stream & beautiful flats are contiguous. We caught a fine turtle & had a pot of good soup.[10] No wood at our camp.   [*Distance, about 17 miles.*

Saturday, May 19th.

Left early. A beautiful morning. Passed over a rolling country. Today we saw a grave in which three emigrants are burried who died with cholera in 10 hours after they were taken. Every day we have passed fresh made graves containing the remains of poor emigrants who have died with cholera on their way to the golden land.[11] Today, as well as yesterday, we had to gather wood and water before we reached camp. We got to our camp ground, which is destitute of wood & water, and labored hard until after dark. Today we passed a great many emigrants.   [*Distance, 27 miles.*

10. Kelly, p. 93, describes a large turtle, ''weighing nearly one hundred weight,'' which was taken by his party in the Little Blue River, not more than two days journey away from the point where Geiger's turtle was caught. Searls, May 26, and Sedgley, June 8, mentioned capturing, ''a huge turtle'' and ''a large turtle,'' respectively, in this same region.

11. Nearly all diarists were impressed and dejected by the hastily prepared graves which, in some cases, lined the trail. Wistar, May 7, noted, ''There is quite a populous graveyard at the crossing of the Blue.'' On the incidence and principal causes of mortalities, see above, pp. 55–61. McIlhany, *Recollections*, p. 21, said, ''Nearly every day we saw graves on the road. At each place there was a path running out diagonally from the trail. It was made by people going out to see who was buried there, and then another diagonal path came out to the road further on.''

Sunday, May 20th.

We were rather late out of camp today, owing to difficulty in catching the mules. It rained today. We came to the Little Blue & crossed above the regular ford. It seems but a branch. About two miles from the Little Blue we came to the Big Blue.[12] This is a stream of beautiful, clear water and is very palatable to a thirsty man. The stream is about 40 yards wide, deep enough to touch the wagon beds, but is neither swift or rough. On either side the banks are rather steep. About an hour before reaching this water one of our wagons upset, smashing the bows but doing no other damage. Two of our men were in it but escaped with little damage. Near this river we found the lava or rocks formed by some volcanic eruption. The ground was covered with the rocks. From St. Joseph to this place the road is good & easily found—plenty of wood, grass & water. The camps have no names but those given them by each emigrant party.

We got into camp 2 miles from the Big Blue[13] about 4 o'clock P.M. and commenced lightening our loads. We threw away a large lot of horse shoes, all the boxes, lard & many other things. We are now fairly on the road. Many are complaining and if chance offered would like much to return. We have been vexed & delayed. Our teams are young & unbroke & the men do not feel as much interest as was to be expected. Our company is too large. The country is not so

12. Geiger's nomenclature is confusing, but an analysis based on maps and contemporary journals makes his meaning and his actual route clear. What he calls the Little Blue could not have been that stream, for the Little Blue lies to the west of the Big Blue, which the company had not yet crossed. Probably Geiger's ''Little Blue'' was a minor tributary of the Big Blue. He appears to be correct in calling the next stream the Big Blue. However, when he reached the actual Little Blue, he had wrongly applied its true name to another stream, and he therefore called it the Republican Fork. This suggests that he may have used Joel Palmer's *Journal of Travels over the Rocky Mountains* (Cincinnati, 1847), for Palmer had also called it the Republican Fork (Reuben G. Thwaites, *Early Western Travels* [Cleveland, 1904–1907], XXX, 45). This does not mean that they mistook the ''Republican Fork'' for the larger Republican River which lies farther west, but that both streams ran through the territory of the Republican Pawnees. This tribe had probably taken their name from the larger stream, but gave it, in turn, to the smaller.

13. The Big Blue flows south from southeastern Nebraska, across northeastern Kansas, and into the Kansas River. The St. Joseph road intersected this stream near what it now Marysville, Marshall County, Kansas.

much rolling—more plain. We are about 1 mile from the Big Blue. [*Distance, about 12 miles.*

Monday, May 21st.

An early start gave us a good march today. Just as we drove out from camp, Comegys broke a fore-wheel to his wagon, but as we had saved one from the destruction of yesterday it delayed us but little. In nine miles from camp we struck the Independence Trail and fell in with a Missouri Company, of 40 wagons & 130 men. Passed them. Water has been scarce—mostly in puddles. Left the Little Sandy to the right & after some 8 or 10 miles struck the *Forks* of the *Republican Fork.*[14] All the trees & hollows here indicate the Forks. Tonight we encamp on one of the forks. Water good, & wood & grass plenty. We have been ascending all day.

This morning we put our arms in order & made every precaution against the Indians. We are now in the Pawnee country—the most hostile of the tribes.[15] There are two other parties encamped in sight. Rumors reached us of a fight between the Pawnees & emigrants some distance [in] advance.[16] An express has been sent for U. S. troops. We chased a wolf today but did not catch him. This has been a hard day's drive.

Some rain fell. There has been so far a stiff breeze on the plains every day. The stream on which we are encamped is Timber Creek. From the junction of the Independence & St. Jo roads, water is scarce. A cut-off of two or three miles can be made by keeping every left hand road.

[*Distance, 26 miles.*

14. Actually, the Little Blue (see note 12, above). This stream rises in southeastern Nebraska and flows in a southeasterly direction emptying into the Big Blue in Marshall County, Kansas. The emigrant trail, having crossed the Big Blue north of this confluence, moved up the north side of the valley of the Little Blue for about 60 miles into southeastern Nebraska.

15. The Pawnees, a major tribe of plains Indians of Cadoan stock, lived primarily in the valley of the Platte. The emigrants feared them for their warlike and "murderous" disposition. See McCoy, June 6; DeWolf, June 13, 17; Long, May 11; Wistar, May 27; Kelly, p. 63; Hackney, May 18.

16. On the incessant and usually baseless rumors of Indian hostility, see above, pp. 57–58.

Tuesday, May 22nd.

Rather late in starting this morning. About a mile from camp we crossed Timber Creek—a deep & bad crossing. We were fortunate enough in getting in ahead of 50 or 60 ox-teams. We were detained this morning by the splintering of Tavener's wagon tongue. We passed some ox-teams and fell in with a train of 200 wagons which we attempted to pass, but they drove up and we had to relinquish the attempt. At one time there was in view at least 400 wagons. The wind blew very hard all day and the dust was almost unsuportable. The road was hilly & rough, and our stock much fatigued. We went into camp about 4 o'clock P.M. after traveling about 18 miles. To-day we gathered wood & water, but as we found later, it was labor lost.

A few minutes before sundown, Joseph C. Young, of Montgomery County, Maryland, a member of our company, died of typhoid fever.[17]   [*Distance, 18 miles.*

Wednesday, May 23rd.

The clear & shrill voice of our guide roused us early and we prepared for a start. At sunrise the remains of our late comrade, Young, was interred. He was wrapped in his blanket. Without shroud, sheet or coffin, he was laid in the silent grave. He was buried on a hill, commanding a beautiful country. After the performance of this sad duty we started on our march.

A drive of 10 miles brought us to the Big Sandy River. The water is low, dark & of bad taste. The banks are covered with sand. The crossing is good. Here we took in wood & water and after a drive of five miles, halted & put our mules out to feed. This is the *Dry Sandy* & dry enough it is. No water or wood. Remained here until about 4 o'clock P.M. and then started out. In five miles we crossed the Little Sandy, a small & partly dry stream.[18] Passing on five miles we struck

17. On the death of Young, see above, p. 56.
18. Big Sandy and Little Sandy Creeks are tributaries of the Little Blue, flowing into the northern side of that stream in what is now Jefferson County, Nebraska. The Dry Sandy does not appear on modern maps, but its arid condition invites a comparison with Badman's comment, June 23, on Rawhide

the main Republican Fork, and went into camp about 10 o'clock P.M. This is a beautiful stream of pure, good, cool & clear water. The banks are lined with cotton trees & some oak. Yesterday & today the land is more gravelly & sandy. Slight sprinkle of snow. [*Distance, 25 miles.*

Thursday, May 24th.

Just as we started from camp the rain commenced falling, & by the time we had gone a few miles it fell in torrents accompanied by the most crashing thunder & vivid lightning. We are now on the main Republican Fork, which we will follow for 53 miles. The land is good & looks fit for cultivation. Many knouls [knolls] & ridges line the road. Understanding that an emigrant in the rear was selling his brandy, the Quartermaster sent Bradley, Cunningham, M'Kay, Hayden & myself back to purchase some. We started in the rain & rode back about 10 miles. When we reached the place we found a great number of men around the wagons buying brandy at *Fifty cents* a drink. We were unable to purchase what we wanted at even double price, but after riding in the rain so far, we bought 1 quart of miserable watered stuff called brandy, for which we paid $3.00. At 12 o'clock M. we set out to overtake the train, but did not catch up until near night & found them in camp. The storm continued all day & until 12 o'clock at night. The road has been heavy. I counted 400 wagons on the road behind us yesterday.

A man was shot in one of the companies a few days ago by putting a loaded gun in the wagon.[19] Caution & warning. Two gentlemen stayed with us tonight on their way home. I met some Illinoians on their return. Wrote to Stevenson. Encamped on the Republican Fork. [*Distance, 25 miles.*

Friday, May 25th.

Continued our march along the Republican Fork. The road was very bad owing to the rain of yesterday & last

---

Creek: ''it is no creek at all as there is no water in it, but still there is a good place for one.''

19. On the frequency with which accidental shootings took place, see above, pp. 59–61.

night. We passed only a few ox-teams. At 12 o'clock we laid up to graze our mules, and put in a new tongue to Herbert's wagon. About 3 o'clock we again got in motion and travelled until 6 o'clock P.M. & then halted on the bank of the Fork.

The country has been much the same as that passed over on yesterday. The views from some of the hills have been truly picturesque & magnificent. The Surgeon[20] this morning prescribed *Brandy* and it was readily accepted & partaken of by all. Owing to the bad road we made slow progress. Our mess had a fine supper to-night made of 7 large curlews killed by Mr. Slagle. We also put a tongue to Tavener's wagon tonight. The wind blew strong & cold from the west. This night was excessively cold, equal to our November weather.   [*Distance, 16 miles.*

Saturday, May 26th.

Made a late start this morning & slow progress all day. Very cold but no[t] so cold as yesterday. Rained nearly all day. We headed the Republican Fork in about —[21] miles, then crossed the American Fork, where we had much trouble. Had to fill it up with brush &c. Some St. Louis teams stuck & we pulled them out. Here we gathered wood & filled our water casks, as there is neither until we reach the Platte. About 3 o'clock P.M. we came into camp. Our kind & gentle-

---

20. The surgeon of the company was, of course, Dr. Bryarly. One of the most pronounced features of emigrant travel was the high proportion of companies which included a physician among their personnel. Page, in a letter of May 2, declared, ''the Doctors are more numerously represented among the emigrants in proportion to their number among the inhabitants of the country than in any other part of [the] community. Every company will have one or more.'' Searls, May 12, commenting on the abundance of physicians, said, ''if any suffer from sickness, it will not be for want of medical advisers.'' Mention of company physicians, by the diarists, seems to validate this statement, for they are referred to by: Badman, June 24; Delano, May 26; Dundass, June 4; Johnston, May 25; Love, June 17, Aug. 6; Lyne, June 30; McCall, May 23, June 18, 21; McCoy, May 19; Swain, letter, May 6, diary, May 13, 28; Webster, June 30; Wistar, May 18, 21. The company physician received special inducements to travel with his party. He usually paid no membership fee, and was exempted from routine duties of the camp. Wistar, June 2, speaks of a Dr. Gambel who left his company ''and joined a large ox train led by Capt. Boone of Kentucky, who will exempt him from all work in return for his medical aid.'' Also McCall, June 18, mentions a physician who, ''in consideration of medical and other services, was to be carried through.''

21. The manuscript here contains a blank space.

manly guide, Frank Smith, invited me to supper & served up
a fine dish of bacon & greens.

This evening we had a general meeting of the company,
and by a unanimous vote, we took our Guide in as a full member of our company. Our Captain & Lieutenants then resigned and placed the entire command & supreme control of
our company in the hands of Mr. Smith, and declared him
our leader & Captain. He appeared and, in a suitable manner, thanked the company for what they had done.

Tonight we encamp on a high hill, with good grass. No
wood or water. I have heretofore neglected to mention the
plan taken by emigrants to give their friends information
of their whereabouts. It is done by sticking up notices &
cutting names &c. on trees, buffalo skulls, ox-heads, &c.[22]
Our travel has been over a heavy road & hilly country today.
In dry weather after the passing of the American Fork there
is no water for 27 miles.   [*Distance, 16 miles.*

Sunday, May 27th.

This morning the sun rose gloriously sheding his warm
and genial rays on the earth. It was welcomed by all. The
cold, wet weather had been so disagreeable that we all
dreaded the oncoming day fearing it would be as bad as the
one just passed. Our start was rather late, and the road
heavy. The country is hilly. In a few miles we got in sight of
the Nebraska Bluffs, raising their naked sandy tops high
in the clouds. A great many antelopes made their appearance about 10 o'clock. Some Indians were in pursuit. A
number of our men went in chase but were un[suc]cessful,
the fleet inhabitants of the praries distancing them without
an effort. We passed several pools of water occasioned by
the late rains. About 12 o'clock M. we stopped to graze our
mules.

---

22. Many diarists comment on this practice. Long, May 15, said, "We pass so
many notices of companies ahead that I have ceased to take any more notice
of them. Not a buffalo's skull or Elk's antler along the road but has a notice
of some description on it." Also see McCall, May 19; Delano, June 7; Johnston,
May 10, 11, June 3; and Sedgley, July 17.

At 3 o'clock P.M. we again got in motion, and passed over the bluffs to the valley of the Platte,[23] which is one extended plain as far as the eye can reach. The soil is black & sandy with little grass; it doubtless had been eaten off by the cattle. We follow the curve of the river but not nearer than three miles to the stream. There is no wood to be had, but for the present we have good running water.

Passed a company of U. S. troops and went into camp within six miles of old Fort Childs, now new Fort Kearney.[24] Here it was determined to lighten up our wagons, by selling flour, bacon &c. at the Fort. Very warm during the day, but excessively cold at night, with dew like rain. Just as we cross the bluffs & near the river, the old Ft. Kearney road continues the main trail.   [*Distance, 21 miles.*

Monday, May 28th.

Drove up to the Fort, and succeeded in selling some flour, bacon &c. We abandoned a great deal of plunder, such as picks, hobbles & every article calculated to retard our march.[25] The allowance now is about 100 lbs flour & 50 lbs bacon to a man. Up to yesterday 2500 wagons had passed this point, and at least 200 passed to-day.[26] The Fort is at the head of Grand Island. All the buildings at the Fort are made of Sods taken from the prarie, and look comfortable,

23. The Platte, so named by the French because of its breadth and shallowness, is the largest tributary of the Missouri.

24. Fort Kearney on the Platte, not to be confused with the earlier fort of the same name on the Missouri, was established near Grand Island on the south side of the Platte in 1848 by Lt. W. P. Woodbury. It was intended to provide protection for emigrants and to prevent Indian hostilities, and it remained in use until 1871. Although it was named for Gen. Stephen W. Kearny, the spelling of his name was inadvertently changed.

25. The only other known diary of the Charlestown Company, that of Benjamin Hoffman (in C. H. Ambler, ''West Virginia Forty-Niners,'' in *West Virginia History*, III [1941], 59–75) also speaks of lightening the load at Fort Kearney. For a discussion of overloading, and the consequent abandonment of goods by the emigrants, see above, pp. 30, 49–51.

26. In comparison with this number as of May 28, it is interesting to note that on May 17, Tiffany wrote that about 300 teams had passed Fort Kearney; Henry Page, in a letter of May 24, said that 1980 teams had passed there up to the previous night. On June 14, DeWolf placed the number at 4000, and on June 19, Webster noted that 5400 wagons and 3 pack trains had passed the fort.

reminding me much of a Mexican Rancho.[27] We went into camp today about 4 o'clock, 2 miles west of the Fort. We are now in the Buffalo country and some have been seen. It has been chilly today. I must not neglect to state that the Fort is at the head of Grand Island. After we reached camp a gentleman was offered for membership & rejected.[28] We got 15 gallons of whiskey at the Fort.   [*Distance, 10 miles.*

27. Geiger, it will be remembered, had served in the Mexican War. He alludes to this again on p. 103.

28. This person was probably someone who had left the company with which he started, and was travelling alone, perhaps falling in with first one company, then another. For the methods of company organization, and the changes in personnel which characterized most companies, see above, pp. 37–40.

II FORT KEARNEY TO FORT LARAMIE

HAVING reached the Platte below Fort Kearney, the emigrants could now follow this watercourse and its tributaries, the North Platte and the Sweetwater, all the way to the South Pass. As they started up the Platte, they found the road firm, the ascent gradual, though very steady, and the climate genial save for occasional storms. As yet, the hardships and the monotony were scarcely felt.

The Platte proper traverses what is now central Nebraska, but in the western part of that state, the trail reached the forks of the North and the South Platte. The north branch was the stream to follow, but no crossing was feasible at the junction of the streams. Therefore the trail continued for about sixty miles along the South Platte. There were various crossings, but the Lower California crossing, at what is now Brule, Nebraska, was the favored one, and it was the choice of the Charlestown Company. From there, a twenty-four mile journey led to Ash Hollow, where the trail descended precipitately from high bluffs to the south bank of the North Platte. Again the route lay along a watercourse; it followed the North Platte into what is now Wyoming. At the confluence of Laramie River and the North Platte, the trail reached Fort Laramie. There the emigrants threw away their excess baggage and made preparations for the tough going which lay ahead.

The Charlestown Company spent seventeen days (May 29–June 14) on this stage of their journey.

Tuesday, May 29th.

AN early start & good roads gave us a very fair travel today. Our wagons run much lighter than yesterday. Our course today has been up the Platte River, sometimes just on its banks & then off for several miles. The grass is much better than when we struck the bluffs and [the] land looks much richer. The Platte is about a mile wide, [with] some cotton trees on its banks. We nooned today & again started & went into camp near the river. Hauled wood &

water. This is the first time we have used buffalo chips.[1] They burn well. The team to which I was attached ran off today but done no damage. After a beautiful, clear and pleasant day, at night it clouded up and rain fell in torrents, accompanied by tremendous thunder & forked lightnings.[2] Every person got wet—the men were soaked and their beds & blankets completely saturated.   [*Distance, 27 miles.*]

Wednesday, May 30th.

This morning everything was wet & cold and the clamor was loud for liquor, from all parts of the camp, but the Guard only was furnished, and as I was on last night, of course I got a "horn" and it done me great good.

About 9 o'clock we got off & followed the bluff for several miles. It was cold & windy & frequent showers kept us very disagreeable. We passed a number of wagons & emigrants and found among the later Messrs. Hunter & [*name illegible*], two of my old friends. The ground has been rising. The greater part of the day we were in view of the Platte River with its turbid & slow waters dragging their "lazy length" over its sandy bed, which in many places it is two miles wide, interspersed with many islands, ranging in size from 10 yds, square to 2500 acres. Today we crossed Cotton wood Creek, an affluent of the Platte, the water of which is not very good. At 8 o'clock P.M. we went into camp on the banks of the Platte, with good grass but wood very scarce. Carried wood in my shirt 1/2 mile. Our march today has been hard [due]

1. West of the wooded area, dried buffalo dung, known as buffalo chips or *bois de vache* became the standard fuel. Most diarists commented upon their first experience with this novelty. See Backus, May 28; Badman, June 5; S. B. F. Clark, May 24, 29; Delano, May 18; Hale, May 20; Johnston, May 15; Kelly, pp. 104, 187; McCoy, June 11; Morgan, July 30; Orvis, June 15; Page, letter, May 24; Sedgley, June 16; Swain, June 15; Tiffany, May 22; Webster, June 23; Wistar, June 4. DeWolf, in a letter of June 17, said, "You would laugh, I know, to see me going along with a bag on my back gathering Buffalo dung to cook with, but we have to do it. The darn stuff burns fine in a stove."

2. B. C. Clark, Hale, Hackney, and McCall, who were all within three or four days' distance of the Charlestown Company, all describe this storm in their diaries of May 29, 30, and all describe it as extremely violent. Also, see the diary of Delano, who was less than five days ahead, for May 30, 31. The storms of the Platte valley were more severe than most travellers expected, as witness the statement of Tiffany, May 31: "I thought I had seen windy days in Ioway, but after travelling on the Platte a week or two I am inclined to the belief that 'she ain't nowhere.'"

to late rains making the roads wet & heavy, & fatiguing our stock very much.

I must [not] neglect to mention that tonight I supped with our captain, Smith, who had provided a large share of lamb quarters greens, which we eat with an excellent relish. Emigrants should pay attention to this, and [at] all suitable opportunities look for & prepare these delightful greens. Use vinegar & they are [a] sure preventive for scurvy,[3] & strange as it may seem they check the Diahrea. They are to be found in old carrels [*i.e.,* corrals] & camps, or where there has been buffalo carrels. The buffalo, as I am informed by Capt. Smith, carrel their calves at night & whenever danger threatens, the old ones protect the young & weaker.

[*Distance, 16 miles.*]

Thursday, May 31st.

Early this morning we were aroused and ordered to prepare for march. It was cold & the wind blew strong from the west with a drizzling rain which continued up to 12 o'clock M., when we had turned out to noon & graze our cattle. Today we have passed a government train, escorted by one company, Mounted Rifles, who are on their way to Fort Laramie. Since writing, the Government train has passed & we have exchanged some powder for whiskey—a canister of powder for a canteen of whiskey.

After a rest of a few hours we again "rolled out," but with little progress, and after a drive of a few miles, went into camp near the bank of the river. Our wood consisted of some green bushes cut on the road side. It has been cold & raining.

Messrs. Keeling & Crane, who were herding our mules, inform [us] that on yesterday they passed through a settlement of prarie dogs, and as we are now in the vicinity of the "Dog-town" spoken of by Bryant,[4] it is supposed to be the same. A prarie wezel[5] was killed on yesterday. It was most

---

3. Marcy, *Prairie Traveler*, p. 33, warns emigrants of the necessity of guarding against scurvy.

4. Bryant, *What I Saw*, p. 81, described a "village of prairie dogs." Many diarists mention these animals.

5. *I.e.,* Weasel. The description of this animal would seem to indicate a Thirteen-striped Ground Squirrel (*Citellus Tridecemlineatus*).

beautiful[ly] striped with black & grey, & on the stripes were white spots of regular distance & uniform size. [It was] about the size of a large ground squirrel. Today we met a party of hunters & trappers on their way to the States, well laden with skins.[6]

This evening about sunset a most brilliant rainbow was seen, with its bases resting on either bank of the river, presenting a perfect arch just sufficient to span the river. Water is easily obtained in this valley by digging a few feet. In some places it comes up good & clear, but in the holes today the water was rather brakish. The plains are very soft, the ground cutting easily, & our wagons frequently up to the axle. It is said that so much rain, wind & cold has never been before experienced on this route. Neither the "oldest inhabitant," nor "oldest hunter" have seen the like.[7]

[*Distance, 14 miles.*

Friday, June 1st.

This is a beautiful clear morning. The sun rose warm & good. A strong bracing wind made travel agreeable. Our march continued along the river. The Bluffs are much higher, more naked & rugged. The Bluffs are said to have increased very much in size in the last few years, and it is supposed they were formed by the wind blowing the sand over the plains, making lodgments. A gang of 15 or 20 antelopes were seen today, but too far off to shoot at. At 12 M., we have halted to noon & graze our cattle. Salt & salt-peter have been found along the river banks & pools today.

We have seen very few buffalo, but their trails are found at every step. The reason given for their non-appearance now is that the pools & drains have been filled with water

6. Backus, who arrived at Fort Laramie on the same day as the Charlestown Company, describes meeting this "fur train" on June 1. On the appearance of these trains and the regularity with which travellers met them every year, see Paden, *Wake of the Prairie Schooner*, p. 66.

7. In connection with this heavy rain, note the statement of Delano, p. 236: "In 1849, there was more grass than had ever been known before. Traders who had been in the country fifteen or twenty years assured us that they had never known such a plentiful season, and that grass was then growing in abundance where they never saw any before, and they universally said that had not such been the case, it would have been utterly impossible for such an emigration to get through."

by the late rains, avoiding the necessity of their coming to the river. One of the men has just brought in a Pararie wolf [8] but which looks more like a red fox—the same color, but of larger size than those found in our country. A few miles from where we nooned, we came across a spring of pure, good, cold water, which was relished by our boys in fine style. We here filled our casks & were loath to leave the spot. Wood was procured here, & after a travel of a few miles, we went into camp near the river with good grass for our mules. Dug for & obtained water, but it was rather brakish.

About sun down a small party went to the river on a fishing excursion and, in the course of an hour or two, one of them returned stating that a party of Indians were crossing the river. Immediately all hands were preparing their guns, pistoles &c. to give the red-men a *warm* reception. Capt. Smith with a small party went to the river expecting to encounter the enemy. Sure enough, some objects could be discerned in the river making for the shore. Every man was excited. They fell flat to the ground in order to conceal themselves, the better to give a fire. Every gun was charged & every eye gazed eagerly at the *Indians,* who in a few moments advanced nearer, when, lo, & behold, the Indians proved to be six large elk crossing the river. The men imprudently left their hiding places & drove the elk back— thus losing the chance of a good roast.

It may be well enough [here] to give the way in which wood is procured by the lasso. Take a rope with a slip-knot & throw it over the dead limbs of a tree, or if the limbs are too high, climb up & adjust the rope—then catch hold & it is easily pulled down.   [*Distance, 18 miles.*

Saturday, June 2nd.

Today, we lay up for the purpose of resting our stock, which are much fatigued. There is but little rest, however, for the men. Washing & cooking is the order of the day. These are the *great works,*[9] whilst some are busily engaged

8. The "prairie wolf" of early western travellers was the coyote, as it is now called. Johnston, May 9, spoke of a "coyote or prairie wolf."

9. The importance of washing and cooking came as a revelation to many emigrants, who had thought of the journey in terms of adventure rather than

in writing, reading, cleaning guns, pistols, &c., others shooting at mark, some fishing, & one or two singing & fiddling. We have shod some mules & horses. This morning early, a tremendous large *wolf* passed near our camp, but he escaped the rifles of our marksmen. The day has been pleasant & clear & all look happy & joyful. We have been living high today. Lambs quarter greens, stewed peaches, rice & molasses were served up by every mess. Some have had peach pies.

Whilst our stock were grazing, and some few men reposing about camp, the poetic talent of our President, B. F. Washington, Esq., was brought into play & produced the following beautiful & feeling lines which I have taken the liberty to copy into my book, feeling assured that they will be read with interest & pleasure:

TO MY NATIVE STATE

Virginia, O Virginia, still thy valley fair I see,
While each hour with "weary step & slow" I'm wandering from thee;
As visions of departed years come swiftly o'er my mind,
They bring to me each hallow'd spot which I have left behind.

'Tis not because thy hills are green, thy valleys fair to see,
Thy forests clothed with varied tints & fill'd with harmony,
'Tis not because thy skies are bright as Italy's in hue,
Or on thy distant mountains rests a veil of shadowy blue,

---

of domestic chores. Delano, June 3, wrote, "Rather than have dirty clothes accumulate, I resolved to try my hand at washing. A number of us took our dirty shirts, and going to a pond near by, commenced our laundry manipulations, for the first time in our lives. It was no trouble to throw our clothes into the pond, and rubbing in soap was not much; but when it came to standing bent over half a day, rubbing the clothes in our hands, trying to get out the stains—heigho! 'a change came o'er the spirit of our dreams,' and we thought of our wives and sweethearts at home, and wondered that we were ever dissatisfied with their impatience on a washing day."

James Lyne, in a letter of May 4, wrote, "I have improved in all the arts pertaining to man's vocation, but in sewing, cooking, or washing, must confess myself at fault. I have always been inclined to deride the vocation of ladies until now but must confess it by far the most irksom I have ever tried, and by way of taking lessons in sewing, have often examined your stitches in my work bag. And then, the cooking. I wish you could take supper with me that you might judge & patern from the hardness & durability of our biscuit. I must at some time send you a receipt for making a lasting sort."

'Tis not that thou hast ever been fair Freedom's dwelling place,
Whence warriors brave & statesmen too, a noble lineage trace,
Nor is it that the fire first burned, thy sacred hills upon,
Whose light with hallow'd radience now to all the world hath gone.

Ah no, not these, nor other charms my muse might well proclaim,
Which throws while now I think of thee, a magic round thy name;
There's something more enchanting still that bids my Spirit flee,
O'er all the weary waste of miles betwixt myself & thee.

Just where a smiling landscape looks upon thy mountains blue,
Where met the waters on their way and swept their barriers through,
There dwelt a maid whose sunny face, & soul of guileless love,
Around my youthful heart a chain of sweetest bondage wove.

I woo'd her & I won her & it boots not now to tell,
The shadow after shadow that upon our pathway fell;
We stood beside the alter & the priest pronounced us one,
And I felt that I had all the world in her whom thus I won.

And now four years have nearly passed since on that happy day,
My stormy youth subsided to the peaceful calm of May;
And cherubs two have bless'd my home—as noble boys I ween,
As ever round the alter of domestic love were seen.

And thus I thought my cup of bliss was full & I would glide,
With sweet contentment, peace & love, upon life's onward tide;
But ah! a change came o'er me & I have left my home,
A wanderer to a stranger land, mid howling wastes to roam.

Upon Pacific's distant shores is heard a startling cry,
A sound that wakes the nations up as swift the tidings fly;
An El Dorado of untold wealth—a land whose soil is gold,
Full many a glittering dream of wealth to mortal eyes unfold.

O gold! how mighty is thy sway, how potent is thy rod!
Decrepid age & tender youth acknowledge thee a God;
At thy command the world is sway'd, as on the deep blue sea,
The Storm King rules the elements that roll so restlessly.

And see, the crowd is rushing now across the arid plain,
All urged by different passions on, yet most by thirst of gain;
And I, my home & native state, have left thy genial shade,
To throw my banner to the breeze where wealth, like dreams, is
　　made.

Near the river were picked up a corn mortar, doubtless
left there by the Indians. It was of the size of those used by
country druggists—also, a human skull, and many bones. At
night we had a difficult job in catching & picketing our mules.
For two or three days back the roads have been bad owing to
the late rains. The road near the Bluffs is much better, but
water is scarce. In fact, from where we strike this valley up,
so far wood has been very scarce & the water bad excepting
here [and] there is a small well & occasional spring. Wood
can be obtained from the islands in the river & along its
banks—also in the bluffs, but it is difficult to procure at best.

Sunday, June 3rd.

We made a fair start this morning & soon passed a number of wagons who had got in our advance whilst we [were]
resting on yesterday. Our mules were much refreshed &
strengthened by the rest & "rolled off" with ease & spirit.
The road today has been good, excepting a few deep ravines.
An excellent spring of cold water was found today in a
ravine about 8 miles from our last camp.

An emigrant party on yesterday killed a fine buffalo &
gave chase to a small herd to-day. From several companies
we hear of men missing, who have gone hunting & doubtless
lost their way. Emigrants should be careful in relation to
this, & ought never to lose sight of their trains. Many murders have & doubtless will yet take place from such a cause.
The Indians hide about in the bluffs & ravines and attack
small parties, sometimes killing, and at other times robbing
the prisoners of their guns, clothes &c., and inflicting severe
lashes, [before they have] turned them loose to find their
friends or perish on the wild & desolate plains.[10] At 12

10. Wistar, pp. 66–71, tells an exciting story of riding away from his party,
encountering Indians, and being furiously pursued by them.

o'clock M. we have stopped to noon & graze our cattle. The valley here is very narrow and the grass indifferent.

We nooned today & laid up for five hours and then made a start for a long drive. We came across a good spring & filled up our canteens. Our course has been off near the bluffs. At 11 o'clock P.M., we encamped near a pool of bad water, with indifferent grass, about 6 miles from the crossing of the Platte. Our object in driving after night was to pass the trains who had gotten ahead of us on yesterday. Besides, it was a clear moonlight night & travel [was] more agreeable than during the day.

Dr. Bryarly & myself, being in advance of the train, left the road in search of a Government train to get a ham of bacon. On approaching the river, shouts & huzzas from the emigrants attracted our notice & we dashed to the river, where we found the[m] firing at a large buffalo bull. We took a hand in the sport, & the animal soon fell dead, pierced by about 15 balls. He was very large—1000 lbs. nett—and made the eleventh killed that day on the bottom. He was not fat. After taking enough for our messes, we left for camp and overtook the train, which had halted to repair the tongue of Mr. Moore's wagon, which had been broke. The country looks poor—sandy & arid hills.   [*Distance, 32 miles.*]

Monday, June 4th.

Made a late start. After a drive of a few miles we met a large party of Sioux Indians mounted on ponies—some very fine. Among them were some fine looking men & a few very beautiful young squaws, who would compare in regularity of features & symetry of form, with the most of our ladies. Many [,however,] were almost naked, rather dirty & disgusting. We endeavored to trade for ponies, but they wanted flour, &c., which we could not spare. A number of us obtained mocasins. Some of their garments were most beautiful[ly] & tastefully worked. Many of them had on pants & coats obtained from traders & emigrants. They all ride well & both men & women set astradle of the horse.[11]

---

11. Probably no single community of Indians was mentioned by emigrant diarists more frequently than this assemblage of Sioux near the crossing of the

About 11 o'clock A.M. we reached the river and Capt. Smith halted us about 3 miles from the old ford, which is now washed out and rather dangerous. Capt. Smith & Dr. Bryarly endeavoured to find a safe & suitable ford. They attempted to cross, but when within a hundred yards of the opposite shore, the Captain's horse got into a quicksand by which he was near losing his animal as well as his own life, which determined him to seek for another crossing lower down the stream.[12]

About 2 o'clock P.M. we drove down the river a mile, and commenced crossing. The river was about one mile wide, some places deep & a great portion of the bottom sandy. The large rope was attached to the wagon and the men laid hold and pulled hard. Most of us were stripped off to the shirt & drawers. The water in no place of the ford was above the crotch. Liquor was freely distributed and a few got a little "how come I so"—but it was of great advantage. By sundown we had crossed all our wagons & mules, & went into camp.

To-day's work has been excessively hard & both men & mules were completely worn down. Emigrants should always take the precaution of fording on a horse before driving in their teams. We had no wood and were compelled to use buffalo chips.　　　　　　　　　　　　*[Distance, 11 miles.*

South Platte. See Johnston, May 21; Backus, June 3; Doyle, June 5, 6; Dundass, June 5; Lewis, June 6; Tiffany, May 20; and Wistar, June 7. It is notable that where the emigrants scorned most Indians, they were prone to recognize the Sioux as a little more trustworthy and notably cleaner and handsomer. The women, especially, won admiration. Most lyric of all accounts is that of Kelly, pp. 127–136. Also see Johnston, May 21, and Delano, June 4. Long, May 26, showed mixed impressions: "The women, some of them, are rather good looking, though the majority were old and ugly with their papooses wrapped in their blankets on their backs. The men were very anxious to trade for anything, whiskey in particular. One of them had the impudence, after my giving him a piece of tobacco, to ask me to give him my coat for said piece of tobacco." The Sioux were a confederacy of Plains tribes, extending from Minnesota to Powder River and from the Canadian border to south of the Platte.

12. The general prevalence of quicksand in the streambeds of the Missouri Valley was one of the major hazards of the trail, and it was never safe to attempt a crossing with animals until the ford had been tested. See Marcy, *Prairie Traveler*, pp. 74–75.

Tuesday, June 5th.

Made a good start and travelled with ease. The roads were good. Met with a large party of Sioux Indians, the same we saw on yesterday. Passed through an encampment belonging to them, of 200 lodges made of skins & reeds. We estimated the number of Indians at 1500. The Chief, *Bull Tail*,[13] made his appearance dressed in a most fantastical manner, rather on the military order. They had at least 2000 ponies, and we succeeded in trading for six of them— we exchanged mules. From Capt. Smith's notes, I extract the following:

"To-day we took a farewell view of the south fork of Platte River, and took a northerly direction across the high range of bluffs to the north fork of Platte. Here we saw a large number of buffalo, most of them, however, on the opposite side of the river, and the ford was rather deep to venture after them. Emigrants crossing the South Fork, should keep the dividing ridge for 10 or 15 miles before descending into the valley of the North Fork—distance by this route, about 16 miles. No wood, and water scarce."

This[14] afternoon Doctor Bryarly & our Indefatigable Guide being in advance, were attracted by the sudden appearance & swift foot of two animals coming over the bluffs and descending towards them, which upon approaching was discovered to be a large grey wolf pursuing what they supposed to be a bear. Chase was instantly given, the wolf taking the hint, & prefering the back track while Bruin pursued the even tenor of his way towards the river, it being distant one mile & a half. They gave him chase, not so much to protect him from the wolf as to supply themselves with fresh meat, & soon ascertained it was too fleet of foot & too large for Mr. Bruin.

13. Bull Tail was principal chief of the Brulé Sioux. He had been present at the council held by Col. W. S. Harney with the Sioux near Fort Laramie in 1845, where he spoke for his people. Maj. Osborne Cross, in 1849, mentioned his presence on the Platte, speaking of him as "the celebrated Queue de Boeuf." (Settle, ed., *March of the Mounted Riflemen*, p. 83). Doyle, June 5, also speaks of this chief.

14. The remainder of the entry for June 5, although written in the third person, is in the hand of Dr. Bryarly.

338693

The Doctor with his spirited & blooded horse "John" came in hailing distance of the gentleman first, and not being acquainted with the appearance of the different ages of the "Varmints of the Plains" hesitated some moments before charging upon him, supposing it might perhaps be some animal which would turn the attack upon him. He however, to use his own expression, patted his pet, looked at his revolver, & charged resolutely upon the unknown, firing, which took effect in his ham. Then the excitement commenced, Mr. Bruin having been discovered to be no other than a buffalo calf six months old. Strange to say, although deprived entirely of one leg, he kept up his pace nobly for half a mile, receiving several shots—which disabled him but slightly. The Doctor & his horse, however, seemed to tire of the sport & with mutual feelings dashed upon the tenacious animal & hurled him to the ground, the Doctor springing from his horse & cutting his throat before he could recover from the shock.

The chase was witnessed by all the train, who were so much excited as to be almost tempted to leave their mules & join in. All that were mounted went pell mell towards the chase, but came up only at the death. It was found to be a very fat one, & served to feed all of the messes, and was enjoyed much by everyone. The Doctor & his horse are becoming quite notorious as hunters, they having helped to kill the first buffalo ever seen by them, & killing, themselves, the second.[15]   [*Distance, 24 miles.*

15. Until they reached the diggings, nothing held such universal interest for the emigrants as the first sight of buffalo and the first opportunity to hunt these animals. Backus, June 3; Badman, June 6; Brown, June 15 (also see 17); Dundass, June 2; Hackney, May 31; Johnston, May 17; Lewis, June 3; Long, May 8; McCoy, June 16; Morgan, Aug. 2; and Sedgley, June 18, all comment on the first observation. Others who mention seeing or hunting the animals include: Bruff, June 23; Caldwell, June 3; Delano, May 31; DeWolf, June 18; Foster, June 3, 8, 13; Hale, May 29; Kelly, pp. 84, 105–119; Love, May 27; Lyne, June 30; Pleasants, p. 30; Searls, June 15; Swain, June 16, 20; Tiffany, May 25; Webster, June 26; and Wistar, May 27 *et seq.* Kelly, although an enthusiastic huntsman himself, spoke of other emigrants as "buffalo maniacs," because of their inordinate fondness for hunting. Lewis was unusual in that he expressed pity for the beasts. Johnston, May 18, and Foster, June 8, 13, commented on the wastefulness of the slaughter. Wistar, June 20, speaks of an area which, at first, appeared to be covered with timber, but upon approaching closer, he found a great herd of buffalo "in countless numbers."

Wednesday, June 6th.

This morning was cloudy and damp. After a drive of a few miles we struck the bluffs and continued our travel for several miles. The rain commenced falling & continued to pour down in torrents accompanied with crashing thunder. It rained for several hours & everything was completely saturated. Towards evening it cleared off & the sun came down warm. We encamped this evening on the river bank with good grass, but had to use buffalo chips. This morning Dr. Bryarly's pistel accidental[ly] went off & came near wounding two men.[16] About daylight yesterday & this morning a lunar rainbow made their appearance.

[*Distance, 20 miles.*

Thursday, June 7th.

It was a clear & pleasant morning. We made an early start. The roads bad, and after a hard drive nooned within 8 miles of Ash Hollow.[17] We laid up about five hours and then rolled out. Passed a large number of teams & found several springs of good cool water, near which we left the river and ascended the bluffs. The road very bad & bluffs steep. In a short time we struck Ash Hollow, where the main trail from the South Fork (traveled by Bryant)[18] meets us. A large number of ash trees grow here, from which it takes its name. The hills are sandy & traveling difficult. Several fine springs of water are here found. We procured wood & drove on, passing many camps & a small party of Sioux Indians. We drove on until 11 o'clock P.M., & halted on the bluffs with good grass. For three days past the roads have been heavy. The bluffs are naked & sandy & the whole country presents a desolate appearance except near the river. We have been much teased & severely bitten by the buffalo gnats which swarm in thousands around us.[19]

[*Distance, 25 miles.*

16. On this near-accident, see above, p. 61.
17. Ash Hollow, on the south side of the North Platte in what is now Garden County, Nebraska, was the accepted point at which the trail reached the North Platte. A steep descent, from bluffs 400 to 500 feet high, caused many emigrants to remember and comment upon it.
18. Bryant, *What I Saw*, p. 97, describes this crossing.
19. The buffalo gnat is a small black fly of the genus *Simulium*. Bryant,

Friday, June 8th.

Rather a late start and our road was over a sandy & desolate country. The wheels cut in deep & the mules were nearly exhausted. Passed what by some are called Castle Bluffs. They are, however, only bleak sandy hills, but little resembling castles or houses of any description. The whole country is sandy & presents a rather desolate appearance. Pools of water are frequent and the trail is oftener near the river. Encamped one mile from Spring Creek, a stream of clear, but rather warm water.   [*Distance, 17 miles.*

Saturday, June 9th.

The morning set in with a drizzling rain & the day continued misty & cloudy, with now and then a little sunshine. The trail is much better & continues to improve. No wood since we left Ash Hollow until today, when we got sight of a growth of cedar or pine on a distant hill. Nooned today on Tower Creek, eleven miles from Spring Creek. The water is clear, cool & good. A difficulty in relation to a mule took place here. Moore refused to let McKay have a mule for his team. Evident signs of dissatisfaction appeared, & many spoke of a general "*bust up.*" Tower Hill was near but the rain & mist hid it from our view. The road has been good & we passed several small streams doubtless occasioned by the late rains. Two miles from Tower Creek, on the right hand side of the trail, a few hundred yards from the road, is a spring of the best water I have yet tasted on the plains. We encamped to-night on the rising ground about a mile from the river & had good grass, with an abundance of wild oats. Strong south wind & some rain.   [*Distance, 17 miles.*

What I Saw, p. 121, declared, "Our mules as well as ourselves suffer much from the myriads of buffalo-gnats." The *Daily Missouri Republican*, Aug. 28, 1850, said, "On the Platte, the most detestable thing in creation is the buffalo gnat, a very small, diminutive insect that, before you are aware of its presence has bitten your face, ears, and neck in a thousand places." Quoted by Settle, ed., *The March of the Mounted Riflemen*, p. 97.

Sunday, June 10th.

A clear morning and fresh bracing wind made us feel pleasant & good after a rainy night. We had a full view of Court House Rock,[20] which as we approached assumed more the appearance of some rude old structure. It but little resembles the dome of the Capitol at Washington.[21] It represents somewhat an old fort, but struck me as resembling muchly the Bishop's Palace at Monterey, Mexico. It is not of solid rock; it is a sand hill, or rather a sand bank, with an occasional layer of soft rock, rather soft, which has been shaped by the action of the rains upon it. It is a prominent object & easily distinguishable. Upon the south side there is a stream of clear water which winds around the Castle & then the bluffs & crosses near here.

From it we have a view of Chimney Rock[22] in the distance. Had yesterday been a clear day we should have seen Chimney Rock at a distance of thirty miles. It resembles at a distance a large hay stack with a pole running thru it, but upon a nearer approach looks more like the huge chimney of some old furnace. Its base occupies nearly half a mile and gradually tapers to the end. Some three years ago it was over 400 feet high, but the heavy rains have beaten it down and it is not now so high.

The Chimney Rock is composed of the same material as that of the Castle. The Chimney stands solitary & alone upon a small eminence in the centre of a gap formed by two large bluffs. A great many names are cut, and at least 1000 more are painted upon the Chimney, & among the rest was found the name of Capt. Smith, cut there in 1845. We went into camp within four miles of Chimney Rock with good grass & pool water.

When we drove up & correlled it was clear and pleasant,

20. This notable landmark on the trail, located in what is now Morrill County, Nebraska, is a rock and clay formation estimated to be 250 feet high and an acre in area. The fur traders gave it this name probably because of its fancied resemblance to the courthouse in St. Louis.

21. This is an allusion to Bryant, *What I Saw*, p. 99, which described the rock's appearance as ''not unlike that of the capitol at Washington.''

22. Chimney Rock, in what is now Morrill County, Nebraska, is a limestone and sandstone formation, rising in the form of a cone and terminating in a tower-shaped structure.

but in half an hour it clouded up. By sundown the horizon was darkened with portending clouds. The thunder burst forth in deafening peals & the lightening played & flashed in the heavens, assuming shapes & colors never before witnessed—with a strong S.W. wind, and then poured down the hail in torrents. The ground was covered like snow. The tents were beaten through and the wagon covers almost riddled.

Our mules being picketed, they began to race & jump, and in a few minutes we had a perfect stampede. Many of our mules broke loose & one ran to the bluffs. After the storm subsided we went in search of, and obtained, our mules. Capt. Smith and a small party went to the bluffs for wood and were caught out in the storm. They took refuge under their horses, but it was but a poor protection, and after they got into camp, an examination of their backs proved that they had been severly pelted & much bruised. The storm subsided about 8 o'clock P.M. It was the most terrific I ever saw. Although the hail was not larger than hickory nuts, it fell thick & heavy.[23]   [*Distance, 22 miles.*

Monday, June 11th.

Remained in camp until 12 o'clock M. for the purpose of drying off our goods, &c., &c. We remained in view of the Chimney Rock [and] many of our boys visited it. We drove out & kept the road along the bluffs passing Chimney Rock, & we then came in view of a row of naked bluffs, five in number, representing castles & old buildings. They presented a truly grand & magnificent view, assuming many different shapes as we approached. By general consent the range was called Castle City. Upon either side of the road, bluffs were in view, presenting a scene of rare beauty, wonder & magnificence. After a drive of fifteen miles, we encamped on the river bank. Plenty of good grass. Our camp was near a ravine from the bluffs, where we procured good wood, which

23. On this same day, Backus, who was within a day's journey of the Charleston Company, wrote, ''At 6 o'clock P.M. one of the heaviest storms we have seen on the plains commenced and continued for 3 hours—hailstones fell as large as wallnuts & the thunder & lightning were constant and terrific.'' Hale, June 11, also commented on this storm, and Hackney, June 10, told of a yoke of oxen being killed by lightning.

had drifted. A deer was killed by a man named Davidson, and brought into camp. In the *partial* & prejudiced distribution of it, our mess was left without.   [*Distance, 15 miles.*

Tuesday, June 12th.

Made an early start, and after a drive of about 3 miles left the river & took the bluffs, which we followed. These are called Scott's Bluffs.[24] In about 8 miles we came to & ascended a very high ridge near the top of which we found several small springs of cool water—as cold as ice. Here there is a store, blacksmith shop and trading post, kept by a Mr. Roubadoe,[25] who has been living with the Indians for 13 years. He is married to a Sioux squaw & has several children. For goods of every description he charges the most exorbitant prices, & for work, truly extortionate. For instance if an emigrant finds the mule shoes, nails &c. & puts the shoes on, he has to pay $1 per pair and everything in proportion.

Here we cross a steep dividing ridge, from which far in the distance can be seen something like mountain peaks, and [these] are believed to be a part of the Rocky Mountains, called Laramie's Peake. From here we have a sandy road & barren country to Horse Creek,[26] a stream of good water, but sandy bottom, an affluent of the Platte. Today we had some hail and rain—the road heavy. Encamped here.

[*Distance, 26 miles.*

---

24. Scott's Bluff, on the south side of the Platte, in Scott's Bluff County, Nebraska, was a formation which took its name from a trapper named Scott, who died here after being abandoned, while ill, by his companions. They reported that they had cared for him until he died, but the later discovery of his bones some miles away from the alleged place of burial led to an exposure of their treachery. See Bryant, *What I Saw*, p. 104. Scott's story became a familiar item in the lore of the trail. Washington Irving, *Rocky Mountains* (Philadelphia, 1837), pp. 45–46, was perhaps the first printed version of this story.

25. Antoine Robidoux, one of several famous brothers prominent in the early West, kept his blacksmith shop from 1848 to 1852, and was mentioned, along with his squaw wife, by many emigrant diarists. See Brown, June 25; Doyle, June 15; Hackney, June 10; Johnston, May 27; Long, June 2; Searls, June 25; and Tiffany, June 4. See also the editorial note by Georgia Willis Read and Ruth Gaines, in *Gold Rush, The Journals, Drawings, and other papers of J. Goldsborough Bruff* (New York, 1944), I, 480, n. 139.

26. Horse Creek is a tributary of the North Platte, flowing into that stream from the south in Scott's Bluff County, Nebraska.

Wednesday, June 13th.

A clear, cool morning. Made a late start. Just before we drove out, a man in a neighboring camp was most cruelly beaten for stealing, & turned out of the company.[27] A drive of a few miles brought us to the Platte, which we had left since we took to Scott's Bluffs. It is much narrower here than at any place I have before seen it. The road has been sandy & hilly. Good grass and plenty of wood. We have travelled all day along the Platte, & encamped on the river with wood & grass. [*Distance, 16 miles.*

Thursday, June 14th.

This day we made a drive to noon on Larimie's Fork,[28] where we found a large number of teams. This is an affluent of the Platte—very narrow, but deep. Here we had to block up our wagon bodies to keep the water out. Our teams passed over with ease. This water is good & cool, as also is the Platte. Much better than where we first struck it.

Near the west bank of Larimie's Fork is old Fort John, now deserted. One mile from this is Fort Larimie, a trading post for some time belonging to the American Fur Company, but which has recently passed into the hands of the United States.[29] The building is made of *adobes* or sun dried brick,

27. Comparable instances where men were punished for crime by being turned out of camp are given by Brown, June 20, and Lyne, June 30. Both of these cases involved men who had shot others, and Lyne regarded the punishment as inadequate, especially since the offender was allowed to take mules and a pack. In 1846, the Donner Party had punished James Frazier Reed similarly, though he had killed in self-defense.

28. Laramie's Fork or River, originally the fork of the trapper, La Ramée (Fourche a la Ramée), flows northeastwardly into the North Platte. The confluence is in Goshen County, Wyoming.

29. Fort Laramie, located near the confluence of the Laramie and North Platte Rivers, in what is now Goshen County, Wyoming, was the successor to a trading post built by William Sublette and Robert Campbell, and named Fort William after the former, in 1834. Soon after, it was purchased by the American Fur Company and its name was changed to Fort John, after John B. Sarpy, an officer of the company. Later, the company built a new edifice nearer the river and also called it Fort John, but "Fort John on the Laramie" became, by popular usage, Fort Laramie. It was only twelve days after the Charlestown Company passed, that the United States government purchased the fort for use as a military post. It was maintained as such until 1890. See Leroy R.

the main building two story high. The others, which form a square, are only one story high—made on the Mexican plan. A Mr. Husband [30] is now head man, as agent of the American Fur Company. Several Indian squaws with half breed children were found there, and a number of Mexicans. There is nothing enticing or pleasing about the place. They were destitute of all articles of trade except jerked buffalo meat. We found here a young emigrant who had been accidentally shot in the thigh—he was not dangerous[ly wounded.] There were no Indians about, they having gone to war with the Crows.

The roads fork at this place, but come together in a few miles. Take the lower or right hand road. A gentleman from St. Louis was injured so much today by the running off of mules that it is thought he will die. Encamped on the river about 4 miles from Ft. Larimie.   [*Distance, 17 miles.*

Hafen and F. M. Young, *Fort Laramie and the Pageant of the West, 1834–1890* (Glendale, Cal., 1938).

30. Bruce Husband had been left in charge of the fort for the American Fur Company in the spring of 1849, when the officially appointed manager, Major Andrew Drips returned to Missouri. Hafen and Young, *Fort Laramie*, pp. 132–133. Bruff, July 10, and Kelly, p. 155, also mentioned Husband.

III FORT LARAMIE TO SOUTH PASS

West of Fort Laramie, the trail entered the Laramie Mountains, and as it did so, the emigrants began to experience a roughness of terrain and a degree of aridity not previously encountered. The insufficiency of forage and the presence of alkali, which was poisonous to the cattle, made the last stages of the journey along the North Platte very difficult. About 110 miles beyond Laramie, however, the trail left the river at a great bend in its course. A brief waterless stretch led to a tributary which General Ashley had named Sweetwater, in grateful recognition of its superiority to the alkalized waters of the North Platte. This cool, clear, and sparkling mountain stream flowed down from sources which were within sight of the South Pass, and the emigrants were able to advance up the valley, until they stood on the threshold of the Continental Divide. An imperceptible rise made easy their journey through this historic portal of the West and into Oregon Territory, which lay beyond. This passage from the Atlantic to the Pacific Basin had an important emotional value to most emigrants.

The Charlestown Company crossed the South Pass fifteen days after leaving Fort Laramie (June 14-June 29).

Friday, June 15th.

AFTER leaving camp we crossed the bluffs over a steep and sandy road and in 4 miles struck the river. Following it a few miles, we again took to the bluffs, altho there is a road up the river. We are now in the Black Hills[1]— deep cuts, short turns & sandy roads, with a stunted pine growth. From the point we last left the river it is 12 miles over a dry sandy country without a particle of water, when you come upon what is called Bitter Cottonwood Creek[2]—

1. The term, Black Hills, was not confined, in the days of overland travel, to the mountain range of southwestern South Dakota and northwestern Wyoming which now bears the name, but was extended to include the Laramie mountains. It was in this broader sense that emigrant diarists used the term. See Read and Gaines, eds., *Gold Rush*, I, 482, n. 143.

2. Bitter Cottonwood Creek is a tributary of the North Platte, flowing into that stream from the south, in what is now Platte County, Wyoming.

good water. Here you follow & cross this stream several times & pass by a spring & stream called Timber Creek. We did not pass the Warm Spring,[3] having kept the ridge road, leaving the spring to our right. Encamped on Bitter Cottonwood Creek, near a good spring about 28 miles from Ft. Laramie. Clear warm day. 　　　　　　[*Distance, 24 miles.*

Saturday, June 16th.

At 4 o'clock this morning we were aroused, and were soon in motion. Followed up and crossed Bitter Cottonwood Creek, & this making the third time we have crossed it. The roads were good for 9 miles, where we came to Willow Spring, (by some called Heber Spring). Here we halted 1 1/2 hours for breakfast. This place is 7 miles from where we last cross Bitter Cottonwood Creek. We again set out, and after a drive of 8 miles over a bad road & through the most hilly, desolate, sandy & barren country I ever saw, we came to Horse Shoe Creek, a stream of pure, clear, cool water, one mile west of which we went into camp near a spring of cold water on the side of the first bluff from the river. It is called Smith's Spring, named by our guide some three years ago. This evening we cut off about 2 feet of our wagon bodies & coupled up the wagons shorter. We also threw away all the worthless plunder we had. Clear, warm day. Since we left Larimie, we have been in sight of L[aramie's] Peake.

[*Distance, 17 miles.*

Sunday, June 17th.

Laid up today to rest our mules & also to shoe some of them. This morning we discovered some buffaloes in the bluffs near our camp, & several of us went in pursuit. After striking & following the ravines & bluffs, we got in sight of several herd & gave chase. After [a] warm, excited & close race we succeeded in downing a large bull. We continued our pursuit but had to return without farther success. Packed & took into camp sufficient for our boys, and left the remainder. A party, however, went for & got more. The buffalo weighed

3. The Warm Spring or Springs, mentioned by several diarists, rise in Platte County, Wyoming, and flow northeast into the North Platte.

1000 lbs. We saw immense numbers of antelopes, but they were so timid & fleet that we could not get near enough to kill any of them. One gang of fifty elk, young & old ones, were in view, but effort to obtain one was futile.

For several days back we have had good hard roads, but very hilly, with now and then deep sand & some rocks. Since we left Ft. Laramie wood & water have been abundant, with one exception, already noticed. From the deep ravines & cuts in the hills, with the large quantities of trees washed up by the roots & floated to the vallies, it is evident that violent & tremendous storms prevail in this country.

Monday, June 18th.

Started before day, intending to go to La Bonta River[4] to breakfast, which we supposed 8 miles off, but missing the road, we travelled for 15 miles before striking it. The road has been over high hills & through deep hollows. The hills hard, but very sandy in the bottoms. Nooned on La Bonta River, a stream of clear water, but not very cool—about 30 feet wide & shallow. After crossing this stream we continued to ascend & descend high bluffs & in five miles crossed a small stream, an affluent of the La Bonta, where we got wood & water, and then drove into camp about 2 miles west.

Today we have been among red sand or red hills, with very short grass. On the hills we noticed hundreds & thousands of large crickets or grass-hoppers of every color & hue. They were called by some Buffalo Grass-hoppers.[5] Marble Creek is the name of the stream last passed.[6] Here we found a beautiful speciman of variegated marble, also soda & salaratus. Hearing that liquor was for sale—went back. $12 per Gal.
[*Distance, 20 miles.*

4. La Bonte River is a tributary of the North Platte, flowing northeast into that river in Converse County, Wyoming. Thwaites, in *Early Western Travels*, XXX, 64, n. 39, declares La Fourche Boisée and La Bonte to have been different names for the same stream, to which he also attributes Big Timber as a third name, but this would appear to be an error.

5. Love, May 27, one day after crossing the South Platte, had written, ''Here the grasshoppers is so thick you can't keep them out of your face.''

6. Joel Palmer mentioned Marble Creek in his Table of Distances from Independence, Mo., in his *Journal of Travels over the Rocky Mountains*, (1847). He also mentioned Big Timber Creek, which Geiger calls Timber Creek (p. 109, above).

Tuesday, June 19th.

Very early this morning we started, but unfortunately broke a bolt pin, and was thus detained. Passed a large conical hill, 200 feet high and of nearly solid rock. We nooned today on A La Prele River,[7] a narrow & swift stream. Grass very short. In 8 miles we came to & crossed Fourche Boise River, banks high, water good & but little or no grass.[8] In 4 miles we reached the Platte & went into camp. Grass tolerable. Wood & water plenty today. In nearly every valley we found good water and in one or two places excellent springs, among them one of sulphur.

[*Distance, 23 miles over the Black Hills.*

Wednesday, June 20th.

A very cold & unpleasant morning. Roads good & our course was along Platte. In about 5 miles we reached Deer Creek,[9] a small stream of clear, good water. Crossed & went down to the [Platte] River, where we found several hundred wagons, which were to be crossed there. Our Captain determined on crossing at this point. We lashed our two sheet iron bodies together, & after unloading our wagons, commenced crossing the river with our luggage &c. It took us until after night, several times our boat washing below the landing. A young man named Drenner, from St. Clairsville, Ohio, in attempting to swim a mule over the river, was thrown off & drowned. Seven men have been drowned in attempting to cross the river in the last week. One wagon went on a raft several miles before it could be stopped. Caught some fine fresh fish today. Several hundred wagons here, busy at work crossing day & night.[10]

[*Distance, 7 miles.*

7. A tributary of the North Platte, flowing northeast into that stream in what is now Converse County, Wyoming.

8. Clayton and Ware, in their guides, both mention Fourche Bois, which was probably the stream now known as Boxelder Creek, Converse County, Wyoming.

9. Deer Creek is the largest tributary of the North Platte between the Sweetwater and the Laramie. It flows into the North Platte in Converse County, Wyoming.

10. The principal crossings of the North Platte were this Deer Creek crossing

Thursday, June 21st.

Owing to the confusion and derangement caused by yesterday's business, we did not start until 11 o'clock. We followed the river as near as we could, being sometimes compelled to leave it for a mile or two. Our road was over high bluffs of sand & sage wood. It was hard on the mules. Every mile we found emigrants rafting the river. Passed several fine grass spots, and drove into camp on the bank of the river after a hard & wearisome march of 10 miles. Wood & grass good.　　　　　　　　　　　[*Distance, 10 miles.*

Friday, June 22nd.

Left camp early & continued to follow the river for some distance, when we had again to take to the sand hills. Found many persons at different points crossing the river. The river can be easily rafted anywhere above Deer Creek up to the Old Ferry. Passed the lower Mormon Ferry, which had crossed over 900 wagons at 3 dollars each.[11] This morning a lady from Missouri was safely delivered of twin children, [while] encamped on the riverside.[12] Rumor says a woman

which the Charlestown Company took, and the Upper or Mormon Ferry crossing, twenty-eight miles beyond. Loss of life at these crossings far exceeded the loss by drowning anywhere else on the trail. On this point, see above, p. 56, and Paden, *Wake of the Prairie Schooner*, pp. 192–194. The diary of Benjamin Hoffman, June 20, also notes the use of the metal wagon beds, and adds, ''We crossed at the mouth of Deer Creek about 30 miles below the regular Mormon Ferry, in order to cut off as many teams as possible. There are 150 ahead of us now. . . . There have been several men drowned while crossing at this place.'' McIlhany, *Recollections*, p. 18, also describes the experience of the Charlestown Company at this point: ''Our head teamster and the guide examined the crossing and they concluded that we could ford the river without using the boats [an error of memory]. We put ten mules to a wagon. It was quite a tedious and tiresome task.'' McIlhany also mentions the drowning of a young man in another company.

11. The Mormon Ferry was first placed in operation in June, 1847, when the Saints arrived at this point ahead of the emigration, with few provisions, but with ''a skiff of sole leather that would carry 1500 or 1800 pounds.'' The Mormons set their charges at $1.50 per load, but recognizing the indispensability of their service, insisted upon payment in commodities at a rate which grossly undervalued the goods. See Edward Eberstadt, ed., *Way Sketches, containing incidents of Travel across the Plains . . . by Lorenzo Sawyer* (New York, 1926), p. 39.

12. Childbirth on the overland trail was not an unusual occurrence. DeWolf, Aug. 11, and Bryant, *What I Saw*, p. 91, both mention instances. Owen C. Coy,

& seven children were drowned today by the sinking of a boat. A man was found in the river, with a bullet hole in his head, $87 in money, & three pistols with the initials "W. C."

Passed in view of Heart Island, which is so called from its striking resemblance to a heart. After a drive of about 12 miles we took a final leave of Platte River and its beautifully singular valley, & took to the ridges over a barren & sandy country destitute of timber, & with no water save lakes strongly impregnated with *alkali*. From where we left the river, it is near 15 miles to good water, over an exceedingly bad road. We watered at the last point on the river, and after a very severe drive encamped on a high bluff with poor grass and no water. Our wood consisted of wild sage, which burns very well. Our mules were much fatigued.

[Distance, 23 miles.

Saturday, June 23rd.[13]

Started this morning at 5 o'clock. A beautiful morning but promising to be very hot when a little farther advanced. We rolled 11 miles over a very hilly & barren country and nooned at 10 1/2 o'clock. Our mules travelled very slow, probably owing to the short feeding they have had for several days, they not having had a good pile of grass since we left the crossing of the North Platte. We nooned in a little valley upon the right of the road. There is here one of those Poisonous Springs which we have heard so much about. This is the second one we have passed, the other being just before we left the Platte. They have a dark black scurf upon the surface & around the edges. They are quite strong with sulphur & their poisonous effect is attributed to the combination of sulphur, copper & alkali. The water is not injurious to persons, but they have not much inducement to drink as both the smell & taste is very disagreeable. Some of the animals drink it with impunity whilst others are killed in an hour after partaking. We saw several dead oxen in the

in his two books, *The Great Trek* and *Gold Days,* lists a number of surviving pioneers who had been born on the trail.

13. On this date Geiger ceased to keep the diary, and the remaining portion is entirely in the hand of Dr. Bryarly.

vicinity, and one, having drank heartily while we were there, was left dead upon the field.[14]

We started again at 1 o'clock, the sun being most powerful, which soon began to show effects upon our mules. Two miles from camp we came to a fine alkali spring, on the left, very cool & pleasant, & quite palatable, 1/4 mile farther to another of very pure clear sweet water. We rolled five miles from our nooning & came to "Willow Springs."[15] This is one of the regular encampments, but there being not a sprig of grass in the vicinity, we watered and rolled 1 1/2 miles & encamped upon the side of a hill, where there was a little grass, but precious little.

In the afternoon, a herd of some 40 buffalo was seen descending a hill immediately to the road. Chase was instantly given by the General (Mr. Smith Crane) & his party. Mr. G. Cunningham (an excellent marksman) taking the lead soon came along side of a fine cow &, with a six shooter, soon brought her to the ground. They gave farther chase but came up only to some very large old bulls, which they cared but little about. The General came up immediately & the excitement depicted upon his countenance is said to have been truly interesting. They cut off as much as they could, & joined us in camp, supplying each mess with a sufficiency.

The teams were much fatigued & many mules completely given out when they arrived in camp. The men were generally in low spirits at the prospect of our mules giving out. It was quite distressing in particular to see our friend Locke, whose mules were among the number that failed. Our friend has been quite desponding for some time at the prospect of being left in the mountains in the snow. He had one mule, his leader, which he had bragged upon very often, & upon which he seemed to have put his main dependence, his fondest hopes. Today, melancholy to relate, "Poor Kit" gave out & poor Locke raised his hands heavenward, & in a most dis-

14. Dundass, June 26; Foster, June 24, 26, 30; Hale, June 25; Doyle, July 1; Orvis, June 23; Searls, July 10; Sedgley, July 9; and Hackney, June 24, all mention the presence of dead cattle and all blame the alkali water. All of these observations are made between nine and thirteen days after leaving Fort Laramie, which means that all were made at approximately the same place.

15. Willow Springs rise in Natrona County, Wyoming, and flow into the North Platte from the northeast.

tressed voice exclaimed, "There, poor Kit's gone, by God." [16]

The appearance of the country is still sandy & broken, presenting a roughness, from the sage bushes. We used this sage for fuel (artimisia). It burns like pine but with a much brighter light. We enjoyed a pleasant camp except the "Peace & Plenty" mess which yet thought of [the] lamentable state of Poor Kit.   [*Distance, 17 miles.*

Sunday, June 24th.

The day was ushered in most beautifully and everyone looked in cheerful spirits. The morning & evening here are strikingly delightful, & instead of the depressing & languid

---

16. By all odds, the worst sufferers on the overland journey were the draught animals, who perished by thousands. At best they were taxed to the utmost, and in many cases they were mercilessly overdriven, but there are many other instances in which their owners developed a genuine affection for them, and attempted to mitigate their suffering. Some illustrations follow: Foster, June 24, Aug. 31, speaks sadly of the loss of oxen, Old Jolly and Old Buck. Page, letters, May 8, 13, speaks of his two oxen, Jack and Jerry, as being "tractable & easily caught & handled." Badman, June 21, notes, that "this is the 1st day that Ether of our mules has fag'd but this day Joseph has fag'd so we had to put Jimmy in the place about 2 m[ile]s before we encamp. The balance of our mules names are Billy & Coley, & our oxen names are Rum & Brandy." On June 22, he added, "our Billy mule has the distemper verry bad"; on July 8, "started with our mules looking like the Devil. Jimmy is very sick caused by drinking [alkali] water." Pleasants, p. 81, tells of an emigrant who shared his last water with a pet ox dying on the desert. McCall, June 24, said, "The rough roads and scanty pasturage begin to tell upon our patient cattle. They bend to the yoke with a will when called upon, and most faithfully perform every labor imposed upon them. Dudley has the finest team. His wheel cattle, a pair of the largest size, stoutly built and perfectly white, are a full team of themselves. His leaders are lighter and cherry red, carrying their heads high and with a cheery air, step as lightly as if only out for a lark. . . . Our wheel oxen are not so well matched. One is a dark brown, with those concentric wrinkles about his dark eyes, indicating nerve and spirit. He has proved himself the master-spirit of the whole herd, and feeds at the head, where the choicest grass is found. He bears the name of "Jim." His mate is red, and of less mettle, honest and easy-going, but no match for "Jim." His former owner called him Charley, and the name has been retained although another member of our *personnel* family [McCall's horse] bore the same title. . . . A daily association for two long months with these uncomplaining, quiet servants, in the midst of their toils, and in their peaceful hours of rest, has awakened such a strong sympathy among us all, that their brown sides are not marred by whip or goad. They are as docile and quiet as lambs. Our Wisconsin friends drove on the lead of one of their teams a yoke of heifers. They are as trim and gay as country lassies, and give them a goodly supply of milk for their table."

feeling that you experience at home in rising early in summer mornings, you feel here rather elated than not, strong, & active & with buoyant & cheerful spirits.

The mules came up filled well, & after *a hasty cup of coffee* we started upon our journey. The country still presented the same broken, barren appearance, with an occasional ravine, or, as the mountaineers say, "Kanyon," in which you can generally find a spring of some sort. Four miles from camp I was attracted by a placard, which on reading, described a delightful spring up a very pretty valley to the left. Some of our company went to it and found it what it was represented.

The roads were a little harder than we have had them and we made three miles. Two miles from the spring above mentioned, we came to another on the left, immediately on the trail. This was rather alkalic. We understood here, that just half a mile farther in the prarie was another of those poisonous and alkali springs, where the night before, 40 head of cattle was poisoned, but which were saved by administering lard.[17] They were so much recruited as to be able to proceed on their route in the afternoon. This is rather novel & I do not yet understand the chemical change.

Five miles farther brought us to noon, upon a beautiful, pure & clear little creek running alongside of the road for more than a mile. We nooned here 4 hours. We had around

17. Swain, July 18, says, "This morning we . . . found our cattle sick from the effect of drinking of the saline springs. We doctored them by giving them large pieces of fat pork & had the good luck not to loose [*sic*] any of them." Delano, July 10, speaks of administering a "dose of bacon" to the cattle. Bruff, Aug. 3, also describes this form of treatment. Marcy, *Prairie Traveler*, pp. 124–125, discusses this matter, as follows: "In the vicinity of the South Pass, upon the Humboldt River, and in some sections upon other routes to California, alkaline water is found which is very poisonous to animals that drink it, and generates a disease known in California as "*alkali*." This disease first makes its appearance by swellings upon the abdomen and between the fore legs, and is attended with a cough, which ultimately destroys the lungs and kills the animal. If taken at an early stage, this disease is curable, and the following treatment is generally considered as the most efficacious. The animal is first raked, after which a large dose of grease is poured down its throat; acids are said to have the same effect, and give immediate relief. When neither of these remedies can be procured, many of the emigrants have been in the habit of mixing starch or flour in a bucket of water and allowing the animal to drink it. It is supposed that this forms a coating over the mucous membrane, and thus defeats the action of the poison."

our camp many rattlesnakes, rather small, but very viscious looking devils. We took some fish with our net & had a palatable meal, after which we enjoyed a siesta & rolled again. The roads continued hard & in a few hours, after travelling 8 miles, we encamped upon Sweet Water River about two miles below Independence Rock. We had good grass—the best since leaving the Platte—a beautiful[ly] situated camp, a good cup of coffee, & after[wards] a delightful snooze.   [*Distance, 19 miles.*

Monday, June 25th.

Was presented to us in all her most bright & glorious colours. We breakfasted, and soon the order was given by our most indefatigable Guide to "Hook up." Two miles brought us to the Great renowned *Independence Rock*.[18] We were much disappointed when it was first pointed out to us, for we expected to see (never having had a description of it except as the Great Independence Rock) a spire, pyramid or shot tower looking object, but on the contrary, it was one large mass extending over perhaps four or five acres & being 150 to 200 ft. high. The exterior was broken by many deep crevices, extending in some places half through. Between the crevices, on the outside it was smooth. From this reason it has been chosen since the passing of the first white man, as a registering & publishing post. Thousands of names are upon it, some painted well, others tarred, and many cut in the rock. You can here see names from not only the U.S., but from all parts of the world. From the top you have a fine view of the valley of the Sweet Water, both above & below. The road comes close to the south base of it & here immediately crosses the river. This crossing is altogether optional however, as you can cross it at any place the bank is not too bluff for you to get to it. Sweet Water River is some 40 yds. wide, generally 3 ft. deep, pure, clear, cold, [with a]

18. No other landmark of the trail was quite so well known as Independence Rock, a spectacular boulder in what is now Natrona County, Wyoming. Here countless emigrants inscribed their names, so that the rock became, in Father De Smet's often-quoted phrase, ''the Great Register of the Desert.'' The name is sometimes attributed to Frémont, but John B. Wyeth had used it as if it were accepted terminology as early as 1833. For discussion, see Edward Eberstadt, ed., *Way Sketches*, p. 42.

sandy bottom & strong current. It is very tortuous in its course, describing horse-shoe bends every two hundred yards.

Four miles from Independence Rock we came to *"The Devil's Gate."* [19] This is the most remarkable freak of nature I ever saw. It is the passing of the Sweet Water River through a mountain of solid rock. From the water below to the top of the rock is by measurement 400 ft., & being more than a hundred yds. wide. The rock presents the appearance of being split asunder, & this being the only outlet for the river it rushed through and went on its way to its mother home. The breadth across is 50 yds.

Four miles from "The Devils Gate" we nooned four hours, and started again and encamped at a bend of the river where the road leaves it for several miles. We had grass to the mules' knees, and they now seem to be improving fast.

We came up to a Government train bound for Bear River, to establish a garrison for the better protection of the emigrants to Oregon & California. They had 50 wagons under the command of Maj. Simonson. I joined the train after we had corralled & was delighted to meet some old friends, Lts. May, Addison, Irwin & Mr. Stevenson.[20] We road together

19. A narrow gorge more than three hundred feet deep, by which the Sweetwater River passes through a range of hills which lies across its path in what is now Natrona County, Wyoming. This spectacular physical feature was another of the accepted landmarks of the trail.

20. In 1846, Congress had authorized the raising of a regiment of 10 companies of Mounted Riflemen for the purpose of garrisoning posts along the Oregon Trail. The regiment was created in accordance with the act, but was sent to serve in the Mexican War, before it ever saw service on the frontier. Bryarly probably met some of the officers in Mexico. In 1849 the Mounted Riflemen marched to their garrison posts in the West under the command of Major Osborne Cross, but an advance party under the command of Brevet Major John Smith Simonson was sent in advance to take up a post on Bear River. It was this advance party in which Bryarly met his friends.

John Smith Simonson, a native of Pennsylvania, had been appointed Captain, Mounted Riflemen, May 27, 1846; Brevet Major, Sept. 13, 1847, for gallantry at Chapultepec; later, Colonel, May 13, 1861; and Brevet Brig. General, Mar. 13, 1865; died Dec. 5, 1881. Julian May, a native of the District of Columbia, was appointed 2nd Lieutenant, Mounted Riflemen, May 27, 1846; Brevet 1st Lieutenant, Aug. 20, 1847, for gallantry at Contreras and Churubusco; 1st Lieutenant, Oct. 31, 1848. John McL. Addison, a native of Virginia, and Caleb E. Irvine, a native of Tennessee, were both 2nd Lieutenants of this regiment. Settle, ed., *March of the Mounted Riflemen*, pp. 275-277 and *passim;* Francis

some 6 miles farther & came to the river again. On rising the hill, we saw for the first time the snow-capped Wind Mountain. We were attracted by a smoke up the mountain on our right side, and all had very considerable curiosity to know from whence it came. Maj. Simonson being something of a *"Tourist"* volunteered to go with anyone. Lt. Irwin offered to accompany him, & they started. They returned in the evening reporting the smoke to be from a large quantity of drift wood which was on fire, & which was found to have been set on fire by some of the deserters of the evening before. They found a pair of U.S. pantaloons, straps &c.[21]

One mile farther the Government train halted & went into camp. I was the guest of Lt. May & [Mr.] Stevenson and was most hospitably received. We were fortunate enough to find some nice sprigs of mint upon the river, & soon were at work with our tools, knocking up one of those nectar drinks, a Julep. The invitation being extended to other officers of kindred spirits, after supper they assembled and with talking of friends at home, of days gone by, of hair-breadth escapes, of the journey over the plains, and with an occasional draw upon the blue pitcher, a bright fire, & that indispensable article, the life of a camp fire, "a Pipe," we whiled away some half dozen hours in almost complete forgetfulness of the many deprivations of the plains, & only broke up our levee when reminded we had but three hours to sleep before reveille.

The neighborhood of Independence Rock is the great battle ground of the Indians. This is the favorite spot for their bloody "set to's," & many terrible battles have taken place here. When the war party of any tribe feel like tigers, or very pugnacious & pugilistic & bloody, their skins trimmed in all their paraphernalia of war, [they] go to the valley of the Sweet Water, near or about the Rock, to look up a fight. Here, if they happen to meet another party upon the same errand, they instantly make battle. The oldest mountaineers confirm this & say many most bloody engagements have taken place in this way.

B. Heitman, *Historical Register and Dictionary of the United States Army* (Washington, 1903).

21. The last two sentences of this paragraph appear on a separate page at the end of the journal, with a note indicating that they pertain to this passage.

Our guide pointed out to me the exact spot at the base of the rock where two emigrants some years since left their guns & ascended for the purpose of scribing their names & were surrounded by Indians & taken. The circumstances as told me by Mr. Smith were these. It was the Oregon emigration of 1844. Two men with it, by name Hastings & Lovejoy, [went] ahead of the train some distance for the purpose of ascending the rock before it came up.[22] They imprudently left their guns sitting against the rock at its base & went up. They scarcely got up before the war whoop of 250 Indians was heard & they were described by the men as jumping up from every sage bush & bunch of grass. The men were the more surprised because they had examined, as they thought, well, all around the place for fear of these self-same fellows. They were still more surprised when they saw their own guns pointed towards them and ordered to come down. They came down and were seized by the Indians & treated with the greatest indignity. The young Indians spit in their faces, pulled their ears & nose. They were stript & whipt most unmercifully & driven thus towards the train which, so soon as they perceived them, corralled. One Indian snapped a pistol three times at Lovejoy's head, but his time had not yet come. They demanded a most exorbitant ransom, in provisions, for them, which had to be paid, and they were released. This taught them however, never to stray too far from home. Lovejoy is now Mayor of Oregon City, & Hastings is one of those who with Sutter, just invited the emigration to California.   [*Distance, 15 miles.*

Tuesday, June 26th.

Early this morning after leaving my friends, I "layed to" upon the road to await our train.[23] It came up soon & I found all expressing some anxiety about my absence last evening. After rolling 9 miles we nooned on good grass on the river,

22. Hastings and Lovejoy were Lansford W. Hastings and Amos L. Lovejoy. Lovejoy was prominent in early Oregon affairs, and later accompanied Marcus Whitman on his famous ride. This episode at Independence Rock is fully described in Hastings, *Emigrants' Guide*, pp. 11–17.

23. While Bryarly had traveled ahead of his company, it had re-crossed the Sweetwater River "to shun the sandy roads and dust and also to get away from the number of wagons. The sand is from 6 to 10 inches deep and almost hot enough to cook eggs." Hoffman diary, June 25.

at a point where the road leaves for some distance. On one side of us at noon we had the "Sweet Water" Mountain, the highest point on the left of the valley, & on the opposite side, the Two Dome Mountains, situated near the river & some 10 miles from each other. They have been thus named from their shape. This chain of the Rocky Mountains seem to take their origin from the Devil's Gate & run west towards the larger range. They are solid rock, having no such thing as herbage of any kind upon them. Occasionally you can see water coming from some of the numerous crevices, 100 ft. from its base & trickling gracefully & gently down.

In advancing close to the base, one's ears is saluted with a terrible & singular sound, which upon closer approximation astonishes you in the shape of thousands & thousands of our common swallows. They build their nests of mud, which sticks very securely to the rocks, always picking out the under part of a projecting one for protection from the weather. One particular rock or mountain, seeming to be a favorite, from the number of nests on it, was named by us the Swallow Rock.

After nooning 4 hours we again hooked up and started with renewed vigour. After leaving the river 6 miles, we again crossed it, & found two roads, one, the old trail, which went through the "Narrows" as they are called & requiring to cross the river twice in two hundred yds. The Narrows is where the river passes between two mountains, the space between entirely taken up by the bed of the river, the distance being 100 yds. The other went around some five miles farther, avoiding these two crossings, but having very heavy sand all the way.

We chose the old trail on account of our mules. On approaching the pass, we met many ox teams returning to the other road, not being able to cross as the river was too high for their wagons. However, we, nothing daunted, & knowing no such thing "as fail," [24] pushed on. We came to the crossing & found it very high, which required our beds to be

24. In the lexicon of youth, which fate reserves
   For a bright manhood there is no such word
   As "fail"

   Edward Bulwer Lytton,
   Richelieu (1839) Act II, Sc. 2.

propped up to save them from the water. At the regular crossing you had to travel up the bed of the river some 75 yds. This was very hard for our mules, being up to their backs in water & pulling against the current, & determined our Guide to make another inlet, opposite the old [one] coming out on the other side. Rocks were rolled down from the mountain over us and filled into the river. Trees were felled & layed along with dirt over them for a road. After a couple [of] hours of hard & active work it was, as we thought, completed. The first team was driven on the first step from the edge, & sent mules, men, & wagon into five ft. [of] water with a strong current. After some difficulty, the men all getting drenched, having been compelled to jump in the river, they were extricated with only a good ducking. This of course determined us to hold to the old crossing, which after considerable noise & confusion was passed. The river was again to be crossed two hundred yds. below. Still keeping the blocks under their wagons, this was also soon done, the men going in the river after having once got out, like muskrats.

By direction of the Guide, I picked a camp on the side of the river at the crossing, and we corralled. The mules were turned to good grass & the men, after partaking heartily of my usual prescription for a wetting, retired.

[*Distance, 18 miles.*

Wednesday, June 27th.

Made rather a late start this morning, having found that some of our wagons beds had leaked, & wet some of our groceries. Seven & a half saw us again upon the road, which here leaves the river, taking to the bluffs & hills for two miles, and striking it again [in] 7 miles, when we again cross it. The other road keeps upon the south side. From our last crossing, the road makes a long stretch of 15 miles before striking it again. If you are late in the day, it would [be] prudent for you to fill your casks, in case of not being able to reach the river to camp.

We nooned 3 miles from last crossing 4 hours, and rolled to the river. Not being able to get any grass nearer than two miles of the crossing, we went thus far on our route & encamped on a hill with poor grass. There was very little of interest in today's route. It was the same appearance of country as for some time past. The Wind Mountain was in view all day, & it, together with the dead oxen on this side of the road, was the only things to relieve the monotony of our march. The weather & hard driving now begin to show but too lamentably upon the ox teams. We saw twelve dead ones during the day, and many driven along, some with the foot entirely worn away [?],[25] must soon follow in the same path The south-side road came into the other, 10 miles from our last crossing. The south road was represented as a bad one, it being a road [*3 words illegible*] up to the hubs.

[*Distance, 24 miles.*]

Thursday, June 28th.

Having very short grazing last night, we made an early start for the purpose of making a long noon when we should come to good grass. The road follows up the river, only leaving it in one place from the old road, which went over a considerable hill to avoid crossing the river twice. Six miles from camp is a very cool pretty spring on the right, 50 yds, from the road. The spring was surrounded with [a] great many gooseberry bushes which were full of fruit. They were green, but were eaten with considerable gusto. We met here also a party of trappers, some of whom intended to return to the States.[26] They were carrying a mail back, receiving 50 cents a letter. They had then some thousands of letters. I stopped long enough to write two, & committed them to their charge. We rolled 2 miles farther and nooned. We stopped at the branching of two roads—one of which,

25. On the prolonged journey, it often happened that the hoofs of the draught animals would become very badly worn. To avert the danger of their being worn away altogether, emigrants sometimes made ''boots'' or ''moccasins'' for the animals by fastening pieces of hide over their hoofs. See Delano, May 30; Wistar, June 22.

26. Hoffman's diary for this same day noted that, ''We met with a party of trappers today who say it will be impossible for us ever to reach California as the grass gets shorter and shorter every day and will give out entirely in 500 miles farther. They say also that there are teams 300 miles ahead of us that will not get through. This has thrown a gloom over all of us, as we have not now more provisions than will last us through providing we have nothing to stop us.''

to the left, kept on the river and in one place went directly in the bed of it for 4 miles. The other kept over the bluffs & does not strike the river again for 16 miles.

We, after nooning 4 hours, took the right hand road, ascending immediately a very steep & winding hill. The first two miles were very hilly & rocky & rough, being on a very great ascent the whole way. The road then was very hard, good, & descending. On starting we filled our casks with water, intending to make the 16 miles to the river, but after rolling 8 miles, coming to *good grass, wood, & water,* we determined to "lay to" for the night. We had a most delightful encampment, high grass, good wood, and a spring of water, cool as though it had ice in it.

Four miles from starting this evening, in a kanyon there was a spring to the right, with a little rivulet crossing the road. This water was colder than any ice water I ever drank. Farther down the same kanyon, large quantities of drift snow were found. It was quite a luxury and was used by the company in great quantities. The Wind Mountain is still in sight, 30 miles, & no doubt these very cold springs that we have spoken of, is the welling of the snow from them. Just opposite our encampment was a beautiful grove of green cottonwood. This is the first large trees we have seen since leaving the Platte & was pleasing & cherishing. The ox teams are still leaving their traces behind, making the atmosphere occasionally hideous! We came up to the Government train before they had started, & rolled in before them.[27] They prepared to go the 16 mile stretch & passed us at noon.

[*Distance, 16 miles.*

Friday, June 29th.

Not caring to be in a hurry to leave such good grass as we had, we did not make a very early start this morning, but let our animals grase until 6 & then rolled out. The road was up & down hill, & crossing several streams, the first, some 5 miles from our starting and coming direct from the "Wind Mountain" was named by us the *Wind River*. The second,

---

27. Backus, who was two days' journey behind the Charlestown Company, wrote on June 30, "passed today a *Government Train* of 40 mule wagons on their way to *Bear* River Valley."

2 miles from the last, the reason for which it came being filled with ice, was named the *Ice River*. These streams are not particularly mentioned by any traveller before, & I doubt not [that] in regular seasons [they] have no water but they are now running from the very hard winter & very wet spring, as, in the recollection of the oldest trappers, such wet weather was never seen before. Eight miles brought us again to the river. Here the road that comes up the river comes in & also crosses.

The Government train was encamped on the river, having layed up for the purpose of tightening their wagon wheels, which were about falling to pieces—the very hot sun & sand causing them to shrink from the tires. We crossed & nooned on the hill opposite the crossing. In this vicinity we found many horned frogs.[28] This & the vicinity of the crossing of the South Platte are the only places we have seen these curious little animals. They are smaller than our toads and have quite a small delicate head. The horns come out from the body, being from an eighth to a quarter of an inch in length.

We found here some trappers who have been laying at this place for two weeks for the purpose of trading with the emigrants.[29] One among them, was a very intelligent fellow, by name Rogers. He was a Frenchman, and a most remarkable looking man. Tall, fine figure, carrying himself very erect, with an immense head of hair hanging in curls over his shoulders, and as black as the Indian Squaw's whom he had for his wife. Their mode of getting through life is I think rather captivating than not. They seem not to have a care, & are free from the petty annoyances & scandal of civilization. Money is no object, nothing to sell for it & nothing to buy with it. Game of all sorts in abundance, & when it is driven from one point they follow it, changing at the same time their lodges and consequently their homes.

Rogers entertained us with some amusing stories of the emigrants that he had encountered in his rambles. Being out

28. *I.e.*, horned toads. The term frogs was not uncommonly used. See Bruff, July 15.

29. On July 1, Hackney, who was at about this same point, a day's journey from the South Pass, wrote, ''found a company of traders hear done some trading with them one of them told me he had not been in the states for 18 years they all had indiane wives with them.''

hunting he saw an emigrant creeping up to an antelope. He
halted until he shot & killed it & then rode up toward him.
The emigrant turned & saw him & with one bound he leapt
upon his horse & bolted from him like an arrow. He evidently
took him for an Indian, which was very natural at a little
distance, but if he had allowed him to approach a little
nearer he would have found him, although a man dressed in
skins yet they were not cut in the rude stile of the Indian,
with the buckskin shirt & legins, but he would have seen a
tall, fine open countenanced gentleman, with skin pantaloons
in gaiter stile, & coat of the same, in the present sack style
of the States. He [Rogers] hallowed several times for the
poor frightened fellow to stop but the wind was blowing in
an opposite direction, & he could not recognize a white man's
voice, & thinking of ten thousand Indians, away he went,
never once turning his head. Finding the dead antelope was
truly deserted, [Rogers] skinned it & packed it on his horse.
In a short time he came up to another emigrant, who had
also been out hunting. He [the emigrant] turned & saw him
some distance behind, & kept walking straight ahead without turning his head once, having made up his mind, as
Rogers expressed it, to meet death with[out] seeing it, if it
was to come. He [Rogers] rode up alongside & spoke to him.
He was equally as much startled, indeed more, to hear him
speak English than if he had spoken Injin. He [Rogers]
asked him where his train was, but the fellow was so frightened he could give no satisfactory account of himself. Leading a mule, he [Rogers] invited him to mount & ride with
him to his lodge, which was immediately on the road, &
[where] he could see his train and join it when it passed.
The man hemmed & hawed for some time, & at last, rather
from the fear of offending than desirous to go with him, he
mounted up. In mounting, the mule was rather skittish, &
he [Rogers] offered to hold his gun until mounted, but he
declined, saying he guessed it would not be much in his way,
& he held on to it, although it was with great difficulty that
he got on with it in his hand. The truth was, he was not yet
sure he had not fallen into the hands of the Philistines. Only
a few minutes before, having made up his mind that death

was inevitable, & meeting instead, one who seemed to be kindness itself, he was completely overpowered & could not understand his position. In the course of the ride to the lodge he [Rogers] found out that he belonged to the same company as the one did who[m] he scared from the antelope. He told him the circumstance, gave him half the animal, & dispatched him to his train which was then passing. We bought a very fine mule & some buffalo meat & skins from them [these trappers]. They all have their wives, & some, not satisfied with one, have two. They perchase them from their fathers, a young squaw being valued at a good horse.

We nooned 4 hours & started for the dividing ridge of the South Pass, it being distant from this last crossing of the Sweet Water 10 miles. We here take an affectionate leave of this beautiful river. We have traveled up it 104 miles, & in its whole course it scarcely varies one foot either in breadth or depth. We enjoyed some delightful camps upon its banks & have endulged in some luxurious soliloquies. I confess I have formed quite an attachment to this captivating little stream & almost think I could pass my days in contentment & happiness upon its beautiful banks.

The road this evening was hard & firm & we soon rolled these ten miles, which brought us in the middle of the *Great South Pass of the Rocky Mountains*.[30] Here is the dividing ridge from which flows the waters to the Atlantic & Pacific.

There is here a large, fine, clear spring, which is called the Pacific Spring. In fifteen minutes walk you can drink from the flowing waters of both the Atlantic & Pacific Oceans. With a little imagination, you can extend your arms, one over the vast waters of the Atlantic & the other over those of the Pacific. These waters reach the Atlantic by flowing into Sweet Water, thence into the Platte, thence the Missouri, Mississippi, & Gulf of Mexico & Atlantic. Those of

30. The South Pass through the southern end of the Wind River Range of the Rocky Mountains was so-called because it lay to the south of the passes earlier made known by Lewis and Clark. This easy passage across the continental divide had first been crossed from west to east by the returning Astorians in 1812 (see above, p. 19) and from east to west by Thomas Fitzpatrick (Broken Hand) in 1824. Captain Bonneville took wagons through in 1832. When the Oregon Trail opened, the Pass became the gateway to the Far West.

the Pacific commencing at the beautiful spring, runs to Green River, thence Colorado River in California, then Gulf of California & Pacific.

Persons generally have a very erroneous idea of this South Pass. It is generally supposed from its being called [a] Pass, to be a narrow pass, a place with high steep ragged, rugged, ugly, black, sharp, & threatening rocks on each side & above, with the steepest hills to ascend & the most dangerous precipices to descend, and being most dangerous to man or beast. You never formed an idea so far from the truth. The Pass is 19 miles wide, & through a little valley. The ascent is so gradual that it is scarcely perceptible. We commenced ascending from our very start from the States, & we are now 9000 ft. above the level of the sea & coming to this point more than 1000 miles would divide into a very imperceptible grade. The truth is, if you were not told, you would not know you were either in the Rocky Mountains or in the South Pass. On the left side of this valley of the Pass is some high mountains arising immediately from the edge of the valley. They are different, however, from those we have seen for some time back, being covered with some grass, and the little ravines being filled with green cottonwood. On the right we have the Wind Mountain, distant from us now about twenty miles. We found the valley filled with wagons & stock, & it was with difficulty we found a place to form our correll & then was obliged to drive our mules 2 miles for grass.   [*Distance, 25 miles.*

IV SOUTH PASS TO FORT HALL

WEST of the South Pass, the Rocky Mountains dominated the scene, and the emigrants found themselves passing through a region that was not only extremely difficult for travel, but geographically confusing. At first they were in the watershed of the Colorado, but they quickly passed from this region to the Bear River valley, which is a part of the Great Basin. But after only a few days there, they crossed over to Fort Hall, on the Snake, and were thus in the drainage basin of the Columbia River.

They reached the first affluent of the Colorado River system when they arrived at Pacific Springs, just beyond the South Pass. Originally, the trail had followed this watercourse southwest toward Fort Bridger, and had again turned north along Bear River. But the haste of the '49 migration had given popularity to a variant route by way of Sublette's Cut-off, which moved due west, intersecting two affluents of the Green River, namely the Little Sandy and Dry Sandy. Beyond these, a waterless stretch of about forty miles brought the emigrants to the Green River itself, which flows south into the Colorado. After achieving the difficult crossing of this stream in what is now Lincoln county, Wyoming, the emigrants continued across country, remaining in the watershed of the Colorado until they had crossed the upper reaches of Ham's Fork, which flows southeast into the Green. From that crossing (also in Lincoln County), it was less than a day's journey into the Great Basin. An easy divide carried the emigrants over into the valley of the Bear River, where they again struck the trail from Fort Bridger.

The journey of the Charlestown Company lay through the Colorado watershed for an interval of nine days (June 29-July 7).

Saturday, June 30th.

THIS is a stretch today of 20 miles without water, from the Pacific Spring to Little Sandy River. The ox teams are all looking badly & the poor drivers have faces long & demure. Many of them started last night at 12 upon this stretch. We rolled out, after filling our cask & canteens, at

4 1/2. The roads being on a descent, & hard & firm, we soon
came ten miles to Dry Sandy river. This has no water in it
in the dry seasons, but now it is quite a stream. But you
must not, (so the Mormons say) either drink yourself, or
allow your animals to drink it, as it is very injurious.[1]
[However,] both the guide & myself allowed our horses,
which were quite thirsty, to drink freely. We have not yet
seen any bad effect from it. We kept on & at 11 o'clock came
to Little Sandy.

We counted 50 wagons in the road before us. The road was
most awfully dusty & the stench from the dead oxen rendered it rather obnoxious. This day has given a panic to the
ox drivers. The oxen are strewed along the road, as mile
stones. We have rolled today 20 miles & passed 20 dead
ox[en]. We much pity those coming a few days behind us
as the horrid smell in this close climate will, I much fear,
cause even sickness among them. There is, in many places,
no such thing as going around them, but [one] must follow
the road, and many of the poor oxen have scarcely hauled
themselves out of the track of the wagons.

We had a pleasant march, however, & I was struck particularly with the unusual spirits of everyone. Even our friend
Locke was once more happy, as "poor old Kit" was once
more "himself again" and was again leading with head &
tail erect. I passed by our friend on the road, & with laugh-
ing, shouting, and an occasional taunt at old Kit such as,
"& you Kit, what are you about, I'll warm you directly," he
looked the personification of contentment.

We nooned 3 hours on Little Sandy & rolled 6 miles to Big
Sandy. Five miles before you come to Little Sandy there is
a road which takes off to the left, which is the Mormon Road,
striking the old trail some distance lower down.[2] At the Little

1. This allusion clearly shows that Bryarly had used Clayton's *Latter-Day
Saints' Emigrants' Guide* (see above, p. 21), usually called the Mormon Guide,
for it lists the Dry Sandy (p. 16) with the comment, "the water brackish, and
not good for cattle."
2. At this point, the original Oregon Trail swung southwestward (left) toward
Fort Bridger, on Black's Fork of Green River. There the emigrant might leave
the Oregon Trail, continuing southwestward to Salt Lake City (hence the term
Mormon Road), in which case his route did not again meet that of the other
California emigrants until he reached the City of Rocks (see p. 161, below) at
the head of the Humboldt Valley. If he continued on the Oregon Trail, how-

Sandy the old trail takes off. But few have travelled it this spring, those going the old trail taking the upper road. Nearly all the emigrants however have gone Sublette's cut-off, which commences at the Little Sandy. We encamped upon Big Sandy. Here commences the great stretch without grass or water, which is the difficulty of the cut-off. At this Big Sandy you leave water & grass for a 40-mile stretch. For four or five miles the banks of the stream are covered with wagons & stock recruiting for this great march. We intend laying by until tomorrow at noon and then taking this 40 mile "bug bear."

The sun has been most suffocatingly hot in the middle of the day for some days, & our herdsmen, who are exposed to it the whole time, have all been taken sick, and are now suffering with a burning fever. They were taken within 24 hours of each other. I have been called to see several emigrants who are suffering from the same fever & cause.

[*Distance, 26 miles.*

Sunday, July 1st.

We are now laying on the Big Sandy River. We remained here until 2 P.M. when we once again "hooked up" and were on this "Jornado." [3] We had a very pleasant camp, although much exposed to the sun, which during the middle of the day was very oppressive. Some amused themselves fishing while others were busily employed "Fixing Up" as they say, such as washing, drying, packing, &c. We remained thus

ever, his route from Fort Bridger lay northwestward until he reached Bear River. Going first southwest then northwest, he would have described a wide arc, but would have gained the advantage of following watercourses.

Emigrants who desired a quick journey were impatient with this detour. Such impatience led William Sublette, in 1832, to attempt a short cut due west (right) across the waterless expanse. Captain Bonneville's wagon party followed his route successfully that same year, and Sublette's Cut-off became the accepted road, except for those who were going to Salt Lake.

Hoffman's diary, this date, said: "We travelled about six miles when the road turns off to Salt Lake. . . . About one half of the emigrants are taking this route."

3. The Spanish term, *jornada* (a day's journey), had come to signify a considerable distance which must be traversed without water (and, therefore, in one day, if possible). It had been adopted by the American pioneers in this specialized sense.

long here for the purpose of recruiting & traveling at night.
There was two hundred wagons along the stream in sight &
they all seemed to have come to the same determination
about starting, as they drove out just as we did.

After filling our casks & some of our gum clothes-bags
with water, supplying ourselves with sufficient to give them
[the animals] a gallon a piece, & having cut a little bundle
of grass for each, we started. We rolled until the moon was
nearly down which was 1 o'clock & then piquetted out. We
then gave our animals some grass & a little water, & then we
"turned in" to remain until daylight. The road for three
miles was a solid mass of wagons.

[*We traveled 25 miles.*

Monday, July 2nd.

At daybreak after a hasty bite we rolled again. During the
morning I saw a great deal of grass—better than any we
have seen since leaving the Platte. These hills, indeed the
whole of this 40 miles, are represented as being very barren,
but we found it covered with the shrubbery peculiar to the
country & in many of the ravines excellent grass. The morning was quite cool, which was most fortunate & favorable
for us. The last 20 miles is up & down hill, some of them very
steep, it being necessary to let the heavy wagons down with
ropes to prevent their utter destruction. Just before you
arrive at the river you have the last but not least of the hills
to descend. It is nearly three miles from the summit to the
bottom, which is at the long looked for *Green River*.[4] We
drove immediately to the river where we encamped for the
purpose of crossing as soon as we could get our pontoons
loaded.

We found many wagons waiting for their turn at the ferry.
This ferry is owned by a Frenchman who had started for
"The Promised Land" with two small pontoon beds and

4. Green River, a tributary of the Colorado, had been a favorite resort of
the fur-traders since the time of Ashley's first expedition. Bancroft later attributed its name to a member of Ashley's Company, but the existence of a
member bearing this name has not been proved, and it appears that the Spanish
had already named it Rio Verde because of its color. The Charlestown Company crossed this stream in what is now Lincoln County, Wyoming.

came to the conclusion he would stop here & establish a ferry, not so much for the accomodation of the emigrants as for the desire of monopoly. He charges $8 a load, & it takes three loads to one wagon. However, they *must* go across, & consequently the ferry is engaged for 4 days ahead. All the streams that we have crossed upon this side of the mountain have been muddy, while those on the other side with the exception of the Platte were clear. The Green River is about 150 yds. wide, with a strong current, & 10 ft. deep. It is unusually high at present. Generally it is fordible.

We had much difficulty in getting our mules upon the opposite side. They would strike across but would get frightened at the strong current & return to shore. After driving them in several times, with howling, whiping &c., we at last succeeded in crossing all but some 20, which had to remain upon this side with nothing but the sage bushes for food.

In the afternoon several of the officers of [the] Government train rode up to our train, having left Big Sandy in the morning. Their train was also on the road. I invited them to take a camp-fire supper which they did. Afterwards we discussed the Sublette Cut Off and the difficulties of crossing Green River. At 12 we parted, they to look for their camp, and I for my lonely couch upon mother earth.

[*Distance, 20 miles.*

Tuesday, July 3rd.

Our guide with his usual energy was at work early this morning, getting our wagons, baggage, &c., across the river. The day was spent in hard, fatiguing, & laborious work. Once our boats were carried 2 miles down the river by the current & wind. It was found impossible to cordel it up the stream, & it was proposed, as the most expeditious plan, to bring the boats back over land. The wagon was taken out—[the one] that was in the boats—and put together, & the boats put upon it, & brought up. We finished crossing at sundown. Having met some Missourians, formerly of our county of Virginia, we loaned them our boats, for which they seemed very gratified, as otherwise they would have been compelled to await their turn, which would have detained them several

days. We were offered $500 for our Pontoons, & two
[wagon-]beds in their place. We would not take it as there
is yet a possibility that we may again need them. This morning in getting over our last mules, we lost one, which, we
concluded, had cooly and deliberately committed suicide.
It did not attempt to swim, but allowed its head to go under
immediately on its going in the water & neither turned [to]
come out, or struggled to save himself, [in] the least.[5]

In the afternoon Mr. Washington, Keeling & myself
visited the Government camp, it being at the lower ferry,
some few miles from our crossing. We supped with them &
after a pleasant "tete-a-tete" drifted towards our camp,
having promised to dine with them on the morrow.

Wednesday, July 4th.

This is the glorious Fourth. The first dawn was ushered
in by a noise from our six pounder, which reverberated,
echoed & reechoed from hillock to hill, until the very earth
itself seemed to tremble in fear at such strange noises. We
determined to remain upon the banks of Green River to
spend the Fourth. Every one was in excellent *spirits* & all
that seemed wanting was a little *"ardent"* that they might
pledge to each other: "The day we celebrate." Our accom-
modating Quartermaster soon furnished the needful, & a
happier set was not collected together in the "[E]stados
Unidos" than was ours.

The little Big Gun was considerable of a curiosity upon the
plains "this far out." The emigrants both at the upper &
lower ferry hurrahed whenever it was fired, & many came
to look at it.[6] Mr. Washington & Keeling & myself left our

5. According to the Hoffman diary of same date, this was the first mule which
the Charlestown Company lost.

6. Celebration of the Fourth of July was the major festivity of the overland journey. Frémont's party had observed the day in 1842, and the precedent
probably dates back to the earliest trappers. McIlhany, *Recollections,* p. 23,
describes the festivities of the Charlestown Company somewhat more fully than
Bryarly does, and his account may well be quoted here: "The next day was
the Fourth of July, and there were a great many emigrants there [on the Green
River] resting. Up and down the stream they were camped about, three thousand
strong. We rested all that day engaged in cooking, sewing, and washing. Tom
Moore, from Harper's Ferry, Virginia, was selected as orator of the day. He
stood on a large stump and had an Indian pole in his left hand to steady him-

camp about 12 for the Government camp, to fulfill our engagement of yesterday.[7]

self with. He had his right one free to make gestures with. Being the Fourth of July, our quartermaster issued whisky rations. Some had more or less, and some didn't have any. Those are the ones that didn't drink. We hadn't had our little cannon out of the wagon since we started, and we concluded that we would take it out that day and chain it to the stump. Moore felt pretty good, feeling the effects of his whisky, and everytime that he would say anything patriotic would touch the little cannon off, and the echo would bellow up and down the valley. The Indians, when they heard that cannon, would not come anywhere near us.'' The Hoffman diary, in Ambler, ''West Virginia Forty-niners,'' also describes these festivities and especially the firing of the cannon.

Other diarists who mention the commemoration of this day include Backus, Brown (p. 142), Bruff, Dundass, Hackney, Johnston, Kelly (p. 254), Long, McCall, McCoy, Royce (pp. 22–23), Searls, Sedgley, Tiffany, and Webster (nearly all of whom mention the firing of arms), but perhaps the fullest and most interesting account is that of Swain. He describes ceremonies which began with the playing of the ''Star-spangled Banner,'' and continued with the reading of the Declaration, the delivery of an oration, and the playing of ''Hail Columbia,'' after which the entire company marched into a ''hall'' ''which was formed by running the waggons in 2 rows far enough apart for the covers to reach from one to the other forming a fine hall covered by the waggon covers, thus forming a comfortable place for the dinner table which was set through the center. Dinner concisted of ham & beans, boiled and baked, biscuit, John cake, apple pie, sweet cake, pudding, rice, pickles, vinegar, pepper sauce, mustard, coffee, sugar, and milk. All enjoyed it well & after dining the toasting commenced.'' Swain remained through five of the toasts and then left before ''reason was out and brandy in.'' Also, see the discussion in Read and Gaines, eds., *Gold Rush*, I, 479, n. 135.

7. Bryarly, McIlhany, and Hoffman all omit reference to the fact that, while on the Green River, the President of the Company, B. F. Washington, acted as counsel for the defense in an impromptu trial. Delano, July 4, describes the episode: A man named Williams, going in pursuit of a murderer, had killed the offender. This led to a decision to try Williams, who thereupon employed Washington as his counsel.

''A court of inquiry was organized; General Allen elected chief justice, assisted by Major Simonton [*sic*. See p. 118 above] who, with many of his officers, and a large crowd of emigrants, was present. A jury was impaneled, and court opened under a fine clump of willows. There, in that primitive courthouse, on the bank of Green River, the first court was held in this God-forsaken land, for the trial of a man accused of the highest crime. At the commencement, as much order reigned as in any lawful tribunal of the States. But it was the 4th of July, and the officers and lawyers had been celebrating it to the full, and a spirit other than that of '76 was apparent.'' In the proceedings that followed, Washington became involved in an altercation with the judges; this altercation degenerated into a fight; and the trial finally broke up without any verdict being reached. Paden, *Wake of the Prairie Schooner*, p. 260, gives additional details of this trial but errs in saying that it was the original killer who was set free.

Thursday, July 5th.

This was rather a blue morning. We all looked sheepish &
felt much the need of a little good old Hock & Sherry. After
partaking of a hearty breakfast, we bid a last farewell to our
friends, with many hopes for each others' success & of seeing each other again. They walked to the ferry with us, & in
looking across the river I was delighted to observe my horse
upon the other side. For this consideration I was indebted
to my friend Smith. We learned our train was then passing
on the other side, which we soon joined. It was very hot &
the dust flew in clouds. We nooned at 12 and remained until
3 1/2. We nooned upon the 12 mile run [creek] (called so
from the distance from the crossing of Green River to the
crossing of it.) In the evening, we rolled 6 miles, & encamped
with good grass. In a few miles we had to cross a very high
& steep hill. We took this road for the purpose of cutting
off several miles, but heavily laden wagons would do better
to keep the main road. Upon the top of the hill was a grave of
a lady, the wife of an Oregon emigrant of '47.[8] At the crossing of the creek, we filled our casks & rolled 6 miles to camp.
We saw some emigrants fishing, who had succeeded in taking some very fine trout.[9]   [*Distance, 18 miles.*

Friday, July 6th.

Daylight saw us again upon our trail. Immediately from
camp we descended a very steep hill, which required back
locking. We ascended & descended these cliffs as they came
during the day.

We nooned 5 hours on the side of what the trappers called
"The Big Hill." We had a beautiful brook of water & the
best grass we have had since leaving the States. It was the
bunch grass which is considered the best & as being equal to
grain. We were again upon the road at 3. The hills still con-

8. Backus, July 7, also mentions this grave.

9. Few fish, apparently, were caught in the valley of the Missouri (exceptions
are shown in Wistar, May 20, Webster, July 19, and Swain, July 26) but
many emigrants noted the abundance of fish, and especially of trout in the
streams of the Rocky Mountain area. (*E.g.* see Hackney, July 8; B. C. Clark,
July 12, 15; Backus, July 20; Doyle, July 17; Love, July 3, 16, 17; and Hale,
Aug. 6).

tinued, and at the bottom of each were little streams. From the top to top was about 1 mile. On our left during the evening, the Eutaw Mountains, covered with snow, were in view and [on] the right the old & familiar Wind Mountains.

Every ravine is still filled with snow, which accounts for the unusual supply of water, & convinces one also of the terrible winter that has just past. This is now in July when everything is burnt up at home, while here we can indulge in the innocent amusement of snow-balling, or step over the hill & take a delightful bath with everything green & as cheerful as the beginning of Spring.   [*Distance, 15 miles.*

Saturday, July 7th.

Owing to the very affectionate endearings, whisperings & communings of the musquitoes we were easily aroused this morning & made a start at daybreak. We descended a very steep hill immediately, at the bottom of which we found considerable of a creek. This is called Ham's Fork. It empties into Bear River, & from this is called one of the feeders of the Colorado.[10]

The road after crossing turns to the left & runs down the valley 1 1/2 miles, & then turns again to the right up the steepest hill we have yet ascended. In reaching the top of this we got on the top of a ridge which has been in our sight for two days. The road was hard & firm. We kept this ridge (the grass being excellently good on each side as far as the eye could reach) for 8 miles & then nooned at a slip of woods where we found an excellent spring. This spring has not been mentioned by anyone heretofore, but having found many fragments of a Fourth [of] July dinner which had been held by some emigrants before us, we called it "Independent Spring."

Just before we stopped we saw upon the roadside a fresh grave, which was of an emigrant who died on the 4th of July. We found at the spring some Indians who had assembled for the purpose of trading. They were of the "Shoushounees Tribe" or vulgarly known as Snakes. They are the most powerful nation & more friendly to the "White Man"

10. Bryarly's geography is in error. Ham's Fork enters Black's Fork, which enters the Colorado. Bear River flows to Great Salt Lake.

than any other nation known. They are not so good looking as the Sioux nor so cleanly. Some of them speak a little English, learned I suppose from the trappers, who associate (for their own safety) more with them than any other nation. We traded with them for some ponies, skins, &c. &c., & found them not hard in their bargains. One of us traded two old saddle blankets for a nice pony.

We nooned 4 hours and again started, still keeping the ridge for 2 miles. We then commenced descending a steep hill, upon which the dust was at least 1 foot thick. The wind was blowing immediately up the valley to which the road ran, & it was almost impossible to open your eyes. Many of us had goggles which succeeded in keeping the dust out of our eyes but did not allow us to see through it. Some quarter of a mile down we found a road branching from the main road to the left. This our guide took, which kept more on the bluff & with a more gradual descent to the valley, although in some places we had to "back lock" & to ease our wagons down with ropes. The main road is a half mile nearer, but about half way, there is a regular "break-neck" jumping off place, where it was necessary to unhook the animals, lower the wagons down by hand, & drive the animals around to reach the bottom. All this trouble & detention was saved us by the knowledge of our guide. I doubt not, had we attempted this *"Devil Hill"* or better known as "The Big Hill" or "Sublette's Hill" we would have lost some of our wagons, as others had done before us, as we saw many remnants of such departed spirits at the bottom.

In the valley we crossed a little stream of cool, pure water, & then came up a steep winding hill, from the top of which we came in sight of *Bear River,* distant in a valley below us about 7 miles. We rolled for two miles which brought us to the descent to the Bear River Valley. Having found a good spring, with excellent grass some two hundred yds. from the Valley, we turned out alongside of the road and camped.

[*Distance, 20 miles.*

[At the point where the trail struck Bear River, on what is now the Utah-Wyoming border, the stream flows northwest, soon reaching what is now Idaho, and pointing toward the watershed of the

Columbia. But after about eighty miles, it reverses itself in a great bend, and flows south to Great Salt Lake. The Oregon Trail followed along the right bank for the northerly part of its course, crossing two tributaries, Smith's Fork and Thomas' Fork. At the bend, however, near Soda Springs, in what is now Caribou county, Idaho, the trail left the river, continuing north to Fort Hall, on the Snake.

After leaving the Colorado watershed, the Charlestown Company spent only four days, (July 7–July 11) in the Great Basin (Bear River valley), before crossing to the Columbia watershed.]

Sunday, July 8th.

[A] pleasant rest last night and [a] spirited start this morning. Rolled 7 miles along the valley, where we found the road turning abruptly to the right about 1 1/2 mile where we crossed Smith's Fork.[11] This is a very deep but narrow stream, & there is four different branches of it. Immediately after, the road is very stony & rough & runs between two cliffs, the sides of which were covered with young hawks & eagles. Some of our men ascended them, & obtained a nice mess of such squabs.[12]

We rolled 4 miles farther & encamped upon Bear River at what is called "The Narrows." Here our guide determined to spend the remainder of the day, which was hailed with three cheers by us all, as we stood much in need of soap & water both for our persons & clothes. We took some fish here such as trout, mullets, &c., &c., which were very fine. I amused myself in the morning by shooting prairie squirels (or as some call them prairie rats) of which we had a most delightful soup. They are the fattest *small animal* that lives.[13]

Being four days from Fort Hall, & having determined to part with some of our wagons there, if possible, we deter-

---

11. Smith's Fork, a tributary of Bear River, was named for Jedediah Smith.

12. Wistar, July 7, speaks of "a kind of large hawk which are fair eating," and Doyle, Sept. 24, mentions soup made from a kind of hawk called a "Pine Turkey."

13. These are the animals now generally known as ground squirrels. Paden, *Wake of the Prairie Schooner*, p. 238, quotes an emigrant who wrote, "Learning that the traders called these small animals (which are so plentiful) squirrels I took the revolver and killed a mess, if they had called them rats they would hardly have been palateable, as it was we relished them considerably."

mined to send two men forward for the purpose of making such arrangements as possible. They were also to see about obtaining some flour, as we fear we will stand in need of more than we have on hand.

The musquitoes were larger & more numerous here than any place we have yet passed. Many of our men who are not used to such plagues of life were much troubled by them, their sting proving very poisonous. We had also the most delectible felicity of tasting for the first & only time "strawberries." They were rather scarce, to be sure, but a couple of handfulls *was quite a GodSend,* & looked like a surfeit.

Two miles above Smith's Fork we again struck the old road, the Fort Bridger road.[14] It has been but little traveled. We could see but three tracks of wagons along it.

[*Distance, 11 miles.*

Monday, July 9th.

Our men who were commissioned as our dispatch was ready at dawn this morning & started for Fort Hall. They were Messrs. Geiger, Kelly & Asquith. The train rolled with them a short distance when they left us for a 50 mile stretch. We passed through "The Narrows" which is the road & river running between the mountains. The road is very level & hard & consequently we rolled quite fast. In three miles we came to a large flat, around which the road ran 5 miles. There was a sort of trail across it which induced some 20 of our men to take it, as the nearer. For half way it was hard & firm, then suddenly became very marshy with a deep slough in the middle.

We that were riding took one way through the marsh, while those on foot took another leading to Thomas's Fork, which we had to cross, & which they determined to shorten the distance by swimming. It was with great difficulty that we at last reached the fork with our horses. They would get mired every ten steps, & [we,] not being able to turn them around, were obliged to battle ahead, our horses plunging & jumping sometimes for 50 yds. at a time. We succeeded at last, however, with jaded & worn out horses, in reaching the

---

14. In other words, this was the end of Sublette's Cut-off, which the Charlestown Company had taken on July 1. See p. 131, above.

crossing in safety, all of us having determined never again to take the cut-offs.

It was here, with feelings of astonishment & regret, that we learned [of] the loss of one of our party who was on foot. It appears that they waded & swam [*one word illegible*] the sloughs & finally came to the river, Thomas' Fork. It was about 50 yds. wide & the deepest part was 11 ft. Some half dozen swam over, & a young man, bold & brave, but unfortunately too rash, named Taliferro Milton, of Virginia, was drowned. They said he was but a poor swimmer & he was solicited strenuously by his friends not to attempt it, but he was ambitious & daring and went in. He had proceeded but a short distance, when he strangled & seemed to have lost all his presence of mind, & instead of trying to get [back] to the shore from which he started, his whole aim was to reach the opposite [side]. The water was not swift, but very cold, & no doubt this caused him to strangle in catching his breath quick. A pole was extended to him by one of his friends who was in the water at the time, which he caught hold of, & giving it a quick jerk as soon as he caught it, he pulled him under and nearly strangled him also. This he done twice & was twice pulled under the water by him, & then he ceased to struggle, & sank in 10 ft. [of] water. He was much liked & beloved by every member of the Company. He was ambitious, energetic & daring. This perhaps was a fault with him, & to this must we attribute his irreparable loss. He was always among the first to volunteer his services for anything called for & the last to give up & cry *rest*. He was from Jefferson County, Virginia, and 19 years of age, with father, mother, & sisters, who, it is said dote upon him as their only son & only brother. We sympathise from our hearts with them. May "their loss be his gain." [15]

He had a brother-in-law in [the] Company, who was deeply affected & was truly distressed, for he said his wife loved her brother so dearly. We crossed the Fork & passed around near the place of the accident and corralled. By tying upon a cord some large rock-fish hooks with a very heavy rod, throwing it out & dragging it in, we succeeded after a

15. The drowning of this young Virginian is also described in McIlhany, *Recollections*, pp. 20–21, and in the diary of Benjamin Hoffman.

few trials, in bringing him to the surface there. I examined him closely to find if there was possibly any hope of resuscitation, but alas it was too late. The spark was out & his spirit had taken its place among the numbered. We wrapped him in a blanket & carried him to camp. There was no timber anywhere in the neighborhood that we could get to cover over the grave to effectively protect it from the wolves, & we determined to take him with us until we reached the river again, which was distant 7 miles, where we could obtain high ground & plenty of timber. He was accordingly dressed in his best suit & put in the sick wagon.

We started at 3 P.M. & immediately ascended a very steep & long hill & then descended another equally as long & steep. In the 7 miles, we ascended & descended four of these hills, being three-fourths of a mile in length. The last one brought us again to Bear River, where we encamped. There was three hundred wagons before & behind us during today's march. It was a beautiful sight to see them climbing up & down the aclivities & declivities. It seems that laying by on Sunday evening dropt us back in the middle of the emigration. They are very much together now, they having started [*one word illegible*] from Green River.

[*Distance, 20 miles.*

Tuesday, July 10th.

At the first dawn of day we carried the remains of our departed friend to his grave. His blanket was his only winding sheet & his coffin. Being wrapt in it carefully, it was sewed nicely all around. This was the best we could do—such a thing as a coffin upon the plains was impossible. The grave having been dug last night & logs prepared to wall it in, we buried him solemnly & with almost tearful eyes. I officiated in the want of anyone else to do it, & read the burial service over him. His name, place of residence, &c., was carved neatly upon a board which made his tombstone. The grave is upon a high point of a bluff 200 yds. from the river & half a mile down after striking the valley.

We rolled out immediately after, & the road being most excellent & keeping the Bear River valley, we soon made 12 miles, when we nooned upon a very pretty little rivulet. We crossed several of these little streams this morning, none of which has ever received any name. The largest is considered 12 miles from the bluff, & is sometimes called the 12-mile Creek. Fort Hall is called 110 miles from it. I visited some trappers encamped on the side of the road with their lodges, squaws, &c. There was also some 50 Indians with them. They belonged to the Shoa Shounnies.

I found one of these trappers very communicative & intelligent.[16] He said he had lived among this tribe for 25 years. He was married & had several children. When asked if he had no desire to return to the States he almost smiled in contempt. There was one trader among them who had his wife with him from the States. She was associating with the squaws & seemed to have imbibed all their modes & tastes of life. I addressed her with the common civilities of the day, when she turned away as though the nearer approach of a white man would contaminate her.

This tribe is the only one which bury their dead. I saw two graves near their camp & enquired if they were emigrants, when I learned they were those of the Indians. One was a very sudden & distressing death & occurred a few days since. An Indian boy traded his pony with an emigrant for a gun. He took it in his lodge, where his mother & sister were, and was examining it with all Indian curiosity, when it went off, shooting his sister through the breast & killing her instantly. She was tall, graceful, & the most beautiful squaw, it is said, in the whole tribe—of her tribe and other tribes. Many trappers, traders, & white men of all sorts had made advances to her, but she was true to her first love, which was with the son of the Chief, & who was then absent on a hunt. He was represented as being a bold & noble fellow, the pride & envy

16. These trappers were almost certainly of the group over which the famous Peg-leg Smith exercised leadership, and indeed it is likely that the trapper mentioned was Smith himself, for he often told emigrants that he had lived with the Indians for 25 years. For other references to Smith, see Bruff, Aug. 15; Hale, July 16; Hixson, June 26; and McCall, July 16. Also Paden, *Wake of the Prairie Schooner*, pp. 272–273, and Read and Gaines, eds., *Gold Rush*, I, 524–525. Smith's true name was Thomas L. Smith (1801–1866), but the necessity of an amputation which he performed himself gave him his familiar name. For a brief summary of the life of this famous mountain man, freebooter, trader, and trapper, see Settle, ed., *March of the Mounted Riflemen*, p. 150, n. 165.

of the tribe. They had taken a wigwam together but a few months previous, & as the trader remarked, he never saw such affection & respect among the civilized. They expected him in every hour & he [the trader] said he feared much he would mourn & starve himself to death, this being a favorite & common mode among them of showing their deep grief & dispair.

In the afternoon we rolled 12 miles farther & encamped in a pretty little valley 1 mile from the road, upon the river. We followed the same Bear River valley until 1 mile of camp, then we left it [and] passed over to the bluffs. We were ordered by our Captain to piquette our mules this evening instead of herding them as usual, & to prepare for a start at 1 A.M. After a supper upon prairie squirels I corralled for a snooze.   [*Distance, 24 miles.*

Wednesday, July 11th.

We were aroused this morning (as we all thought) in midst of a sweet sleep. It was a beautiful moonlight night, & everything was tranquil, in deep repose. By taking a cut, three miles brought us upon the road, which ran in a beautiful valley, skirted on each side by beautiful rolling mountains, the verdure extending up to the very tops without a rock or a shrub to break the velvety surface. Twelve miles brought us again to the river, & to the *well-renowned* "Soda Springs,"—by some called "Beer Springs." We arrived here at day break and coralled. The teams that we had been with for several days, expressed very great surprise, in passing all this morning, to find us before them & snugly & pleasantly layed up in this delightful spot.

The whole surface of the earth for miles around shows the effects of an immense [volcano] or many volcanoes. Along this, as we named it, "Lava Spring Valley," the earth is covered with charred irruptive stones. In many places the earth is bursted up as with an irruption very lately. In other places the rocks & earth are completely split open, & you can look as deep down as the eye can penetrate. Down many of them you can distinctly hear running water, all showing that some day [a] *"long time ago"* there was at least a great commotion in these parts. I cannot attempt to account for the many different freaks, irregularities, & the remains of departed times that we saw at this place. I will only tell it you, & you can form your own opinions.

The whole valley, however, is the most interesting spot of earth that I ever beheld. Here is a grand field for the geologist, minerologist, naturalist, & any other kind of "ist" that you can conceive. The road crosses here a little creek which empties, 200 yds. from the crossing, into Bear River. Immediately at its crossing we found two springs both of which were Soda.[17] They arose at the edge of the water. Upon looking farther, we found a great number of them along the banks, and also, from the bed of the creek & river, you could distinctly see the little springs shooting up. A little farther, some 200 yds., you find one covering a quarter of an acre. This is called "The Boiling Springs." It boils up from crevices in the rocks in a thousand different places, making the surface foam & hiss, as boiling water. At the lower part of the spring, the water descended again in the ground, this being the only outlet. This was also Soda. In fact the whole earth seemed to be saturated & filled with this water, & it is bursting out from every crevice & hole that you can find. The greatest curiosity of all, however, is what has been named "The Steamboat Spring." This is situated upon the edge of the river, half a mile from the first spring. Out of a solid rock, with a hole 1 foot in diameter, gushes forth the water, foaming, whizzing, sizzling, blowing, splashing & spraying. It throws it up from two to three feet high. There is a little intermission of a few seconds every now & then, which makes it resemble more "The Palaces of the Deep." A few feet from this large one are two smaller ones, which are phizzing away all the time and somewhat resemble the scape-pipe of a Steamer. This large one has also a suction power. Some one around reached a cup into it, when it was immediately drawn from his hand into the hole. He, however, delved down for it, & found it the length of his arm in, & required a considerable jerk to get it out.

This lava water is pleasant to drink, & when mixed with

17. The various hot springs named here, especially Soda Springs and Steamboat Spring, were mentioned by almost all diarists, with varying degrees of amazement. Long, July 7, wrote that the water of Soda Springs "tastes precisely like some of Tom Rutherford's pop after the effervescence has gone off."

an acid, effervesces prettily. It has been analyzed by many, but I do not now remember all of its constituent parts. *The most however, from the deposit around, is Carbonate of Lime.* Fifty yds. from the Steamboat Spring, just upon the side of the river, was two springs, one foot and a half apart, one of which was a beautiful clear spring which was very good water; the other was perfectly red & was copperish. There is another spring somewhere in this vicinity, which is told me of by our guide, which is certainly the most remarkable one yet. He says that some years since, having lost his cattle, he went out to hunt them, when becoming very thirsty he started to look for water. Having found a little trickling in a ravine he followed it up to quite a large spring, which, upon approaching, he was surprised to find himself suddenly almost suffocated. He stopped a moment and then proceeded a few steps farther, when he thought he certainly would fall if he took another. He immediately stepped back some paces, where he could look for the cause of this singular phenomenon and, when in looking more closely at the spring, he was astonished to see, around its edge, numbers of dead birds, rabbits, frogs &c. He did not approach nearer, having attempted it several times & found it would certainly take his breath.

To the right of the road is the remains of what Bryant speaks of [18] as "the remains of an old crater." But I beg leave to differ with him. So far from being any thing like [there] having been a trace of fire about it, it has every appearance of being formed by water. It is upon a knoll which covers about one acre. The whole of this knoll, being some 50 ft. high, is of a yellow appearance, resembling at a little distance yellow clay. Upon arriving at it, however, it presents a different appearance. It was slimy, shining, & greasy, and when walked over had a hollow sound. We took some of our horses on it, & in some places [it] not being strong enough to bear them, they broke through, showing a scurf or crust of a few inches thick. The whole hill was but a shell, & when broke through, it was a hot whiteish mud, soft &

18. Bryarly appears to be in error here, for Bryant had taken the Mormon Trail to the Great Salt Lake, far to the south of the area through which the Charlestown Company was travelling.

tough underneath. Wherever it was broken, water came out in a stream. Upon this hill was a round hole some 6 ft. in diameter, with a wall, solid & smoth, both inside & outside, coming up above the earth around some 3 ft. The inside was filled up [with]in four ft. of the top with dirt, stones, & rubbish. Twenty feet from this, on the same mound, was a small [k]nob, 4 ft. high & 10 ft. in circumference. On the top of this, from a hole 6 inches in diameter, pushed forth as pretty a little stream as you ever saw. It bubbled up beautifully, and was warm with a sweetish taste. From the top, it flowed in a sheet over this little [k]nob & leaving a deposit of a whitish scum which, on closer examination, proved to be saleratus.

There is no doubt that the whole of this hill has been formed in this way. Everything around proves it so. There is not a volcanic stone in a half mile of it, but the grass is good, being green & thick, up to the very base of the mound. You can trace the deposit of this same substance of which the hill is composed, wherever the water runs. Half a mile from this is another hill of the same appearance, but the water has ceased to flow from it, but you can distinctly hear it running underneath. From the opening on top, instead of water, there is a pungent gas escaping, rather sulphurated & ammoniacal.

I examined all these different places with considerable interest, & confess I was fully repaid, & think it would almost repay one the trip across the plains to spend some weeks on this spot. It is a matter of astonishment that no Indians or mountaineers or adventurers have ever settled upon it. It is in [a] beautiful valley, fine water & plenty of large timber. The only drawback whatever is the injurious effects of the Soda water upon stock, which I think might, by a little care, be easily prevented. Some of our men were so much pleased with it as to determine at some future day, if fortune should fail them, to return to it & be hermits.

[The departure of the Oregon Trail from the Bear River Valley at Soda Springs had always presented a problem for emigrants to California. For the Oregon traveller, the next goal was Fort Hall, to the north, on the Columbia. But for the "Californians," the Fort

Hall road was a wide detour, and they had always felt an impulse to leave the Oregon Trail at the bend of Bear River and strike due west toward the Humboldt. The Bidwell-Bartleson Party had attempted this more direct route in 1841, but had met with such hardships and difficulties that for the next eight years, California emigrants were content to follow the Oregon Trail to Fort Hall. When the Charlestown Company passed, therefore, the Fort Hall route was the only route. The Forty-niners, however, were extremely eager for quick transit, and only a few days after the Charlestown Company turned north, a party led by James Hudspeth and J. J. Myers attempted a short cut due west (p. 159, n. 5, below). This attempt succeeded; the bulk of the migration followed; and Hudspeth's or Myer's Cut-off became the principal route to California.

The Charlestown Company were probably among the last of the Forty-niners to go by way of Fort Hall. They reached the Fort three days after leaving Bear River (July 11–July 14) and sixteen days after leaving Fort Laramie (June 29–July 14).]

We layed at these springs until 2 P.M. All the different messes cooked & baked bread for several days, having found that the water made it rise beautifully without the addition of anything else. Everyone drank very freely of the water, and after filling our casks for the purpose of making bread, we rolled. The road was very rough. Ten miles brought us to another spring of the same sort. It was on the right of the road coming from a high bluff. This is some times called Soda Pool. The water from the spring runs into a basin which has formed by the crystilisation of the water at its edges. It is 25 ft. in diameter & the wall around is 2 ft.

Two miles farther brought us to several springs of clear cool water in a very pretty valley. This is a regular encampment and many [were] encamped, but we, not having traveled any in the morning, determined to go farther. We rolled on, the road still keeping the valley, to a little brook, where we encamped. We got in camp at 9 o'clock, and it was very cold. It was sufferingly cold during the night and all the water around was frozen.   [*Distance, 33 miles.*

Thursday, July 12th.

When I awoke this morning my bed clothes were covered with a thick hoary frost, but having taken unusual exercise yesterday I did not feel the cold. We travelled up a little stream during the morning called "Tulocks Fork." It is a clear, pure, little stream & contains fine trout. Two miles after [the] crossing of [this] fork we encamped, or rather nooned, upon a little rivulet. We found here some Indians. They were poor & we done no trading. In the afternoon, 2 miles from noon, we crossed the dividing ridge between the waters of Bear River & those of Columbia River. The road was very hilly and those [hills] very steep. Four miles farther brought us to "Lewis Spring," the headwaters of Columbia River. It is [a] very large spring on the left side of the road & gushes out of the rocks. We followed this spring branch down two miles & encamped upon the side of a hill with plenty of wood, grass & water.   [*Distance, 17 miles.*

Friday, July 13th.

Our road this morning was very dusty & in two hours after starting [we] could scarcely distinguish one another. The country this morning was very barren, not even sage bushes. No grass on either side, but the sand was oppressively hot. We rolled 13 miles to noon. This is the first real hot day that we have had, in fact it is a perfect Mexican day. We met an express this morning from Oregon City "en route" for the troops destined for that place.[19] We had a few minutes conversation with them & we understood that they were desirous to obtain the troops as soon as possible to protect the women & children from the Indians, the men all having gone to California. We learned also that the cholera & much of other sickness was at the mines, & [that], on this account they were rather deserted for the time. The report was still confirmative of the abundance of the Dust. We saw also, to-

---

19. Oregon City was the capital of Oregon Territory, which at that time extended east as far as the Continental Divide. The first territorial legislature met there on July 16, 1849.

day, the Mormon mail, which passed us at a good round pace.[20] We got no news from them whatever.

After two hours rest we again started, the road becoming sandy in a short distance & continuing so for 7 miles. This is decidedly the heaviest piece of road that we have yet had. The dry, black, heavy sand was up to the axles the whole way, making one continuous drag. We got through it after a fashion safely, & came to a very large bubbling, boiling spring called "The Big Spring." It is distant from Fort Hall 6 miles. We here encamped, it being yet early in the afternoon. A few minutes after being in camp, our dispatch met us on its return from Fort Hall. They confirm the news of the sickness in California & say that many of the emigrants are going to Oregon. They succeeded in getting a sufficiency of flour &c.[21] The road from here is represented as being horrid in the extreme, not saying anything of musquitoes.

[*Distance, 19 miles.*

Saturday, July 14th.

There being 150 wagons around us, we moved at daybreak to get upon the road before them. We soon encountered a marsh & slough which was very trying to our mules, many of them going down in the mud up to their very nose. The road is through a swamp & these sloughs are every 200 yds. Our guide informs me that heretofore this has always been a smooth, hard, excellent road, & the vast amount of water

20. Leroy Hafen, *The Overland Mail, 1849–1869* (Cleveland, 1926); Oscar O. Winther, *Express and Stagecoach Days in California* (Stanford University, 1936); and other authorities, make no specific mention of any service known as the Mormon Mail. At this time, all United States government contracts for mail to and from California, were for ocean carriers; not until 1850 did the government let a contract for mail service between Independence and Salt Lake City; not until 1851 was this service extended from Salt Lake City to Los Angeles. Butterfield's Overland Mail first operated in 1858, and the Pony Express in 1860. Long before carriers under Federal contract had entered the field, however, private enterprisers were locally and casually active. In the earliest days of overland travel, eastbound fur traders carried letters, at a fee, for westbound emigrants; later, a number of private express companies were locally important.

21. Hoffman's diary for this day says that the company's delegates "succeeded in purchasing 700 weight of flour at 8 cents a pound. As to the information as to the road on to Fort Sutter, they gained none."

now here is accounted for in the same manner as it has been during the trip. I have been much in a musquitoe country, but confess I never before saw them in their glory. They were so thick you could reach out & get your handfull. We tried to tie up our heads & faces, but they would creep in wherever an opening was left. Our horses & mules were literally covered with them & you could scrape them off by handfulls. After 4 hours of splashing, plunging, & draging we arrived at "Fort Hall," it being distant from the start, 6 miles.

Half [a] mile before you reach the fort, you touch upon the bend of a river. This is Lewis's Fork or Snake River,[22] one of the tributaries to the Columbia. It is, at this point, 120 yds. wide & looks very deep, but not with a very strong current.

Fort Hall [23] is still in possession of an English fur company, "The Hudson Bay Fur Company." It is built of *adobes,* but has more wood about it than common, & consequently retains its original shape better than they generally do. It is much the same looking ranch as Laramie's but is not as large or as high. It has a fine court in the centre, with a fountain of water in the middle. There is an entrance on the south side & one on the north. Around the inside are little rooms with one small window to each, which are to keep their furs & fur stores, trading shops et cetera. The upper story, with a portico on the north side and steps running from the court, is the apartment of Capt. Grant, the English Agent. On the west side of the Fort, 150 yds. dis-

22. This principal tributary of the Columbia was first named after Meriwether Lewis, by his associate in the Lewis and Clark expedition, but the name of the Snake Indians of the region was the one finally adopted.

23. Fort Hall, on the Snake River in what is now Bingham County, Idaho, was built in 1834 by Nathaniel J. Wyeth and named in honor of Henry Hall, of Boston. The Hudson's Bay Company purchased the fort in 1837. When the Idaho region passed into control of the United States by the Oregon Treaty of 1846, the rights of the Company at Fort Hall and other posts were guaranteed, and the Company continued to operate the post until 1855. It was a vital way-station on the Oregon Trail. The chief agent at the fort between 1841 and 1852 was Captain Richard Grant, who was vividly described by Bruff, Aug. 24. See C. J. Brosnan, *History of the State of Idaho* (New York, 1935), pp. 84–86, and Read and Gaines, eds., *Gold Rush*, I, 529, n. 298. Thwaites, in *Early Western Travels*, XXX, 86, n. 62, gives the name incorrectly as James Grant.

tant runs the Snake river, which furnishes water to the Fort. On the opposite side is a slough which extends around the back part of it, making a moat around except in front.

Capt. Grant has been at this station for 25 years. He first came in the employ of the Fur Company, & has remained in it ever since. He has become identified with Fort Hall. He has been married twice, his last wife being a squaw. I met his son, Mr. John Grant, who was about 20 years of age, & a very gentlemanly & intelligent gentleman, although raised in the wild woods & dressed in skins. The Captain himself is a most remarkable looking man. He is 6 ft., 2 or 3 inches, high, & made in proportion, with a handsome figure. His face is perfectly English, fat, round, chubby, & red. His hair is now getting in the sere & yellow leaf & his whiskers are also turning grey.

There was many Indian lodges around the fort & many Indians. They are not good looking or cleanly & are also poor. We succeeded however in getting a few skins & a couple of ponies. There was here many traders, this being the headquarters for both their startings & returnings. They are generally Frenchmen, & the most of them came out many years ago in [the] employ of the Fur Company, having joined in St. Louis, which was first settled by the French. We succeeded in getting some nice milk & also a fried chicken, which carried us so far back, "to days that's past," that we were quite low spirited.

After getting our flour on board we rolled away, the road being better than this morning. Three miles & a half brought us to Portneuf or Pannack [24] River, which we crossed, it being up to our axels. The river was 75 yds. wide, pure, clear water, with a gravelly bottom. Half mile, we encamped on the side of the river. Having mules that required shoeing & wagons to be repaired, we determined to spend the evening

---

24. Here Bryarly confuses the Port Neuf with the Pannack (or Bannock, after the Indian tribe) and assumes that they are alternative names for the same stream. Actually, he was on the Port Neuf, and when next day he came to the Bannock he did not know what to call it. Ware's guide distinguished between the two streams, but Bryarly, who had access to a copy of Ware (see entry for July 19) failed to notice the distinction. Note that on July 15, he repeats the error.

at this place. We saw some very large fish[25] in the stream
and drew a seine, but, owing to the moss covered bottom,
took nothing but a bucket of lobsters or craw fish. These we
"parboiled," & those [of us] that had lived in fish country or
on water courses enjoyed them very much, while others were
standing around with mouths turned up in awe at such wolf-
ishness. The Pannack river runs down the valley for twenty
miles & empties into Snake River above the American Falls.
In many places where the river makes bends, they come
within a quarter of a mile of each other.

[Distance, 6 miles.

25. Bryarly's comment on the size of the fish invites comparison with Hoffman's statement, this day, "I saw fish in this river fully ten feet long. We
rigged up a small seine but caught only some small trout and fall fish."

V FORT HALL TO THE SINK
OF THE HUMBOLDT

FOR about sixty miles west of Fort Hall, the "Californians" continued along the Oregon Trail, traversing the difficult terrain on the south bank of the Snake, and crossing its tributaries, the Port Neuf, the Bannock, Fall River (Beaver Creek), and others. At Raft River (not mentioned by Bryarly), however, the road to California left the Oregon Trail, after utilizing this route for more than two-thirds of the total journey.

After the failure of the Bidwell-Bartleson Party to find a satisfactory route west from Bear River in 1841 (see p. 148, above), California emigrants had continued on the Oregon Trail to Fort Hall. The party of Joseph B. Chiles and Joseph Walker in 1843, did so, and thence made their way into California, but they did not open a desirable route. In 1844, however, the party of Elisha Stevens likewise went to Fort Hall and was there met by Caleb Greenwood who acted as guide into California. His route was so good that it enabled the party to keep their wagons, and these wagons were the first that went overland into California.

Greenwood's route became the basis for subsequent overland travel. In following this basic route, the Charlestown Company was to leave the Snake at Raft River, move southwest up that river, and up its tributary, Cache Creek. From the headwaters of Cache Creek, the road ran westward, across country, until it struck Goose Creek, another tributary of the Snake. Moving up this watercourse to its source, the emigrants entered what is now Elko County, Nevada, where they crossed over for the second time into the Great Basin, and approached the headwaters of the Humboldt.

Sunday, July 15th.

I THINK this valley should [be] named Musquitoe Valley, instead of Fort Hall Valley. They disturbed us very much, not allowing us scarcely any rest. The morning broke beautiful & clear, & light saw us once more hooked up & off. Our road continued down the valley for four miles, crossing and recrossing them [sic] often. In many places, they looked smooth, quiet, & peaceable on top,

& upon entering you found them dirty, ugly, *take in sort of places,* your horse going the first step over his back & requiring the assistance of ropes to drag him out. We here came to a stream, larger than either the Snake or Pannack river. We crossed this and ascended a steep cliff to the ridge. This road is a new one, having been made by the Emigration this spring. The old road went down the valley, which is 20 miles long, but on account of the flood of the early spring was impassable. This ridge was covered with artemisia, & in other respects [was] a sandy, barren place.

The road was very dusty & dry, & run along the edge of the bluff overlooking the valley. Upon the opposite side you had in view three well marked, very distinct buttes, being distant from one another perhaps 10 miles. In the valley you had in view the Snake River or Lewis Fork of Columbia, being nearest the opposite bank, then the Portneth or Pannack, taking this name from the Pannack Tribe of Shoshonees who reside principally upon it, then we have in view the last stream we crossed, which has no name & comes from a large spring half a mile above our crossing. From one of my friends finding this fact out I have named it Washington's Spring. We rolled 4 miles farther & nooned upon a little stream, where we had a difficult & dangerous crossing. We made a floating bridge of willows, similar to those made by Gen'l Taylor of corn stalks, & passed over in safety. The weather today was suffocatingly hot. The grass commences to look parched & our animals do not eat it with the same relish.

Four o'clock saw us again in motion, & we rolled upon the same ridge 7 miles, when we descended the bluff, & came to a beautiful bottom, which is part of Musquitoe valley. Two miles farther brought us to [the] edge of this bottom, where we encamped in the headquarters of the musquitoes. No one can conceive of the annoyance of these devils incarnate until they have experienced what we did at this camp. Our animals were very near stampeding from them & our guards were so busy saving their own eyes, that it was almost impossible for them to watch the animals.[1] [*Distance, 17 miles.*

---

1. Most emigrants complained bitterly of the sufferings inflicted by mosquitoes, and Badman, July 22, declared that ''they bite as if they had never

Monday, July 16th.

Last night we were regaled with music during [the] night. With the cornopeans of the musquitoes, & bass roar of the American Falls, buzzing of the buffalo [g]nats, interspersed with an occasional "solo" from a burro, the night passed off in wakefulness & watchfulness. It required but little time or trouble to arouse the camp, but every one was but too eager for an excuse to leave their ungrateful blankets.

We left the Musquitoe Valley & four miles from our start we came to "The American Falls"[2] on Snake River. The distant rumbling of these Falls broke the monotony of our march yesterday evening & last night, & we felt anxious to see them. The fall was about 30 ft., & reminded one of a miniature Niagara. The first fall was on the opposite side, & it extended half way across the river, it being 200 yds. wide at this place. The half on this side, after tumbling over the rocks, very similar to the rapids of the Niagara, it then fell the same distance as the other side. In one place in the middle of the Fall, was a round hole in the middle of the rock, through which the water rushed with great velocity, & throwing the stream some distance forward of the sheet of water coming over.

The road along the river continued dusty, being in many places up to the mules' knees, & raising in such clouds that the drivers could not see their leaders on the road. For several miles up the river were [a] succession of falls varying from 1 to 5 ft. The banks of the river here is well marked, being of high rocky bluffs, resembling those of the beautiful Hudson River. Six miles from [the] Falls, the road passes through two "Buttes" of solid rock with just space between

seen a human Being before." These complaints became especially vivid when the emigrants reached the Bear River valley. *E.g.*, see Backus, July 16; Hackney, July 21; Kelly, p. 244; and Long, July 3. Long tells how his party "concluded to *Funk*" the mosquitoes: "so one of the boys made an amateur chafing dish and lamp out of a little tin bucket, a tea cup of fat, with a taper, and a tin plate for the dish, on which we burnt tobacco, oil peppermint, oil aniseed, camphor, red precipitate, and in fact, some of everything that our medicine chest contained."

2. The American Falls, in what is now Power County, Idaho, are said to have been so named because a party of American trappers were swept over them to their death, in the early days of the fur trade.

for the road. One & [a] half miles farther we nooned upon
the river, with good shade of the pines. The sun was most
oppressively hot & we nooned 6 hours for the purpose of
making [our] march in the cool of the evening. We succeeded in taking some fish—which were fine—the salmon
trout.

We rolled in the evening at 4 o'clock, the road leaving the
river at our start, [a] half mile to our right. Five miles
brought us to Beaver Creek.[3] From the creek we ascended
the steepest hill we have yet encountered. The crossing also
was bad. The Creek is a succession of *dams* distant 50 yds.
from each other. They extended as far as the eye could
reach. These dams are supposed to have been formed by the
beavers, and have become petrified. Five miles farther, the
road bids farewell to the Snake River & strikes off to the
left. Here also "The Oregon Trail" strikes off to the right &
leaves us alone in our glory, with no other goal before us
but Death or the Diggins.

The road was most unaccountably bad, with chucks just
large enough for the wheels to fit tight in, & the dust raising
& hanging over in a cloud, with not a breath of air stirring to
drive it off. Five miles farther we encamped on Cache Creek,[4]
in a narrow, sandy, sagey valley. This [creek] is named for
the french word cache—to hide, the emigrants & traders
both to Oregon & California having hid or buried a large
amount of goods upon it. There is supposed to be a vast
amount laying here at this time which has been buried for
years & years.   [*Distance, 27 miles.*

Tuesday, July 17th.

This morning we were astonished at not hearing our usual
summons "To Horse," & lay for some time basking in the
sunshine of a bright, fresh, clear & glorious morning, won-

3. This tributary of the Snake was named Fall Creek, by Frémont in 1843;
Ware also spoke of it as Fall Creek, and it is known by that name at the
present.

4. Bryarly first wrote "Cachia Creek," then struck through it, and sub-
stituted "Cache Creek." In later entries, he uses the form "Cachia." The
stream is now sometimes called Cassia Creek (see Paden, *Wake of the Prairie
Schooner*, p. 321, and Thwaites, *Early Western Travels*, XXX, 90), but the
term Cache Creek has remained in general use.

dering what could be the cause of such unusual sluggishness. Laying thus, pondering over the many new & delightful scenes that I have so much enjoyed in the last two months, and coming suddenly to myself & my present position, I arose with excited feelings to be enlightened upon such an unusual thing as being allowed to let the sun catch us in our blankets. I was agreeably surprised, & yet regretted it myself, to understand we were to spend this delightful morning in camp. Thank God we had no musquitoes last night, & we arose fully refreshed.

Our Captain had determined last night to leave one of our wagons, or rather to mend the remainder with it. A committee was appointed to decide which was to be the victim. With no little delight did our ambitious teamsters learn that the wagon with the best team was condemned. It was duly unpacked & its load distributed in shares to each of the others, & the wagon distributed in parcels to repair the damages of others. I also came in for my share of spoils. *I* succeeded in getting first choice for two mules & *of course* I chose the best. One of my choice[s] very much annoyed my friend Geiger, who was most anxious to get it from me, but the sick must be attended to first, & I could not oblige him. I rigged four horses with these two additions to my sick-wagon, & promise more comfort to the unfortunate invalids.

The men amused themselves in fishing, bathing, & washing their clothes. My friend Washington was applied to to swap a very dull, indolent, good for nothing Indian pony that he had, for a large, fine, handsome American horse whose back had been made sore by packing. After *some persuasion* he done so, the pony being [worth] $10, the Horse $100.

At 3 P.M., we again rolled, crossing the creek, which was very much cut up. We found here two graves of emigrants to Oregon several years since. The tomb stones were undefaced & the graves untouched. Four miles we again crossed the creek, & keeping up it two miles farther, left it. We then struck off more nearly to the south, while the creek ran due west. We noticed at this point where some persons, and [we] supposed them to be emigrants, had set fire to the grass either by design or accident, & it burnt for several miles on the side of the road & was still burning. If it was [done] by design it was unpardonable. They should certainly think of those who are coming behind them. Six miles of dust, in clouds, thick & impalpable, brought us again to the same Cachia Creek, running now due south. We encamped in its valley, with good grass, wood & water, & *no musquitoes.* In fact, this was the prettiest encampment since leaving the Platte. Here goes off the last road to Oregon, taking directly over the bluffs.   [*Distance, 12 miles.*

Wednesday, July 18th.

The morning broke clear, beautiful, & refreshing. After a good cup of coffee we were off again with spirits buoyant as air. Two miles & a half brought us to Cachia Creek again, which we crossed. The crossing was bad. The road then struck off to the south-west, having been running south for some time. We gradually neared the bluffs (on the side of which we found a good spring). Distant from the creek five miles, was a fine spring to the right of [the] road, distant 100 yds. Three miles brought us *again* to Cachia Creek, or one of its tributaries. Here the road keeps up this branch, in a westerly direction. Three miles we nooned. Many of us took some fine trout, these mountain streams abounding [with] them. At 4 we halted again. The road still continues as dusty as before & runs down between two range of mountains, the valley being not more than 100 yds. wide. We rolled 8 miles when we again crossed this branch of Cachia.[5] During the evening we crossed several little streams of spring water. We here filled our casks & watered our animals, not knowing positively that we would have water for camp. Immediately after crossing we crossed a swamp, which required considerable persevering to get through safely. Three miles farther we encamped on the side of a hill, between two range of mountains which are white in their ravines with snow.

5. It was at Cache Creek crossing that Hudspeth's Cut-off formed a juncture with the road from Fort Hall. The fact that Bryarly does not allude to it implies that it had not yet been opened on July 17. Delano, July 22, indicates plainly that it was not open on that date. Paden, has shown, by using the diary of Henry Mann, that the cut-off was completed on July 24 (*Wake of the Prairie Schooner,* p. 309). If the Charlestown Company had been a week later, it would probably have followed the cut-off, for very few emigrants went by way of Fort Hall after it had been opened.

We came to an ox team this evening which was loaded with merchandise. Many of our men, who were prepared [for the journey] with nothing but fine shoes, & consequently were nearly barefooted, hailed this with delight & were but too glad to pay even $3 per pair for $1.25 shoes.

[*Distance, 23 miles.*

Thursday, July 19th.

With charming spirits we renewed our journey this morning. The road still continued between the two mountains for 4 miles, when we emerged into an open plain which was a marshy valley. Two miles, we crossed a run of water, which I suppose is Ware's "Rattle-Snake" River.[6] The road here runs west until we reached another little stream distant 2 miles farther. Before reaching this we crossed a very marshy place which extends as far as the eye can reach, & which I judge is "Swamp Creek." The road here runs south. Across the other side of the valley which we passed, we distinctly saw the dust arising as from a road. This excited our curiosity very much to know where this road could come from. From some emigrants recruiting at Swamp Creek we learned it was the road from Salt Lake. Three miles we turned again due west, the road passing between two rocky, craggy mountains. The road here for 200 yds. was rocky in the extreme and tested fully the strength of our wagons. There was the remnants of many laying along this little piece of road, which had split upon these rocks. After passing them we nooned. A very pretty little mountain stream ran along this kanyon pass.

The road here lies between high & immense rocky mountains, with not a particle of herbage or vegetation upon them, but being white & smooth upon their surface. Just opposite to where we encamped was one which struck us as particularly curious. It was a perfect face upon the highest cliff around. We nooned 4 hours & rolled again. The road continued between these & around these rocky piles but the road itself was good. You can imagine among these massive

6. This reference proves Bryarly's familiarity with Ware's *Emigrants' Guide*, for page 31 of that treatise describes a certain "Rattlesnake River." The present identity of this stream is not clear.

piles, church domes, spires, pyramids, &c., & in fact, with a little fancying you can see [anything] from the Capitol at Washington to a lowly thatched cottage.[7]

Four miles brought us to the coming in of the Mormon Road. Half [a] mile before striking it we passed through a narrow pass of rock, just wide enough for the wagons, & which evidently has been made by some adventurers before us. Three miles farther we came to another valley. Four miles across this we encamped under a mountain. We found here a pleasant stream of water, & good grass.

[*Distance, 22½ miles.*

Friday, July 20th.

The road this morning ran, soon after starting, through a mountain pass 10 miles. During the whole distance it was up & down hill. Many of them was very steep, but not enough to require back locking. The road also, in many places, was rough & rocky.[8] At the entrance of the pass was a pleasant little spring & fine branch. In the middle was another, equally fine.

We emerged from this pass into a pretty valley, which is "Goose Creek Valley," with Goose Creek running through it. We nooned 1 mile upon this, with good grass & wood. We took some fine trout here, of which we enjoyed our dinner much. Goose Creek is from 10 to 15 yds. wide, & 3 to 4 ft. deep. The valley is half [a] mile wide, but the creek runs frequently close to the bluffs, making the road take for a short distance across the bluff.

7. The rock formations were the City of Rocks. The coming in of the Mormon road meant that the trails again converged which had separated just after the crossing of the South Pass, taking some emigrants by way of Salt Lake City and others by way of Hudspeth's Cut-off or Fort Hall. Among the Forty-niners whose diaries have been used in this study, twelve (Kelly, McCall, Lewis, Johnston, Foster, Doyle, Swain, Dundass, DeWolf, S. B. F. Clark, Orvis, Royce) went by Salt Lake, six (Brown, Sedgley, McCoy, Searls, Webster, Pleasants) went by Hudspeth's Cut-off, and eleven beside the Charlestown Company (Long, Love, Delano, Tiffany, Wistar, B. C. Clark, Caldwell, Hale, Page, Bruff, Backus) went by way of Fort Hall. At this junction point, Lewis, July 19, having travelled the Salt Lake road, recorded his belief that it was 100 miles farther and a worse road.

8. Cf. Badman, July 12, ''These mountains is rightly named the Rocky Mountains. I think no one will dispute their name & try to find another.''

In the evening we rolled up this valley, the road being hard & fine & but little dusty. Our guide being unwell, he requested me to choose a camp. I rode ahead accordingly, 10 miles, & chose one with good bunch grass. There is in this creek many fresh-water mussles. We gathered a peck, which, upon opening, we found to be very fat & large. After much preparation & discussion over them, we had a fine bowl of soup, which, upon these plains was rather hard to beat.

[*Distance, 21 miles.*]

Saturday, July 21st.

The morning broke cloudy & dark, & consequently we did not get off as soon as usual. Last night we had a few drops of rain, which is the first we have had for 6 weeks & which was hailed by us with delight.[9] We rolled along this valley & creek for 11 miles, which brought us to the turn of the road where it leaves the river. We here filled up our casks & went 1 mile farther to grass, & nooned. At the head of the run were several good springs which were rather sulphurated. It was cloudy & pleasant until 8 o'clock, when the sun shone out with redoubled fury.

The men that were walking complained that the sand was so hot it had blistered their feet. Our mess-things were so hot that we could not handle them with any degree of comfort. Having left Goose Creek we struck out due west over hills & down dales, but with smooth & excellent roads. In the evening it clouded up [and] we had a little rain, but not enough to settle the dust. We rolled across these hills 13 miles to Hot Springs in Hot Spring Valley.[10] Here we coralled, with good wood & water, & turned our animals 2 miles to good grass.   [*Distance, 24 miles.*]

Sunday, July 22nd.

The morning broke again cloudy, with a little rain. The road for several miles showed evident marks of a hard rain a few days since. We rolled down this valley during the morning, it presenting equally as barren a prospect as the

9. Hoffman also mentions this as the first rain in six weeks.
10. Better known as Thousand Springs Valley, Elko County, Nevada.

Black Hills. Not a sprig of grass or any sign of water for 10 miles. We here struck out to the middle of the valley, hoping to find some water, but we found naught but pools (an elegant name for mud hole). We travelled on up the valley, 15 miles, where we obtained water sufficient for cooking by diging in the ravine. This ravine extends the whole distance of the valley, & in wet weather no doubt is filled with water.

The sun was most oppressive during the morning & many of our men were suffering much from headache. In the evening we rolled to a beautiful part of this valley, where the water was good & the grass fine. Here we coralled about 4 P.M. During the evening our Captain determined, as we had such excellent grass, to remain until the morrow noon.

[*Distance, 20 miles.*]

Monday, July 23rd.

This morning I indulged myself in an unusual luxury of a knapp after sunrise. The morning was cool, fair, & pleasant, & everyone in camp seemed to enjoy it to their heart's content. We had layed by such a short time since for the purpose of washing, mending, & bathing, that today no one was busy save the blacksmith, but all were seeking out a little shade[11] to corall himself under & take a growl with his friends.

About 10 o'clock, several teams of oxen drove up close to us & coralled for noon. A joyous & happy shout was soon after heard, echoing from place to place around the camp, & upon turning, I observed that a charge was about being made upon these nearby wagons, the cause of which I was yet to learn. Curious for variety, & loving excitement, I soon followed in their wake & was brought up all standing with the rest at the foot of a wagon where I could distinctly hear the clattering of tins, the crack of bottles, & the jingle of money. Murder will out & here was the secret of all: "Brandy at $8 a gallon." Upon the wagon was written "Store & Groceries." [12] It was the first we had seen, the first we had even

---

11. Cf. Badman, June 21, "I am now laying under the wagon for that is the only thing that makes a shade, for there is not a bush nor has not been for near 200 m[ile]s Large suficient to shad a Rabit."

12. Brown, July 7, speaks of a "trading wagon," encountered west of Fort Laramie.

heard of for a long time, & then, that it should fall into our laps so unexpectedly, & that, too, while we were laying by resting. Is it any wonder we all got "Taught"? Well we done so—laughed, talked, chatted, & sang songs, & [with] an occasional "pull at the critter," & time soon slipped to 2 o'clock, when we [were] ordered to hook up & be off.

The country still presented the same barren appearance for several miles, without grass or water. 8 miles brought us to a large fine spring upon the left of the road. Feeling very thirsty, I jumped off my horse & rushed to it & put my mouth down to drink. You can imagine my surprise when I tell you the water was boiling hot—yes really boiling in many places & no mistake. It extends over half an acre, arising from many different parts & flowing to one common stream. You could not bear your hand in it. You could see where snakes & frogs had scalded to death in it. A dog of a neighboring train rushed in, thinking to quench his avid thirst & bathe his wearied limbs, but the moment he touched it, it was ludicrous in the extreme to see his surprise & astonishment, not saying anything of the many quick & successive movements he made to escape from it. Even after he got out he turned his head & looked down at the water as though still doubting his experience of the deception. I had no thermometer, & consequently can[not] tell its exact degree of heat, but I should think it would thoroughly cook any kind of meat in a short time.[13] [In] two hundred yards we came to another spring, & you may imagine I approached it most cautiously. This however was cool—indeed cold.

Our Captain, here feeling "a little indisposed," requested me to go ahead and pick a camp, which I did, three miles farther, with excellent grass, fine water, & greasewood. It was astonishing & surprising, but our men were *uncommonly thirsty* when they came into camp & the first thing every one asked was, "where's the water?" After a good cup of coffee, we turned ourselves in at dusk to corall for the night.   [*Distance, 11 miles.*

---

13. Many travellers commented with wonder on the hot springs, and at least one became convinced that, "Hell ain't far off." See Paden, *Wake of the Prairie Schooner*, pp. 385–386.

Tuesday, July 24th.

This was rather a blue morning. Water, "sweet water," was in great demand & our cool, refreshing & nectar spring was crowded with the "Mourners" who had given vent to their spirits yesterday. With a cheerful laugh from one to another, & a few headaches, we again resumed our journey, many thinking seriously of the great excellency of that band of brothers, "The Sons of Temperance." [14] But each promised himself never to do so more, and with this balm to our souls, "Richard was himself again." [15]

We rolled 6 miles through this "Hot Spring Valley" which brought us to its termination at the bluffs. Here was a little brook of water, cool and pleasant, but no grass. We were now in a mountain pass through which we rolled 9 miles, which brought us to the head of another little creek, which arose & sank as the one in Hot Spring Valley. We here nooned 4 hours. The country around was very barren & sterile; even the sage & greasewood looked stunted. In the evening we rolled 10 miles, which brought us to a narrow pass of the mountains. The valley between being but a few hundred yards, but [with] tolerable grass & sage wood. The road, until we struck this, kept to the side of the mountain & presented the appearance of being made this spring. The water was obtained by diging for it in the ravine, which in high water carries it on down the valley. It was a continuation of the same we nooned upon.   [*Distance, 25 miles.*

Wednesday, July 25th.

The morning was clear & cold, in fact for several nights past it has been quite cold before day, requiring one to pull the blankets carefully over. We rolled out this morning at day break. The road kept the pass in which we encamped, for two miles, & then emerged into a valley. The willows along the ravine which we have been following for several days

---

14. The Order of the Sons of Temperance had been organized as a national society on Sept. 29, 1842, in New York City. In 1850, the society reported 5,894 lodges, with 245,233 paying members.

15. "Conscience avaunt, Richard's himself again."

                    Cibber's version of *Richard III*, Act V, scene 3.

are now increasing in size, & the pools of water in it are larger & more frequent. Five miles down these pools resulted into a pretty little stream with an evident current in the direction we are expecting to find Mary's River.[16] There were excellent camping places all along, & although we had not made our morning drive, we were much tempted to "turn out" to graze. Seventeen miles from our camp we nooned upon a pretty, clear, & swift little stream, putting into the one we travelled down. This we supposed to be Martin's Fork of Mary's.

We had here the best grass we have ever had. There was much clover in full bloom. We nooned here 3 hours, then crossed the stream & rolled. We travelled down this same stream, [which had] increased much in size since morning, & increasing every mile. I think we may now safely call it Mary's River. We rolled 10 miles & encamped in grass up to our horses' bellies. Good water & good wood. We all enjoyed a delightful meal upon sage hens. The most of our men have shotguns, & being very good shots, whenever small game of this kind is to be found, they literally slay them. This morning the firing reminded me of a discharge of musketry. They came into camp loaded. The birds are the size of a chicken & have much the colour & appearance about the head of guinea fowl. They are very fat and tender & certainly are the greatest of delicacies.   [*Distance, 27 miles.*

Thursday, July 26th.

It was again cool & clear. Our overcoats were rather comfortable than not in moving around our campfire, & in riding they were almost indispensable. We got a usual start. The road still keeping the valley, it was good but dusty, & consequently we made good time. Eight miles brought us [to] where the road takes to the bluffs for the purpose of cutting off a point of bluff; otherwise, we should have to go over.

16. The Humboldt River was originally called Mary's River, perhaps after the wife of Peter Skene Ogden. Frémont, in 1845, ignored the existing name, and called it the Humboldt. B. C. Clark, July 21, and Hale, Aug. 7, called it the St. Mary's, and Bruff, Sep. 3, surmised that it was "called Mary's . . . in honor of the Blessed Virgin." If French Catholic fur traders were first to name it, Clark's designation is perhaps the truest rendering of the original name.

One mile & a half brought us to the crossing of another creek, which ran from the northeast, & put into Mary's. This has increased our stream from little pools to a considerable size & now I think we certainly may call it "Marys." [In] half [a] mile we nooned immediately upon the stream.

Our Hunters had success again today, & we again enjoyed a *special* dinner. Three o'clock saw us upon our road again. Still in another valley, the same as that we have just past, we rolled this evening 15 miles & encamped. During the day we have seen signs of the Digger Indians, & indeed, we have seen a placard set by an emigrant stating they had attempted to kill some of their cattle. We have seen the remnants of fishnets set by them, still remaining in the water. These Diggers are considered the meanest Indians in existence. We had good *grass, wood & water* & good spirits, & with all these luxuries, after a pleasant smoke we retired to dream of home & love.   [*Distance, 25 miles.*

[THE hardships of the journey reached their climax as the trail re-entered the Great Basin. The one factor which made transit across this desert area possible was the presence of the Humboldt River, and the emigrants followed it doggedly across the present state of Nevada from its sources to its terminus, where it "sank" into the parched earth. Near its source, it was fresh, cool, and reasonably full of water. But as it flowed through sun-scorched, alkali-impregnated country, it grew progressively warmer to the touch, more offensive to the stomach, and more dreary to the eye. Emigrants detested it, and it made severer demands on their stamina than any other part of the journey. They knew that the worst hurdle of all, the Humboldt Desert, awaited them at the end, and the terrors of this barrier were so great that most of the Forty-niners who reached the Humboldt after the middle of July preferred to risk the alternative of Lassen's Cut-off which struck due west from the Humboldt about fifty miles above the Sink. Distances by this "cut-off" were greater, and sufferings were not less, so it was fortunate for the members of the Charlestown Company that they passed Lassen's Meadow before the cut-off was opened, and followed the Humboldt its full three hundred and fifty miles. They arrived at its "Slough" twenty-five days (July 14–Aug. 8) after leaving Fort Hall.]

Friday, July 27th.

The mornings continue quite chilly & make our mules look badly, being drawn up into almost a knot although [we have] most excellent grass. Upon driving them in, one was found mired, & upon drawing him out we found he had been in that *pleasant* situation so long, & with his many, perhaps desperate, exertions to extricate himself, he had become so exhausted & weak he was not able to travel, & consequently was left and abandoned by us, to become the prey of either the wolves or Diggers (who it is said eat them), or the emigration behind us.

We rolled down the valley 6 miles, which brought us to a narrowing of the valley & the road crossing the bluffs. The road first rises a steep & long hill 2 miles & then takes to a kanyon, through which we passed 12 miles. This road runs very near north & strikes another little branch putting into Mary's, but which is here only pooly. About two miles before coming to it, we passed two springs, the first of which was scarcely drinkable; the other, half a mile farther, was very good. Both of them arose in a marshly alkalic place. In this last marsh was a Warm Spring, or rather, Hot Spring, much hotter than the large one before seen. When we struck the branch, the road turns southwest, which carried us back almost towards our starting point [of] this morning. We rolled down this, being then in a valley 4 miles, where we again struck the river. The pools had become quite a stream before reaching it. We here encamped.

This has been the hardest day's march we have yet had.[17] We did not noon, having neither grass or water for our stock. The dust & heat in the kanyon was almost insupportable. Some idea can be formed of the heat when I tell you that, having a tin canteen of water, it became so hot that I was enabled, with a little ''Essence of Coffee'' that I had in my pocket, to make excellent coffee, which my friend Mr. Gittings (who was riding with me) & myself enjoyed much. Our teams straggled into camp, many of them without their compliment of mules & all nearly given out.

17. Hoffman, July 27, wrote, ''This was by far the hardest day's travel that we have had on the route.''

This point has been a general camping one, & consequently the grass was not very good & [was] hard to find. The ox-teams were rolling in during the night & disturbed our peaceful slumbers not a little. One, in particular, in driving *his Bulls* across the river, passed through our encampment, & had I not awoke & jumped [I] would certainly have been crushed under his mighty feet. Of course then, some compliments passed between the driver & myself.

After arriving at our camp we found we had made a great mistake in coming so far around the bluff. It was one, howevere, that all the emigration had made before us. Some of our men followed the river up & came to our camping place 4 hours before us, it being only 8 miles. They describe it as being as good a road for wagons as any we have seen, requiring to cross the river twice, but good crossings.

[*Distance, 24 miles.*

Saturday, July 28th.

Our mules looked badly this morning. We had fair grass, & little of it. We made a late start & kept down the valley 4 miles, when we came again to a narrowing of it, & when the road took to the hills. It ascended some 2 miles direct & then was broken by hills & dales. These hills are barren in the extreme. Even the sage and greasewood looked stunted. In 7 miles we came to what we called the "Sage Spring." It was a hole dug by some emigrant ahead, & the water of which was quite good. Our guide also found a little patch of grass over the hill & determined to noon, our mules being already, from their bad feeding last night, much exhausted.

I, being anxious to get to the river, kept on. Two miles from [where] the train nooned I found several very excellent springs, but neither wood [n]or grass. The road here commences a gradual descent to the river. In many places the pass between the rocks was very narrow, & it was also rough nearly all the way. Nine miles from [the] spring brought me to the river once again. It was not so hot today as yesterday, but the dust was suffocating. I coralled myself in the shade to await our train. I arrived here at 1 o'clock, & they not until dark. You may imagine I was tired as well as hungry. The train arrived safe although the mules & men both were fatigued. There was not a sprig of grass in one mile & a half of the striking of the river. We drove our tired animals thus far, & here, even, it was worse than it was last night.

Some of our men attempted to make another "cut-off" by coming up the river, but they were decidedly taken in, for they did not get into camp until dark, & said they were walking all the time since 6 o'clock this morning. They thought it 35 or 40 miles.

One can but be struck with sorrow for those coming behind us. Already the grass is so scarce that we will be enabled to get through, if at all, by merely the skin of our teeth, & what the seven thousand teams behind us are to do *God Almighty only knows*.

Indians were seen on the hill tops today. One of our ox-train, mistaking their campfire in the distance for dust in the road, struck out for it thinking to make a "cut-off." He says [that], upon arising a hill just by them, he discovered them sitting by their fires, numbering some hundred. He crawled away cautiously and came suddenly upon twenty more sitting around him, as he said, in a huddle. They asked him for tobacco, which he gave them, & got some water in return. He then left them & had advanced 50 yds. when two came sneaking after him. He instantly stopped, when one ran away, & upon [his] advancing towards the other, he also took flight. The way he [the driver] then broke for camp himself was a caution.

The men who came up the river describe a large, hot, boiling spring upon its banks. It arose some 25 or 30 yds. from the river & ran into the river. It was some 20 ft. in breadth & ran this width into the river direct. It was boiling hot & sent off steam & heat from its surface, which [was] as hot as the scape pipe of an engine. Even after it ran into the river, it foamed & hissed as cold water poured into hot & sent off steam for 80 yds. below, and extending half over the river.   [*Distance, 24 miles.*

Sunday, July 29th.

The grass being very poor, our mules were scattered in every direction in search of sufficient provender, & consequently we made a late start. Our animals looked decidedly bad & the spirits of our men were equally so, which gave us an uncommonly gloomy start, with not even the usual compliment of blessings to the mules upon being grand. We rolled out [at] 6 o'clock & had gone but a half mile when the road branched, one [branch] going down the river upon the opposite side & the other across the bluffs.

Having determined to stop at the first good grass, & somewhat in the hopes of making a cut-off, our guide took the river road, with the exception of my sick-wagon, which, being in advance, had taken the hill road before the other was determined upon. We crossed the river & proceeded down it, going around a point of bluff. We rolled 10 miles, when we nooned, the grass being still very poor. Here we distinctly saw the sick-wagon upon the other side of the river & the road coming down from the top of the bluff. The road across was not more than 5 miles, while that which we came was 10, & we were just opposite. I am happy to say my sick must certainly be convalescent, as they drove 3 or 4 miles farther to cross to get their dinners. This morning one of our herd horses, upon starting, refused to leave his corall for want of sufficient strength to carry him. With many thanks & remembrances for services rendered, poor ''Ridge Back'' was ''left alone in his glory.''

We nooned 4 hours & again ''hooked up.'' In three miles we again came to a branching of the road, one [going] around the river, the other over the bluff. The one over the bluff was found to be half [a] mile while the other was 2½. We preferred the former. We rolled over this & crossed the river. One mile farther we came to some good grass—the first for 50 miles. We, of course, stopped, & it was a pleasure to see the manner our animals enjoyed the grass. Our animals were driven into a point of land in the bend of the river, & had been grazing but a short time when they rushed towards our camp with fright, making everyone jump from his campfire in double-quick time. We rallied out & drove them back, when an antelope came bounding from the bushes & running with sudden bounds & stoppages through our camp. Guns were eagerly called for and seized, and at the first crack the gentleman took the hint, and curled his tail over his back & streaked it most beautifully. Twenty shots were fired at him, but he kept on his way rejoicing.

[*Distance, 15 miles.*

Monday, July 30th.

Having determined to lay by during the day, we all indulged ourselves in a late sleep. Finding upon inspection that we were draging one more wagon than necessary, not having sufficient load for it, it was determined to select the worse one of the lot & leave it.

It was a beautiful, cold, & clear morning, and we enjoyed the rest very much. It is a fact [though] that, after eating & resting, a camp becomes very tiresome to everyone, however beautiful the spot & scenery around may be. Our huntsmen had glorious sport today. In a quarter of a mile of our camp, 5 antelope were killed,[18] not saying anything of the numerous sage hens & ducks. This furnished us all with fresh meat, which was relished greatly. The day was passed with the usual monotony of "laying by," & the night, after regaling ourselves with the joyous violin & our pipe, was passed in golden dreams.[19]

---

18. The terminology applied to animals of the Plains was evidently rather loose, for Hoffman, July 30, spoke of the killing of "five deer."

19. In almost all diaries, the accounts of hardships are balanced by references to the simple pleasures of the journey. One of the foremost of these was music. Thus Swain, June 24, speaks of a "sing." The effect of many voices raised in song, on the still plains, was he says, "electric on me & I suppose the same on the wolves [*i.e.*, coyotes], for they set up a most horrid pow-wow just out on the plains around our camp." Johnston, May 8, also described group singing, and Searls, July 9, wrote, "a number of companies are camped in our vicinity, in one of which are several Ladies. We were treated this evening to a vocal concert from them." Usually, as in the Charlestown Company, a "fiddle" provided the background for vocal music; Lewis, June 4, wrote, "The boys are in fine spirit. We have had a serenade tonight, music from fiddle and camp kettle." Sometimes a banjo replaced the violin (Delano, Aug. 14) but either one was likely to include "Oh Susannah" in its repertoire (Kelly, p. 33), and to be accompanied by dancing. In Delano's company a Negro "jumped Jim Crow" to the banjo (Delano, Aug. 14; B. C. Clark, July 27, spoke of the singing of a Negro guide in a company from Virginia). Sometimes the men danced together in a "stag dance" (Hackney, May 9). On July 24, Hackney wrote, "Some of the Pike County boys paid us a visit tonight they brout a fiddler along with them and we all had a sociable dance among ourselfs." Bruff, Aug. 2, said, "the men sat up some time after supper, spinning yarns, singing, and performing on various instruments of music." Badman, on July 9, described an unusual celebration: a neighboring company "threw away about 20 qts candles & we being on the hill beyond Prospect hill . . . the boys thought they would put on a dance . . . so they bilt about 3 fires with wild sage & lit about 30 candles and they commenced dancing they kept it up until about 11 o'clock." The presence of young girls was rare along the trail and when it

Tuesday, July 31st.

Ice was a quarter of an inch thick upon our buckets this
morning, & just before day, it was chilling cold. An early
start this morning, with fresh mules & drivers, rolled us
along at a rapid rate. We are still in the valley, with high,
bare mountains upon either side but divested of everything
like vegetation. There was no grass, and everything was
parched & dry.

We rolled 10 miles & was lucky enough to find, in a narrow
niche of the river, some good grass, to which we turned our
animals. It was warmer today than it has yet been on our
route. The sun at 12 o'clock was most oppressively hot. We
remained here 8 hours, and started at 5 o'clock. It was determined to start thus late in order to avoid the heat of the
sun, prefering much to travel after night.

Four miles from nooning brought us to another narrowing
of the valley. The road kept immediately upon its banks &
the edge of the bluff. It was rough, there being many large
stones rolled into it. After passing through this *Pass,* we
emerged into a very broad valley which presented itself to us
in no favorable light at this time in the evening. It was
whitish as far as the eye could reach, being covered with soda
& potassa. Towards the bluffs of the right side were sage
bushes, but they were unusually small & the earth around
alkalic. The road keeps the same direction we have been
traveling during the day, but the river bears far off to the
left.

We traveled down or rather across this 9 miles. Here we
again struck the river, but neither grass or wood. We rolled
down this, looking for grass & wood [for] several miles but
found neither. We were at last compelled, on account of our
mules, to corall, with grass parched & eaten over a half dozen
times. Sorry am I to say that many of our men, either from
fatigue or ill nature, growled & grunted much at our night
driving & endeavoured, it seemed, to raise some dissension
to it; but the prime mover (Mr. Asquith) is no longer a rock

occurred, it almost invariably produced a celebration. Thus, Swain, Oct. 14,
"This evening our boys and those of another train laying here together with
the Smith girls had a tall time in the shape of a fandango which lasted till
10 o'clock."

under water. He is known in full, & to prove it, I have only to refer you to some of his acts, which prove the man.

[*Distance, 25 miles.*

Wednesday, August 1st.

On account of our Captain refusing to act as such today, we were late aroused & had a very late start. Everyone looked gloomy at each other, & such anger in the countenances of the most was depicted [as] only to be surpassed by their determined & resolute bearing. Everyone seem[ed] to fear a beginning, and dreaded it. For well they knew the consequences would be terrible. A few of us got together & found on enquiry that this ill-feeling & back-biting, & mean, ill-natured, contemptable slandering was done by a few sheep in wolves' clothes that had crept into our camp. One of the same has been long since known and for this, as well as all other dissensions that we have ever had, to him must we attribute the cause.

Our Captain having again consented to guide us & not mind the barking of these curs, we rolled out at 6 o'clock. The road was down the valley, which presented the same drouthy appearance as yesterday evening. The water in the river is quite muddy, & is warmer & consequently not so good. Our Captain having requested me to be the guide for the day, I rode ahead 10 miles from camp & picked a nooning. I found but a small patch of grass & about this I had quite a contention with an ox driver. In riding along this morning I witnessed a most sudden & singular death. A man driving an ox cart, when in the act of cracking his whip (ruling passion strong in death) fell dead upon the spot. They all, at once, pronounced it sun stroke, but I presume it was a sequel to either a disease of the heart or some disease of the brain.

We passed this morning a grave upon the left of the road of a Mr. Byron, of Bryant's Company from Louisville.[20] He is 11 days ahead of us, & started three weeks [ahead]. We

20. Johnston, p. 17, met Bryant in Louisville, and encountered his company several times subsequently (Apr. 4, 15, 26). Tiffany, June 14, spoke of meeting Bryant's company, with 150 pack mules. Backus, Aug. 3, speaks of "the grave of a member of Bryant's Co. from Ky." Read and Gaines, eds., *Gold Rush*, I, 629, n. 5 gives other references. Edwin Bryant was a native of Massachusetts who had moved to Kentucky and became a journalist. In 1846, he made the over-

nooned 8 hours & again rolled. The road soon left the river, which went off to the left around the bluff, & it [the road] kept [on] over this same bluff. One mile over, & we were again in a similar valley as we had just left. *No grass, no wood, & bad water* is now all we look for.

It was our intention to travel late tonight, but it became cloudy & the moon was obscured, without the light of which we made but a poor out in travelling, & consequently we stopped after rolling 7 miles. In a nook of the river we found some little grass & willows, & we were content. So soon as it was dusk this evening a large fire was discovered upon the very highest peak of mountain to our left. We knew this to be the Diggers & it was a warning to us to look out. It burned for several hours very bright & then gradually disappeared.[21]

We passed today a great novelty as well as a very great curiosity upon the plains. Stuck up on the side of the road was a board with "Grocery" in large letters written upon it, pointing to a sun shade of willows, with a chest, a box with "Tobacco" written upon it, an old pair of wheels with a [wagon] tongue laying here, an axle there, & old iron accordingly thrown around. This was the grocery. It had a peck of hard bread & a quart of whiskey for sale. For the whiskey, he asked only $4. On enquiry, the proprietor [informed us] he had been there 9 days, buying what he could from all the trains passing & selling to others as they passed. He told me he cleared in that time $3.40 [*sic*].   [*Distance, 17 miles.*

---

land journey, which became the basis for his widely-read book, *What I Saw in California* (see above, p. 21). He served as a lieutenant in the California Battalion, as alcalde of San Francisco, and as a witness at Washington in the court-martial of John C. Frémont. He repeated the overland journey to California in 1849. He died at Louisville, 1869.

21. Emigrants in the valley of the Humboldt tended to regard all the Indians of that area as "Diggers"—a wretched, degraded, and despicable tribe, who were held guilty of making raids upon the cattle, at night. In fact, there were two distinct Indian groups; first, the Diggers, whom Captain Bonneville had called Shoshokees, fully as debased, but by no means as dangerous as the emigrants supposed them to be; and second, the Utes, a warlike group, proficient in the art of cattle stealing. Since they usually struck by night, it was natural that their crimes were attributed to the Shoshokees, who were apparent by day. The signal fires mentioned here, and by many other diarists, were probably those of the Utes. See Paden, *Wake of the Prairie Schooner*, pp. 379–380. Read and Gaines, eds., *Gold Rush*, I, 546, n. 2, discusses the signal fires.

Thursday, August 2nd.

Tranquility, peace, & good order being once more established among our very courteous company, we were summoned as usual & got an early start. We rolled quite briskly in the cool of the morning, but as soon as the sun was fairly shining, it was most awfully hot. Still keeping the same valley, and with the same sterile appearance of the country around, we rolled 11 miles & nooned just where the river passes through a kanyon & the road takes to the bluffs. The river has much decreased in size since yesterday & is evidently sinking. The water is still muddy, & neither cool or pleasant to drink, but we have gradually become accustomed to drinking all sort and any sort, & now we scarcely take a second thought whether it is very good or very bad. The grass was very poor, but after considerable time & labour, a ford was made across the river & our animals driven to good grass.

We nooned 8 hours & again rolled. One road went down the river, crossing it twice in a very short distance. The other, which we took, went over the bluffs. This road was not very steep but was deep sand which consequently made it even worse for our animals. We passed over this 5 miles & again struck the valley & the river. We rolled down this 5 miles more & encamped upon the edge of the river. We had but tolerable grass & poor wood, but *sleep was sweet.*

This morning soon after rolling out of camp we came to two wagons coralled upon the side of the road, & on enquiring found the Diggers had stolen all of their animals during the night.[22] They were in a most lamentable & unfortunate predicament, and we felt much disposed & anxious to help the poor fellows. But charity must begin at home, "this far out," as well as in the States, & we could not do it. Several emigrants offered to go with them to look for their animals, but the chances are many against it. This theft accounted for the fire we saw upon the mountain last night. We were prudent enough to be cautious & careful, & lost not one.

[*Distance, 21 miles.*

---

22. Hoffman, Aug. 2, mentions this theft and enumerates the losses as five mules and two horses. For a general discussion of cattle-stealing by Indians in this region, see above, p. 45.

Friday, August 3rd.

It was quite warm last night and the sand that we spread our blankets upon kept hot during the night. The sun during the day makes the sand & dirt so parching hot that it would not cool during the night. We rolled out early, the road keeping the valley & winding some distance around slough & marshes. One marsh in particular has extended over miles & the river itself seemed lost in it. At first we though this must be the Sink (which now is the goal of our fondest hopes), although we ought not to come to it for 100 miles. However, after heading this, we again found the river emerging from it in its same tortuous way. We rolled thus 11 miles & nooned with the expectation of crossing our animals to grass.

Having arrived before the train, & being something of a swimmer, our Captain requested me to make an exploration, upon which, I striped off & done so, & we came to the conclusion we could [cross the teams]. After the mules arrived we tried it, but found they would all mire, & had to give it up. We stayed a couple of hours & rolled on. One mile farther we found an excellent crossing with good grass, & encamped. We have heard of several trains which have lost mules & horses by the Diggers but as yet we have not been molested in the least. Around the head of the great marsh the road turned southwest, having been running for several days northwest.   [*Distance, 12 miles.*

Saturday, August 4th.

The first peep of the sun this morning gave us the unpleasant intimation that when she was a little farther advanced "we would catch hell." We immediately struck the bluff, which was not steep or high above the bed of the river, but the sand (which is the detestation and abomination of our teamsters) was nearly up to the axle, & a dead drag all the way. The road continued thus for 10 miles, when we nooned. We coralled in the sage bushes & drove our animals among the willows to *pick*. We were compelled to do this as our mules had nearly given out, having become "leg wearied" from draging through the deep sand. Having rode some miles ahead, I found a road crossing the river & going up on the opposite side. The road upon the same side was sandy for 5 miles, as far as I went, & seemed to continue [so]. Our Captain being again indisposed, I was requested to be again the guide.

We crossed the river one mile from nooning, & was but too glad to escape from the sand. The road here was splendid & but few teams had passed over it. We rolled in the same southwest direction for 5 miles, when it [the road] turned directly south. Having found good camping, we coralled for the night. On enquiring I found the road crossed the river again one mile from camp, where the road took to the bluffs, which was sandy for fourteen miles, without wood or water or grass. This determined us to "lay by" in the morning to recruit for this *Jornado.*

Our mules are generally in tolerable condition but they cannot stand the drives they could a month since. This failing is not confined to our mules, but to all animals now in our vicinity. Horses, in particular, have failed most signally since leaving Fort Hall. They are poor & weak & I think it doubtful that they will again recruit. I was informed by one of an ox train, that their cattle, which had never drooped before since leaving the States, were now failing fast & [that] they were not able to go more than 12 or 15 miles.

Almost every one came in camp at noon with a "Jack Ass" Rabbit.[23] These animals are at least four times as large as our own. They have ears in a proportionate size of the Jack Ass. Some idea can be formed of the size when I tell you [that] one of common size will make a full meal for our mess of 6, & who are not bad feeders either, but are generally blessed with good appetites.   [*Distance, 20 miles.*

Sunday, August 5th.

Resting, sleeping, eating, & bathing are certainly very pleasant occupations & a most happy way of spending or killing time, but in spite of all these, this *laying by* is tire-

---

23. The long-eared, long-legged hares of the West were almost invariably known as jackass rabbits; apparently this was not contracted to jack rabbit until later, for the *Dictionary of American English* shows the former usage as early as 1847, but does not show the latter prior to 1870.

some. We layed all this morning in camp, & before the time rolled around for us to hook up, it hung heavy upon our hands. Many of our men went hunting & returned laden with the "Bureau [Burro] Rabbits" & consequently we fared sumptuously.

We sometimes, for the want of anything better or worse to growl about complain of having nothing but salt pork.[24] Today part of the Pittsburgh Company came up, & having a friend with it (Mr. Murray), I learned from him that they were out of meat entirely & had not had a taste of it for six weeks. Their sugar, rice, beans, & flour were also out & they had been living on nothing but hard tack & coffee, & coffee & hard tack. They had no shot guns & of course took no game. This reconciled us, I assure you, & we censured ourselves for our past time growling, & [we] find [that], instead of suffering, we have been feasting.

We rolled out at 3 o'clock for this "Bug-Bear" Jornado. Our Captain still continues quite sick, although out of danger, & I went ahead to supply his place. Of late we have had considerable sickness (Diarrhea) in our Company, produced either by the water which is bad, or by the game which we have had in much abundance for some time. Soar throats & bad colds have also been prevalent. Mr. Geiger in particular has suffered much for a few days. They are all, however, now convalescent & look cheerful. During the morning we saw but few teams pass us & these were mostly on the bluff upon the opposite side of the river. The sand there was heavy & deep, & we saw poor fellows trudging along, stopping every hundred yards, some of them to double teams all the way through. We crossed the river & took ourselves to the Bluff. Here we were most agreeably disappointed in finding we had no sand but instead a fine road although dusty. We rolled over this barrenness 16 miles from our camp & again struck the river. Having sent ahead to find a camp before night, we encamped upon the best [spot] we could find, which was poor, as this has been a general camping for all that has past. At dusk, it clouded up and the distant rumble

24. On this day, Hoffman noted in his diary that an inventory of the Charlestown Company's foodstuffs showed only 30 pounds of flour per man, or enough for 15 to 20 days at the most.

of thunder was heard, accompanied with a few flashes of lightening. We congratulated ourselves that we were once more going to have a little rain, but we were too anxious and had congratulated ourselves too soon. It cleared off in the course of an hour and left us with the same old monotonous weather.   [*Distance, 16 miles.*]

Monday, August 6th.

The morning broke clear, pleasant, and beautiful. Upon awaking, my old friend Gen'l Crane was standing over me & saluted me with his very peculiar salutation of the morning, which is certainly original, beautiful, &, this far out, in good taste. The members of our Company will remember this pleasantry for a long time, & no doubt at some future time [it] will serve to recall to the mind of some, when their heads have become whitened by time (that slow but sure coach of deprivations, hardships & pleasures), that [which], perhaps, may never be experienced by any other emigration across any portion of the globe.

Leaving the little valley in which we encamped, we ascended direct the same old bluff of yesterday. We rolled over this through dust & sand one mile & a half, & came into another valley through which the river was still winding its snaky course. The road here was very good &, at times, left the river at a considerable distance to head sloughs & marshes. There was scarcely a sprig of grass, & every part of it was trampled & beaten & cut up by the animals before us, as to almost destroy the remaining roots of what had been. We rolled 11 miles & nooned, turning our animals across the river to pick among and to pluck the green willows. Considering the bad provender, our animals came up well filled.

We again started, after nooning 4 hours. According to reports & to some guide books, we expected to cross the river in three miles, but the road again left the river & took the bluffs. The country here totally changes in appearance. The road passes over the most barren & sterile prarie we have yet seen. In riding over any part of it, that looked perfectly smooth & encrusted, you would leave a cloud of dust behind.

The river was confined between two immense banks, several hundred feet deep. Between these was the river. As it performed its customary windings & twistings, it formed a narrow valley which was generally perfectly barren, but [for] sometimes a few willows & the signs of what had been grass, but which at present was bare.

We rolled along the bluff, tho never coming nearer the river than one mile and a half or 2 miles. Having made our customary drive, & having found a larger space between the banks than usual, with some little grass & willows, we turned into the river & coralled upon the bank and drove our animals down to the river. Very small sage bushes served for our fuel this evening, but we were tired, & our camp was soon [w]raptd in deep & sweet slumber.

Some of our party saw today three Eutaw Indians, on their return from California. They gave a most flattering account (so far as they could be understood) of both the road before us & the gold valley. They have met many teams of both sorts, oxen & mules, & from what they saw they are evidently under the impression that the drivers are entirely of different tribes. They spoke of them as the *Wo haughs* & the *Muros*.[25] [*Distance, 23 miles.*]

Tuesday, August 7th.

Our mules came up this morning looking remarkably well notwithstanding the poor grass last night. Upon hitching up, thirteen of our animals were missing. Search upon the river bottom was immediately made & twelve of them were found two miles from camp, having strayed, I suppose, in search of grass. The other was found *beautifully coralled* in a slough. He was cordelled out[26] but was too weak to stand, & consequently was left to fatten on willows & enjoy the delightful miry baths of the *delectable Humboldt*.

25. Delano, July 29, tells of a group of Indians who had identified the emigrants by the terms which they most freely used; these Indians assured a party that ''there was plenty of grass for the *whoa haws,* but no water for the G-d d--ns.''

26. To cordelle meant to tow or work an object (usually a boat) forward by means of a rope or tow line. This term, widely prevalent on frontier waters, was used as early as 1826, by Timothy Flint. See *Dictionary of American English.*

Still following the same old bluff or ridge, we rolled to the striking of the river 6 miles. The road down to the river is very rough and [crosses] a winding hill, which in many places is very steep. Here I learned that we did not cross the river at all, but [that] 12 miles farther we would again strike it & leave it.

After having the animals watered, we again rolled, the road again going to the ridge. Our mules soon began to show the bad effects of last night's feeding. Six miles from [the] river we turned to the left, & again struck [it], & nooned. We turned our animals to very nice, tender young willows, & they seem to chop them off with much gusto.

We nooned 4 hours & started. Six miles farther brought us to the river. Here we found some hard willows & sage bushes, & nothing else. However, our animals were tired & I coralled them for the night, & drove them to the river to pick what they could. Numerous reports reached us today of the great suffering upon the stretch before us of 65 miles. Report says that 800 to a thousand animals are lying dead upon it, & 100 wagons have been abandoned. However there is equal[ly] cheering news upon the other hand, & that is [that], at the slough, distant from us now 10 miles, there has been discovered, within a few days, grass extending over 5000 acres, & up to the animals' bellies, distant only 7 miles from the slough. If this be true, we are safe, but if not, we can never get one third of our animals through. Indeed, they would not be able to haul sufficient water to last them through in their present condition, not saying anything of their loads. Our Captain is improving & I think is now perfectly safe.   [*Distance, 18 miles.*

Wednesday, August 8th.

I sang out heartily this morning for an early start, but as usual on such occasions, something always occurs to retard you when you are in the greatest hurry. I was anxious to get over this 10 miles to the Slough in the cool of the morning, & to get our mules to the grass as soon as possible. I started ahead, & upon my "Walking Squaw" (an Indian pony obtained from the Sioux), one hour & three quarters brought me to this long wished for goal. Contrary to my expectations, I found but few wagons here, but upon enquiry, [I] found that the "grass story" was true & they had rolled over to it [but] two days before. You may imagine this news was received with joy by me, & my informer smiled to see me smile. This Slough is but a poor landmark to have received such a prominent place in the description of this road. It is nothing more or less than a little ravine, with a few small springs in its bottom.

Leaving word for our teams to water, I rode on to this "green spot in the desert." "Old Squaw," with her nation's instinct, & aided by her natural one, discovered its direction sooner than myself. When four miles from it, she would stop suddenly &, raising her head high, would sniff the breeze & seem to drink in with delight the passing fragrance of the atmosphere. In due time I reached the spot on the plain & found it surpassing anything that I heard, in respect to the quality & quantity of the grass.

I found here some two hundred wagons laying along the edge of the grass & their animals turned to it. Mowed grass also was laying about curing, for the purpose of carrying it with them on the Jornado. After picking out a suitable place for coralling, I went on the road to await the train, which, in good time, arrived & coralled. Our animals were turned on a little flat before us & a guard placed around them to prevent their getting in the mire. It was with delight & almost envy that I witnessed the joy of our almost starved animals when turned loose. They fairly layed down & eat it, or rather mowed it.

Among those guarding was Mr. James Davison from Frederick County, Virginia. He had a double barrel gun in his hand, which he had taken out for the purpose of killing some game for the Captain. He was laying upon the grass &, upon rising, the cock of his gun caught in a bush & went off, sending the contents, which was small shot & a few buck shot, into the abdomen (the right Iliac region).[27] It glanced to the right, fracturing the hip bone & leaving the load just

27. McIlhany, *Recollections*, pp. 24–25, gives a detailed account of this accidental shooting, but, by an error of memory, calls the victim Joe Davis. Hoffman also notes this loss.

under the skin, some few of the shot passing through. I was
in camp at the time, & immediately after the report of a
gun, was heard the cries of "I'm, I'm shot." Upon [our]
looking, he was seen to run a few yards & fall. I ran to him
as quick as possible & found several inches of intestine pro-
truding. I replaced it as soon as possible, & upon examining
the wound found it as I described : one inch of the parietes of
the abdomen was carried away, making it very difficult to
keep the intestine in its proper place. He was layed in a
blanket & carried into camp, where I made a more thorough
examination & dressed the wound accordingly. He has not
yet recovered [from] the shock & I much fear will not. While
there is life there's hope, but I am sorry to say he must die.
He has an elder brother, [a] cousin, & many friends, & of
course is well cared for.   [*Distance, 18 miles.*

Thursday, August 9th.

I was aroused at daybreak, having layed down only two
hours during the night, to come to see my patient, as they
thought he was sinking. I found it was too true, & [at] 5 1/2
o'clock he departed this life after suffering the most acute
agony for twelve hours. He never reacted or recovered from
the shock to the general system, but gradually sank from the
time of the injury until death itself came to his relief.

Having determined to lay here several days to recruit our
animals & to cut & cure some grass for the purpose of taking
it across the "Jornado" for them, we moved lower down the
marsh, where it was better & the ground drier. We coralled
on a beautiful smooth spot with grass six or eight inches, &,
immediately upon arriving, it occurred to us all, "oh what
a nice sleep I'll have tonight!" Two hundred yards in front,
the water from the marsh around collected in a stream &
running beautifully over the long grass, it made a fall of
several feet into a pool. This made a most delightful place
to bathe, & the water itself was better than any we have had
for several weeks. The grass between our corall & this [pool]
was knee high, & the ground dry, & our animals were in view
the whole time. Our men were soon fixing their scythes &
everybody was busying himself to harvest—which, although

[*i.e.* despite] the sad accident that had deprived us of one of our number, still brought a smile to the countenances of our practised farmers & sturdy yeoman.

In the meantime the necessary preparations to pay the last respects to our deceased member were being made. A hill near was chosen as a spot suitable, from its elevation & vicinity to what will always hereafter be the road, to receive his remains. At three o'clock the preparations were announced ready & we took a solemn movement towards the grave. His blanket served him for his winding sheet & a few planks layed over, for his coffin. The funeral service was read & a suitable board [placed] at his head, & thus he was left, each perhaps thinking of the uncertainty of life & death.[28]

This marsh for three miles is certainly the liveliest place that one could witness in a lifetime. There is some two hundred and fifty wagons here all the time. Trains going out & others coming in & taking their places, is the constant order of the day. Cattle & mules by the hundreds are surrounding us, in grass to their knees, all discoursing sweet music with the grinding of their jaws. Men too are seen hurrying in many different ways, & everybody attending to his own business. Some mowing, some reaping, some carrying, some packing the grass, others spreading it out to dry, [or] collecting that already dry & fixing it for transportation. In fact the joyous laugh & the familiar sound of the whetted scythe resounds from place to place & gives an air of happiness & content around that must carry the wearied travellers through to the "Promised Land." The scene also reminds one much of a large encampment of the army, divided off into separate & distinct parties, everybody minding his business and letting other people's alone.

Friday, August 10th.

Our camp continued the same joyous, variable thing during the day. We have perhaps remained longer than the majority, but our animals & men all required recruiting.

28. Backus, Aug. 12, mentions the grave: ''near us is the grave of a member of the *Charlestown Va.* Co. who accidently shot himself.''

As many as five hundred have left since we arrived. It is rather amusing to see the many different manners which necessity has compelled the poor fellows to travel—some packing upon their backs, others driving a half-dead mule or pony before them, laden with a few hard crackers & a coffee pot. [There are] carts of all descriptions, wagons [that] have been divided, one party taking the fore wheels & half the bed, another the hind ones with the remaining half. "Necessity is the mother of invention," & if anybody doubts it, I think it will be convincing to them to be upon this road. Oxen are also packed, the load being placed upon their backs & upon the yoke. They move along very well & keep up a very good gait.

The men have all been busy fixing their grass & repacking wagons. The day was passed with pleasure & enjoyment to all, & at night the exciting violin & the soft melodious flute was heard from the different campfires, giving cheerfulness to everything around, & serving to make us forget that we are two thousand miles from those we hold most dear.

We determined to lay here until tomorrow at 1 o'clock, when we will again take up a line of march, through the Jornado & to California. Discussions of the various routes are heard from every knot of persons that you pass. Reports as various & different as possible is told by everyone, so that it is useless to attempt to make up your mind which is preferable. Today an old Indian was in our camp, who had been several times to California, & who advised us by all means to take the left hand road. He drew the different roads upon a piece of paper, and with his numerous signs & contortions explained the difficulties of one & the excelling of the other, & finally finished by rubing out all but the left road, [thus] showing us that it was the only one to get to California. A little while after, a gentleman came along with a letter from a friend who had gone ahead to explore the different routes, saying take by all means, the old road, the right hand, & that he had ascertained that these Indians had been sent upon the road expressly to turn the emigration to the farthest road to "Pleasant Valley," the left road taking you to Sutter's, 50 miles from the valley, the right, directly to the valley.

VI ACROSS THE DESERT AND OVER THE SIERRA

LIKE some vast, deliberately contrived obstacle course, the trail first exhausted the reserve strength of men and beasts along the Humboldt, and then subjected them to two supreme tests—the Humboldt Desert and the Sierra Nevada. The Desert presented a sixty-five mile stretch of heat and sand, without wood or water, save for the noxious fluid of a single boiling spring. It required fifty-two hours of almost uninterrupted travel to make this crossing. Alternative roads led either to the Carson River, or to the Truckee, which was also sometimes known as the Salmon Trout River. The Charlestown Company chose the route to the Truckee, where they found the respite of cool water and green grass. But they could not linger long while the Sierra crossing still remained. This immense granite barrier required travel up grades steeper and along ledges narrower than any Forty-niner would have believed possible when he left Missouri. But great as were the difficulties, there was also great stimulus, for the ''Diggings,'' the deposits of gold which had drawn men from the Old World and from below the Equator, lay just beyond the ridge. Within a week after reaching the summit, Bryarly and his companions arrived at the ''Diggings.'' Four days later (twenty-one days after setting out across the desert), they arrived at Johnson's Ranch, at which point the company pitched camp, and where it remained until it dissolved and the members dispersed in various directions to seek fortune in the stream beds.

We have seen the Elephant.[1]

Passed the journey of death, safe through the Forlorn Hope.

1. The term ''to see the elephant,'' meaning, in general, to face a particularly severe ordeal, to gain experience by undergoing hardship, or to learn the realities of a situation at first hand, had been current as early as 1835 (*Dictionary of American English*), but it probably reached the maximum use at the time of the Gold Rush. A popular song, was entitled ''Seeing the Elephant.'' Backus, June 23; DeWolf, June 7; Dundass, May 22; Lewis, Sept. 2; Lyne, May 4; Morgan, July 18; and Tiffany, Aug. 18, 19, all used this expression. Searls, p. 7, spoke of his desire of '' 'seeing the elephant' which is but another name for going to California.'' It is sometimes said that the phrase originated with the victims of P. T. Barnum, who paid admission to see an elephant which proved to be a hoax, but the use of the expression in 1835 virtually disproves this explanation.

SINCE Saturday at 2 o'clock, we traveled 65 miles without *wood* or *water* to last evening [Monday] at 6 o'clock.[2]

Saturday, August 11th.

The morning was fair, beautiful, & pleasant. Early, everything & everybody was in active preparation for a start in the evening. Grass was bundled & packed & stowed in the wagons. Loose mules were packed also, & everyone riding an animal had his fodder behind him. Casks & kegs, gum bags & gun covers, coffee pots & tea kettles, canteens, jugs & bottles, *everything* was filled with water & at 1 o'clock the order to gear up was given & at 2 we bid farewell to the marsh & our numerous friends.[3] The road goes direct across to strike the old road some 5 miles. It was a new one, & made through the sage bushes & of course was not very good, but the old road was as smooth as a table & hard as a rock. It passed over what is in high water part of the sink & consequently there was no vegetation save a few sage bushes,

2. The caption indicates that Bryarly wrote the entries for August 11, 12, and 13, on August 14, after the desert crossing had been completed.

3. Even the most laconic and perfunctory journals convey a quality of eloquence as they describe the crossing of the Humboldt Desert. For instance, Andrew Orvis had made the journey as far as the desert with no especial difficulty. But when he had completed four-fifths of the crossing, trouble began: "In 8 miles of the [Truckee] River my horse bigan to fail and I had to go slow but I drove him until within 3 miles of the river. I could not get him any farther. I was over come and tired out. I would travel a little and I would lay down on the sand and rest and the sun shining on me. There is no timber thare. I thought I would never get through and I laide down to kick the bucket; but I thought of home and it give me a little more grit and I would get up and stager along. I was so thirsty my tonge and lips cracked and bled but I was able to get to the water and after drinking a little—I dare not drink much—I felt better. Towards knight, I took some grass and water in my canteen back to the horse. He was in the same place I had left him. I poered water on the grass and he eat and then he went to the river first rate." Other accounts of the crossing of the Humboldt Desert in '49 are: Hixson, pp. 199–210 (very vivid); Johnston, July 16; Long, Aug. 2, *et seq.;* B. C. Clark, Aug. 2–5; Tiffany, Aug. 3 *et seq.;* Wistar, Aug. 10 *et seq.;* Backus, Aug. 13 *et seq.;* S. B. F. Clark, Aug. 11–12; Love, Aug. 13 *et seq.;* Hackney, Aug. 25–26; Lewis, Aug. 22 *et seq.;* McCall, Aug. 27–29; Kelly, pp. 296 *et seq.;* Searls, Sept. 3; Dundass, Sept. 6 (a notable account); De Wolf, Sept. 29–30; Royce, pp. 40–57. The last of these is one of the most intensely felt personal records in American history.

which were upon mounds several feet above the level. Stock
of all sorts, horses, mules, oxen & cows were scattered along,
having coralled themselves in the arms of fatigue & death.
Here for the second time upon our journey we saw the mi-
rage upon these immense white basins. It was a poor example, however, but was very deceiving to those who had
never seen anything of the kind before.

Twelve miles upon the old road brought us to the *Sink,* the
disideratum of long hoped for weeks. "How far to the
Sink?" has been a question *often* asked, & *often* answered,
& *often* heard in the last month. This Sink extends over several miles & is generally grown up with rushes & grass.
There is immense basins however on all sides, which, in
high water, receive the back water. The road keeps in these
basins, which extend over *miles* & *miles* without a vestige of
vegetation, but so white & dazzling in the sun as scarcely to
be looked at. We rolled by this, the water of which cannot be
used by man or beast, [for] 4 miles, & came to some sulphur
springs or rather wells. Here we encamped for the night.
These wells were dug in a slough, & the water was very like
many of our sulphur springs at home. The animals drank it
freely & it seemed to do them no harm. In this slough just
below the spring were a great number of cattle & mules,
which had become mired & were not able to get out & were
left. Some of them were still alive. The most obnoxious,
hideous gases perfumed our camp all night, arising from the
many dead animals around.[4] In the morning some were
found laying immediately by us & in the vicinity 30 [others]
were adding their scents to the nauseous atmosphere. Our

---

4. All testimony emphasized that the dead beasts of burden and the discarded
goods on the Humboldt Desert presented as grim a scene as a field of battle.
The animals here were driven to the utmost limits of endurance, and hundreds
died along the way. De Wolf, Oct. 1, spoke of 500 dead oxen; Backus, Aug. 15,
and Long, Aug. 3, spoke of hundreds; Love, Aug. 15, Hackney, Aug. 25,
McCall, Aug. 29, Dundass, Sept. 6, and Royce, pp. 52–53, were impressed by the
heavy animal mortalities; B. C. Clark, Aug. 5, said, "All along the desert
road from the very start even the way side was strewed with the dead bodies
of oxen, mules, & horses & the stench was horrible. All our travelling experience furnishes no parallel for all this." The general record of horror is
occasionally relieved by the story of emigrants who went to extreme lengths
to save cherished animals or to mitigate their suffering. See McCall, Aug. 29;
Pleasants, p. 81 (on Black Rock Desert); and Paden, *Wake of the Prairie
Schooner,* pp. 432–433.

animals were turned to the grass we brought already dried,
& they seemed [to] relish it much.

We were *past the Sink*.[5] This is glory enough for one day.
I would ask the learned & descriptive Mr. Frémont & the
elegant & imaginative Mr. Bryant, where was the beautiful
valley, the surpassing lovely valley of Humbolt? Where was
the country presenting the most splendid "agricultural
features?" Where the splendid grazing, the cottonwood lin-
ing the banks of their *beautiful meandering stream*, & everything presenting the most interesting & picturesque appearance of any place they ever saw?

Perhaps Mr. Bryant was speaking ironically of all these
most captivating things that he saw, or perhaps he thought
it was "too far out" for anyone else but himself to see. If
not, I have only to say, "Oh shame where is thy blush."[6]

---

5. The Sink of the Humboldt, sometimes called Humboldt Lake, in what is
now Pershing County, Nevada, was a landmark sought by all emigrants. The
"Sink" tended to alter its position in response to the volume of water which
the river carried at any given time.

6. Bryant, *What I Saw*, p. 198, spoke of "numerous . . . varieties" of
"heavily seeded and . . . highly sustaining . . . grasses" along the Humboldt.
Frémont had traversed the Humboldt region on his third expedition, and had
described the valley as "a rich alluvion beautifully covered with blue grass,
herd grass, clover, and other nutritious grasses; and its course is marked
through the plain by a line of willow and cotton wood trees" (*Geographical
Memoir upon Upper California* [Washington, 1848], p. 10). Ware, in his
Emigrants' Guide, p. 32, echoed these descriptions, and stated that the Humboldt
valley was "rich and beautifully clothed with blue grass, herds grass, clover,
and other nutritious grasses."

These descriptions provoked angry comment from many emigrants. John
Caughey gives specimens of this criticism in his edition of Ware's *Emigrants'
Guide*, p. 32, n. 49. Among the Forty-niners, Kelly, p. 295, censures Frémont
for his description, and McCall, Aug. 16, notes that "many are bitter in their
denunciations of Frémont." A particularly biting comment is a verse which
Tiffany, Aug. 5, quotes as coming from the pen of his companion, John Grant-
ham:

"THE HUMBUG"

"From all the books that we have read
And all that travellers had said
We most implicitly believed,
Nor dreamed that we should be deceived,

That when the mountains we should pass
We'd find on Humboldt fine Blue-grass.
Nay that's not all[;] we learned moreover
That we'd get in the midst of clover.

We have travelled along it several hundred miles, from its commencement from a little pool that you could drink up if thirsty, to its termination in the sink. It is so very crooked in its whole course that I believe it impossible for one to make a *chalk mark* as much so. Frequently I have stood & fished on each side of me in two different parts of the river, the distance around being half a mile or more. It is a *dirty, muddy, sluggish, indolent stream,* with but little grass at the best of times, & as for cottonwood, there is not a switch of it from one end to the other. A friend of mine remarked, it was fit for nothing else but to sink to the "Lower Regions," & the quicker it done it the better. He much preferred calling it Hellboldt River.   [*Distance, 23 miles.*

Sunday, August 12th.

We rolled out at daybreak. The road was firm, hard, level, & smooth. In four miles we came to the forks of the road. Here we found many placards, the most of which advised their friends to take the right. The left was but little travelled in comparison to the right, & we took it.[7] We rolled through the same kind of a basin as yesterday and [at] 10 miles we stopped to breakfast, which was cooked with some pieces of wagons we picked up on the road. We layed by until 2 o'clock having given grass & water to our stock, & again rolled. The road continued the same for several miles, when we left the basin forever, the road then being upon a

> Nay, more yet, these scribbling asses
> Told of 'other nutricious grasses'
> But great indeed was our surprise
> To find it all a pack of lies. . . .
>
> But when we to the Humboldt came
> It soon with us lost all its fame
> We viewed it as a great outrage
> Instead of grass to find wild sage."

7. Here, Bryarly appears to reverse the facts. At this well-known junction, the left-hand road went to the Carson River, the right-hand road to the Truckee. The Charlestown Company certainly went to the Truckee, as the rest of the journal shows, and therefore must have taken the right. See statement by John Caughey in his edition of Ware, *Emigrants' Guide,* p. 36, n. 55, and Paden, *Wake of the Prairie Schooner,* p. 404.

ridge with a few sage bushes & rocks. We rolled thus 15 miles, which brought us to the Hot Springs.[8]

Seventy dead animals were counted in the last 25 miles. Pieces of wagons also, the irons in particular—the wood part having been burnt—were also strewn along. An ox-yoke, [a] wheel & a dead ox; a dead ox, yoke, & wheel; & a wheel, dead ox & a yoke, was the order of the day, every hundred or two yards.

These Hot Springs are one of *The* things upon this earth. The pool is some 25 or 30 yds. in circumference & around it are a great number of springs, some placid & luke warm, others sending off considerable steam & hot water, & others again, bubbling & boiling furiously & scalding. The water when cooled was drinkable, but sulphurish & very salt. There was a great number of kegs & casks, boxes & wagon-beds here, which had been used to cool the water by others. These we filled & after some hours our stock drank it. A piece of meat, held in one [of] the boiling springs, boiled in 20 minutes, perfectly done. By putting the water in your coffee-pot & holding the pot over the bubbling, it would boil in a few minutes. In this way many of us cooked our suppers.

Thousands of dollars worth of property thrown away by the emigration was laying here. Wagons & property of every kind & description, not saying anything of dead animals & those left to die. The machinery of a turning machine that must have cost $6[00] or $700. A steam engine & machinery for coining that could not have cost less than $2[000] or $3000, were also laying here, all sacrificed upon this Jornado. These things they say belonged to the notorious Mr. Finley [?] who also lost 55 cattle out of 80.

[Distance, 25 miles.

---

8. Hot Springs or Boiling Springs furnished the only natural source of water on the desert crossing. When traffic was light across the desert, each traveller usually found water left by a previous traveller in casks, where it would cool, and he in turn filled the casks for the next comer. But when traffic was heavy, each party had to wait for its own water to cool. The water, however, was naturally bad, and did not improve when dead animals and other debris accumlated in the springs. Wistar, Aug. 13, relates that his party used coffee to disguise the taste of the water. ''My horse drank a little of the coffee, though he declined the water with decision.'' See McCall's description of these springs, Aug. 29.

Monday, August 13th.

We started this morning [at] 2 1/2 o'clock. The road was again in a basin & was level, hard, & smooth. Soon after daylight our animals showed evident signs of fagging. Four miles from [the] Hot Spring we came to some sulphur springs. They were very salty & not good, but had been used by others. The sun was most powerful, & the reflection from the shining dirt made it most oppressive. We rolled 12 miles, & having come to where we strike the sand which we have been dreading all the time, we stopped to breakfast. Some of our teams did not get in for some time after the others, they having fagged so much as to fall in the rear.

Here we fed the last of our grass & gave the last of our water. Several wagons were here, the animals having given out & were taken to the river ahead to recruit, which we learned was but 8 miles, but deep sand all the way. Several of us started soon after eating & came on to the river & luxuriated ourselves & horses with delicious water. The teams started at 1 o'clock but finding they would in all probability give out or at least be a dead strain all the way, they determined to double teams & bring half over & recruit the mules & bring the remainder today. This was accordingly done & seven wagons arrived safe & our animals watered & turned to good grass. Some remained behind with the wagons & water was packed back to them.

This [is] Salmon Trout [Truckee] River. It is a beautiful, clear, swift stream, & the water is delicious. Large cottonwood trees skirt its banks, which gives everything around an air of comfort once more. In approaching it the trees are seen a mile off, & to the parched, famished, & wearied man & beast they are truly "a green spot in the desert." [9] We are

9. Hackney, Aug. 26, wrote, "we came in sight of truckies river thear was nothing in the whole world that I would have sooner seen at that moment then it its banks wear lined by large cottonwood trees and was quite a contrass to the wide dosolation behind us when we got to the river we could hardly keep our oxen out of it when we drove them in it done me good to see the poor devils drink." Wistar, Aug. 13, mentions the "brays of joy" with which the mules responded when they smelled the water of the Truckee. Later, "Everyone hurried bodily into the water and drank all he could, while urging the others to be careful and not drink too much. Fortunately, Spanish mules never founder,

safely over *the desert,* however, without losing a single
animal, although many are very far gone; but a day or two
recruiting, which we think of giving them here, will put them
again all right. The water of the Hot Spring which was used
freely by both the men & animals affected them most singularly. Two or three hours after drinking, it produced violent
strangling to both. The men in particular were very much
annoyed also by the most violent pain in the urinary organs.
It was truly laughable to see their contortions & twistings
after urinating, which they desired to do every hour. The
mules also seemed to suffer much, but their symptoms lasted
only 10 or 12 hours. Upon examining an old canteen that had
had this water in it, with a grass stopper, I discovered the
evident fumes of nitre, & upon examination found it [to]
contain much, & no doubt these unpleasant symptoms were
caused by it. The dead animals were not so numerous today
although there was yet sufficient to be very annoying from
their perfumes. On the other [Carson] road I am told they
are much thicker, more than half of the head emigration
having taken that road.   [*Distance, 20 miles.*

Tuesday, August 14th.

All night the teams, with loose mules & oxen, were rolling
in, causing a general buzz all night. We layed in camp until
noon, our mules being in excellent grass. They were then
brought up & taken back [on the desert] for our remaining
teams, which arrived in camp at 12 o'clock at night. They
report many more dead animals upon the road than yesterday. Every train that has arrived has lost one or two upon
this last stretch. The weather today was most oppressively
hot & we congratulated ourselves we were not on the parched
desert.

There is two roads here, one to the left on the same side
of the river with a stretch through the sand of 25 miles to
water & grass, the other crosses the river & keeps up the
river through a kanyon 16 miles & crossing the river many
times. From all we have been able to gather, we have deter-

and after drinking all they could, they lay down and rolled in the stream
mixing up teams and harness in joyous confusion.''

mined to cross the river, taking the right hand road. We had today a general inspection of our provisions & find we have only sufficient to last us ten days. This was alarming & our Quartermaster was ordered to look out for more.

Wednesday, August 15th.

All night the starved & famished mules & cattle were rushing through our camp, very much to the annoyance & risk of injury to those sleeping upon the ground. Many teams arrived last night, with the same proportionate loss as those before them. Everyone, without a dissenting voice, cursed the desert, and yet thank God they are over it with their little loss.

The morning was again very hot & we almost dreaded the idea of exposing ourselves to the hot rays of the sun upon the road. Our mules were brought up at 11 o'clock & we again hooked up. We crossed the river & rolled two miles when we came to a sand bluff which was very hard pulling. We passed upon this one mile & a half & nooned, turning our mules across the river to grass, it being the only grass in several miles. Our Quartermaster having made arrangements to obtain some flour & pork from a train behind, the sick wagon was left to bring it when it should arrive. One mile from noon we got off the sand & crossed the river & was soon in the kanyon proper. We passed along this, crossing the river four times in 5 miles. Here night overtook us, & not being able [to] proceed farther, & finding Capt. Smith awaiting us, we pulled out on the side of the road & tied our mules to the wheels, feeding them upon willows & cotton bushes.

Owing to the scarcity of the grass, the Captain determined to keep a camp ahead [of us], & leave [some]one behind at each place to point out the grazing spots, & I [am] to remain behind to take charge of the train. Our herders have been reduced to the ranks, each teamster taking care of his own extra mules, & the other extra ones rode by the men.

A fellow statesman[10] & friend, Mr. Long, having overtaken us today, invited Mr. Washington to accompany him through

---

10. *I.e.*, apparently, a fellow citizen of Maryland or of Virginia.

[to the diggings], he being upon pack mules & expecting to arrive a week before us. I tendered to him [Mr. Washington] the use of my "Walking Squaw" & he determined to accept & started off an hour before us. By the way, the Hot Spring water acted very singularly upon the "Squaw." Soon after arriving at breakfasting on the morning of the 13th at the beginning of the sand, she was taken with violent pain, as though she had the cholic, & very much to the astonishment of all, she was *confined* & brought forth. This abortion no doubt was caused by the water. We know not her history & consequently cannot tell the pedigree of the little one, or whether she herself had been *imprudent* & *slipt her foot,* but who knows but in this, was lost the race of as fine stock as ever the world saw. "Squaw," with her nation's peculiarity, was as much herself again in half an hour as though nothing had happened, & was hitched to the sick wagon & dragged it through the sand to the river. (The power of endurance of some of these ponies is most astonishing.)

[*Distance, 8 miles.*

Thursday, August 16th.

We had a most unpleasant camp last night, & at daylight we were again upon the road. Yesterday evening it clouded up with heavy black clouds, with rolling, rumbling thunder, accompanied with vivid flashes of lightening. In the course of half an hour we were blessed with a hail storm, with a fine shower of rain. This is the first for 7 weeks & we hailed it with delight. Last night it was cloudy & very dark, with distant thunder, & being [in] the very narrow place in which we were, with high mountains upon each side, and only able to see the sky looking straight up, gave it a most dismal and sepulchral appearance, & daylight was most welcomed. We rolled 3 miles & coming to some grass upon a flat we stopped to breakfast. Here we remained 2 hours & again rolled 5 miles, when we came to better grass & coralled for the day for the purpose of waiting for our provision train, as well as to feed our mules.

We crossed the river today 7 times, making 12 times in all. Some of them were deep & very rocky, with a swift cur-

rent, so much so as to take some of our mules off their feet.
It was amusing to see many of our men riding their mules
across. They would do it most cautiously, picking out their
way in every step, but in spite of all this, they would frequently fall, sometimes rolling over [on] their sides & coralling them [the riders] most beautifully in the water. Our
friend Locke, in particular, was riding "a very high mule"
whose legs were "twisted out"—& which landed him most
beautifully in Salmon Trout.[11] The current is so strong that
a man can but with difficulty walk across, & consequently it
is very dangerous to be thrown in. As yet everything has
passed in safety & we hope, with care, it will continue to be
so.   [*Distance, 8 miles.*

Friday, August 17th.

It rained again last night & a very heavy dew also fell.
We started at 6 o'clock & crossed, & recrossed the stream.
Eight miles we nooned, crossing in this distance 8 times.
Here we had tolerable grass, our Captain having picked it,
& left one [of the advance] to point it out to me. We remained here until 2 when we again rolled. In the evening,
we rolled 7 miles, crossing the river 4 times, making in all
22. [24.]

The road between the crossings was sandy in some places,
rocky in others, & very steep both going up & coming down
in others. After 7 miles we emerged in a beautiful, green,
velvety valley, which, upon first coming in view, presented a
most cheering appearance. We here crossed a slough, the
crossing of which was fixed & bridged by our Captain & party
ahead. Before this was done, it is said it was almost im-
passible, each having to be cordelled across. We passed over
in safety & encamped in this lovely valley, with blue grass to
the horses' knees. We passed today two graves; one had
been drowned several days before,[12] the other had died to-

---

11. Cf. B. C. Clark, Aug. 8, along the Truckee: "Some riding mules would
go along picking their way quite cautiously until suddenly the swiftness of the
water or some loose rock plonged horse & rider into the torrent. Up they would
rise again amid the shouts & geers of the spectators with drooping crests & we
may add drooping tails."

12. B. C. Clark, Aug. 10, at about this same point along the Truckee, wrote,
"Last evening a man was drowned here (one of the Iowa Company)."

day. We came in sight for the first time of the Sierra Nevada mountains, or rather of the chain. During the day it has been cloudy, with constant rumbling of thunder in the distance. In the morning we had a very nice shower, & several times during the day it gave us a pleasant sprinkle.

[*Distance, 15 miles.*]

Saturday, August 18th.

It was our determination to lay here until the provision train should arrive, consequently we endulged in an uncommon knap after sunrise. Grass was fine, wood plenty, & water delicious, with a beautiful camp, & we all enjoyed it very much. Grass was mowed & packed, & in the evening we hooked up & moved up the valley 3 miles so as to be nearer the stretch of 15 miles for which we prepared the grass. Two men were left here to conduct the [provision] wagon over the slough & bring them up to us.   [*Distance, 3 miles.*]

Sunday, August 19th.

The provisions did not arrive last night, very much to our disappointment, but today about 9 o'clock it came in sight, when immediately we hooked up & rolled out. We soon left the valley, the road being very rocky with large round stones. In six miles we struck the river, where we nooned, giving some of our grass to them [the animals].

Upon a proposition, the flour & bacon was divided between the different messes, on account of the scarcity of the provisions & thinking that they would be more economical in using them.

We rolled out at 2 o'clock. The road was rough in the extreme & very hilly. We crossed the river 4 times making 26 [28] times altogether. Ten miles we came to the river again. Before striking it we came to large trees of pine, cypress, & lignum vitae. The banks of the river & the sides of the mountain are also covered with them. The valley where we strike the river is narrow, but had excellent grass upon it, but by some person or persons unknown, [it] was burned off & part of it was still burning. We tied up to the wheels & fed

the remainder of the grass we had provided ourselves with
yesterday.   [*Distance, 16 miles.*

Monday, August 20th.

The scenery around us last night would put at defiance the
artist's pencil. It was one of the [most] majestic ones that
ever falls to the lot of man to witness. Immediately upon the
opposite side of the river, the mountain commenced its ascent, covered with large timber of fur, pines of all sorts, &
arbor vitae. They were not thick but presented rather, the
appearance of a grove with good verdure & no underwood.
The valley was narrow but was visible for a mile or more.
In a thousand different places, both on the side of the mountain and along the valley, the trees & grass had been set on
fire. It was a dark night, the clouds having gathered over
very threateningly at sundown, & the bright blazing fires up
the mountain and down the valley, the roaring & splashing
of the river over the rocks, accompanied with the occasional
fall of a tree that had burned through, with the howling of
wolves [*one word illegible*] in their round, all presented a
scene to the wearied & silent beholder not soon to be for-
gotten.

We started at daybreak & crossed the river. The road
turned immediately to the right in a north direction & continued for one mile, when it went in a northwest direction,
ascending a spur of mountain, one of the chain of the California mountains. We ascended this, it being in some places
very steep, & then again coming upon a little table of land
upon which had been good grass, & upon one with a cool but
small spring. After rolling there 5 miles, we opened upon a
beautiful little valley with a very steep hill to descend to it.
We went down in the valley & nooned. This valley is oval in
shape & had plenty of good grass & water in it.

We rolled again at 2 P.M. The road here took a south
direction, having travelled northwest this morning. We
passed along through the woods, which was very large timber of the same description as before described. Occasionally we struck a little valley with good grazing & water. Four

miles we encamped in one of these valleys. At our noon to-day we learned from a gentleman, that the Indians had killed one of his mules with an arrow last night. They were about starting in search of them.   [*Distance, 9 miles.*

Tuesday, August 21st.

It was very cold last night & many of us that had not pre-pared for it suffered much from it. The grass was covered with a white hoary frost, which crackled under our feet. The water in our buckets was frozen to considerable thickness. We started early & rolled over the same kind of road as yes-terday evening, through woods, valleys, & up & down hill, but none very steep. Three miles brought us to a larger val-ley than usual, with a little stream of water coming from the mountains on our right. This is one of the tributaries of Truckee or Salmon Trout. We rolled 6 miles over the same sort of country with high mountains upon each side of us & came to another large valley with a larger stream running through it—another tributary to Salmon Trout. Here we nooned.

Around our camp last night the awful & distressing cries of a panther was heard, first in one place, then soon after in another. The guard came in one after another to double arm themselves for this very formidable enemy, but he did not return too near. Today, one was seen only a short distance from camp, in the road. He stopped & turned to take a survey of those behind, & then trotted slowly away. They had no rifle & consequently did not pursue.

We rolled in the evening at 2 P.M. The road still the same, except a little rougher. Four miles, the road turned left. Here, upon our left, distant some hundred yards from the road was Truckee River in all its glory again, splashing & dashing over the rocks. Here we met one of our advance who informed us we were but five miles from the base of the *great bugaboo,* that which has caused many a sleepless night, with disturbed dreams to the discouraged emigrant, "*The Sierra Nevada*" *Mountains.* We were much inspired & equally rejoiced, [as] we had no idea we were so far on our way. We were informed there was no grass at the base, or near it, & consequently we rolled a mile or so farther & encamped.

We were informed that the cabins of the "Lamentable Donner Party" [13] were also on our road, as well as also [that] the [Pyramid, or Donner] Lake [was] but one mile from the present trail. I immediately started off to look for these mournful monuments of human suffering. One was only 150 yds. from our camp upon the left of the trail. This [cabin] was still standing. It was two in one, there being a seperation of logs between. The timbers were from 8 inches to a foot in diameter, about 8 or 9 ft. high & covered over with logs upon which had been placed branches & limbs of trees, dirt &c. The logs were fitted very nicely together, there being scarcely a crevice between. There was one door to each, entering from the north and from the road.

There were piles of bones around but mostly of cattle, although I did find some half dozen human ones of different parts. Just to the left of these was a few old black burnt logs, which evidently had been one of those [cabins] which had been burnt. Here was nearly the whole of a skeleton. Several small stockings were found which still contained the bones of the leg & foot. Remnants of old clothes, with pieces of boxes, stockings, & bones in particular, was all that was left to mark that it had once been inhabited.

In the centre of each was a hole dug which had either served as a fireplace or to bury their dead. The trees around were cut off 10 ft. from the ground, showing the immense depth the snow must have been. After examining this I

---

13. The Donner Party was an emigrant group of 1846, whose nucleus was the Donner and Reed families from Illinois. This party was persuaded to follow the unfamiliar Hastings' Cut-off south of the Great Salt Lake, as a result of which much time was lost and winter snows immobilized the party near Pyramid Lake in the Sierras. There they suffered fearful hardships; many died; and the survivors were reduced to eating the flesh of those who perished. A succession of rescue parties attempted to carry relief, and forty-seven were saved, but the death of forty others made this disaster a classic warning to later emigrants against the perils of unfamiliar trails, and against the dangers of delay along the route. Bryant, *What I Saw*, pp. 249–265, gives an account (to which Bryarly refers) which was widely read among the emigrants. In this, he explains that Gen. Stephen W. Kearny, visiting the scene on June 22, 1847, ordered the human remains to be buried and the cabins to be burned. Bryarly refers to this fact, below. A vivid and accurate account of the tragedy appears in Bernard De Voto, *The Year of Decision, 1846* (Boston, 1943).

passed on one mile where the road went to the left in a more southerly direction. The old trail went on straight down the valley to the Lake which was distant one mile. I went on to the lake & was fully repaid for my trouble, for it was one of the most beautiful ones on record. It was beautiful, fresh, pure, clear water, with a gravelly bottom, with a sandy beach. It was about 2 miles long, three-quarters wide & confined between three mountains on three sides, which arose immediately from its edge. On the other [side] was the valley by which I had approached it & through which a little stream was passing off from it. I here took a delightful bath & felt renovated.

In returning I came to another of the cabins, but which had been burned by order of Gen'l Kearney. Here also I found many human bones. The skulls had been sawed open for the purpose, no doubt, of getting out the brains, & the bones had all been sawed open & broken to obtain the last particle of nutriment.

Bryant has given a most satisfactory account of the suffering of the unfortunate emigrants of Donner's party & the many trials, deprivations & sufferings, with loss of life [that] runneth not in the knowledge of man. To look upon these sad monuments harrows up every sympathy of the heart & soul, & you almost hold your breath to listen for some mournful sound from these blackened, dismal, funeral piles, telling you of their many sufferings & calling upon you for bread, bread.

There seems to be a sad, melancholy stillness hanging around these places, which serves to make a gloom around you, which draws you closer & closer in your sympathies with those whom hunger compelled to eat their own children, & finally to be eaten by others themselves, & their bones now kicked perhaps under any one's feet. There was also another cabin upon the opposite side of the road, but I did not visit it.

Accompanying the Pittsburgh [Company] was a man by the name of Graves, who was one of the survivors of this party.[14] I conversed with him several times about the road

14. William Graves and Jonathan Graves, sons of W. F. Graves and his wife, had been rescued together with their sisters. Both parents had perished in the mountains.

when meeting with him upon [the] trip, but he avoided & alluded [*i.e.* eluded] any conversation about his misfortune. I was told by a member of his Company, that the night before they came to this place, Graves started off without saying anything to them, & did not [re]join them until after they had passed. He preferred viewing the place of his unprecedented suffering alone, not wishing that the eye of unsympathising man should be a witness to his harrowed feelings.

A meeting of our company was called today & our Quarter-Master was appointed to select two other gentlemen to go ahead of us, to obtain provisions necessary for us upon our arrival, & also to find out all the important information necessary for us to commence operations in the mines. They accordingly, this afternoon, left us, having their provender tied on behind them.   [*Distance, 14 miles.*

Wednesday, August 22nd.

It was very cold again last night, & it occurred to us forcibly that if it was this cold here in August, what must it be in January. Early everything was in motion. In one mile we crossed a little stream to the left, which runs from the Lake. Here we stopped, & cut sufficient grass for a feed. After rolling one mile farther we struck the foot of the mountain. The road was very rough & in many places steep both going up & coming down. Every now & then there was a little table upon which was a little grass. We rolled thus 2 miles when we nooned (or rather rested, not taking our mules out) upon one of these tables. We stopped 2 hours, when we ascended a steep & very rocky road with many short turns around the large rocks & trees. One mile brought us to the foot of the "Elephant" itself. Here we "faced the music" & no mistake. The "Wohaughs" could be heard for miles, hollowing & bawling at their poor cattle who could scarcely drag themselves up the steep aclivity.

We immediately doubled teams, & after considerable screaming & whipping, thus arrived safe at the top. They then returned & took up the remainder with like success. We were but four hours ascending, & we were much disappointed, but agreably so, in not finding it much worse. Certainly this must be a great improvement upon the old road, where the wagons had to be taken to pieces & packed across. We rolled down the mountain 4 miles, the road being rough & steep half way & then striking a valley, where it was good. We passed through a grove of woods & then emerged into a beautiful valley & encamped.

We were all in the most joyous & elated spirits this evening. We have crossed the only part of road that we feared, & that without any breakage, loss or detention. I had but the one & only bottle of "cognac" that was in our camp, & which I had managed to keep since leaving the Old Dominion. This I invited my mess to join me in, & which invitation was most cordially accepted. When lo & behold, upon bringing it out, it was empty—yes positively empty. The cork was bad & with numerous joltings, it had gradually disappeared. This was a disappointment many of us will not soon forget.   [*Distance, 8½ miles.*

Thursday, August 23rd.

We layed in camp during the morning, our mules being in good grass, & not knowing when we would get more. Many of our men went hunting, but one buck only was killed.

We rolled at 2 P.M. & [in] one mile left the valley, the road taking a more southern direction. Here we entered again into a mountain gorge. The road was rougher than we have before seen it, immense large rocks. The road was also up & down hill; one in particular, about 5 miles from starting, was so rough & steep as to have to let our wagons down by ropes. In getting thus far we passed 6 lakes, some upon each side, & of considerable size, measuring several miles in length. Soon after descending the steep hill, we commenced ascending a very steep rough mountain, the road making short turns [on] smooth rock. We ascended to the top of this, which was two miles, & encamped at the base of a very high, projecting rocky mountain with a very pretty valley surrounding it, with good water. This peak of mountain is very remarkable for its roughness, being of sharp slate-stone, [as] also for its peculiar shape & immense heighth. We met today some gentlemen on their return from the "Diggins." Their account of the road ahead is discouraging

—indeed almost appaling—but the news from the "Diggins" is flattering in the extreme.　　　　　　　[*Distance, 8 miles.*

Friday, August 24th.

Our mules were grazing a mile from camp & consequently we did not get them up in time to start as early as usual. Half past six, however, we were again in motion. The road was still the same except perhaps more rough than yesterday. Up & down hill, over rocks as large as the wagon itself, & tumbling & throwing them about as though they had nothing in them.[15] Four miles we came to a very steep rocky one; this, after a fashion, we descended, & struck a little creek with stony bottom. This was Bear Creek or River. Just where we struck [it] there was a little valley, but no grass—still nothing but bare rocks. We nooned here after crossing the river & tied up [our animals] to the wheels.

We again rolled at 2. Everyone is liable to mistakes, & everyone has a right to call a road *very bad* until he sees a worse. My mistake was that I said I had seen "The Elephant" when getting over the first mountain. I had only seen the tail. This evening I think I saw him in toto. I do not know, however, as I have come to the conclusion that no Elephant upon this route can be so large that another cannot be larger. If I had not seen wagon tracks marked upon the rocks I should not have known where the road was, nor could I have imagined that any wagon & team could possibly pass over in safety.

An immense hill to ascend & descend, with rocks of every description, large & small, round & smooth, & sometimes one flat one covering the whole road. You may imagine what sort of a country it is when you cannot ride a horse anywhere but immediately in the track. We were unfortunate in getting behind a large ox-train & consequently were much detained, our wagon having to stop for hours upon the side of one of these steep, rough hills. Upon riding forward I ascertained the cause of the detention to be the unyoking of their cattle & letting the wagons down by ropes. This was truly the

---

15. Badman, July 26, noted, "17m[ile]s over the Damdist mountains I ever see or hird tell of for a wagon to be drove over."

"jumping off" place. They [the wagons] were let down over a large smooth rock. A rope attached to the wagon & then passed around a tree, commanded it perfectly, paying out as much rope as necessary, & checking it instantly if required. The bark of some of the largest trees which had been used in this way was cut entirely through.

The trains ahead of us did not get over until after dusk, consequently we had to stop & remain the night just where we were upon the side of the hill among the rocks. There was nothing for our animals to pick & they were again tied up to the wheels. The rocks were so thick & rough that it was with difficulty I could find sufficient space to spread my blanket. McKay, one of our mess (being now, by the absence of Mr. Washington reduced to four) killed two very fine bucks. They were packed in, & each one of the messes were supplied with a piece. A very large quarter was reserved for ourselves which, remembering our scarcity of provisions, we salted & packed away.   [*Distance, 6 miles.*

Saturday, August 25th.

The men were early at work letting down the wagons over the precipice. Some mules were missing, having been turned loose contrary to order. Search was made, but two mules & [a] pony were not found. After a time & after a fashion our wagons were landed safely below, by the means spoken of yesterday. Once, a wagon came faster than it should, & was very near crushing Mr. Moore who slipt down on the rock. After this we again started, the road getting worse & worse. Three miles brought us to an uncommon steep hill & again very rocky. This was ascended with great difficulty. Half [a] mile farther we struck the foot of another mountain, very steep, but road comparatively good. We rolled up this one mile, there being several little smooth tables. Along & upon two of these were lakes covering one or two acres.

We then commenced descending, which was very steep, with rocks, but not large, & which was accomplished very easily. Here we struck a wood valley & rolled 2 miles when we struck a meadow or willow valley with grass & here we coralled. We passed this morning two old cabins upon our left, which had been burned. They presented, around, the same appearance as those on Truckee Lake, & no doubt was some of the suffering party. The mountain sides were covered with cherries which were bitter & growing upon small bushes [and with] the prickly gooseberry also, which is a beautiful fruit & very good, but rather dangerous & inconvenient to eat. Raspberries were in abundance. They grow upon a vine, the leaf of which is very much like the grape. The fruit is large & has the most delicate flavour.

For the purpose of lightening our wagons, our loose mules were packed & driven ahead. Both the men & mules are "green" at it, & of course there was much confusion before they got off. [*Distance, 7 miles.*

Sunday, August 26th.

The valley we were in last night properly should be called "Yellow Jacket Valley." Such numbers never were seen before collected together. After building our mess-fire, a nest [was] found directly by us. We were anxious to compromise with them, that if they would let us alone, we would not disturb them. They would not agree, however, & opened hostilities upon us, when we thought it prudent "to raze our eyes" to withdraw our forces under cover. Here we quietly remained until nightfall, when the enemy having retired and reposed in their corall with apparent serenity, we blockaded the mouth of their citadel with a chunk of fire & finished by building our mess fire immediately over their strong & deep founded works. In the morning our mules were scattered in every direction having been run off by these Gulliver little varmints.

We rolled at 6½. The road was upon the side of a mountain, but good in comparison to what we have had for some time. Two miles we came to another valley similar to the one we just left. One mile farther the road was as rough as it well could be, down a hill & immediately up another so steep & rough that some of our teams had to double. [As] soon as we arrived at the top of this, which was 200 yds. from the foot, we saw—yes, I think I can with safety say, here—we saw the "Old Gentleman Elephant of all." If I had not seen a wagon going down before me, I think I would have sworn none could, but they were actually & really going down.

It was a hill almost perpendicular, so much so that fear was expressed that the wagon would turn head over heels down. This first was about 75 yds. down; here was a little table; then another hill &c., &c. Four of them brought you at last in a valley with a beautiful spring, a fine stream, & plenty of grass. This is Bear Valley.[16] By taking out the leaders of our teams & back locking & every other kind of locking, & [by] attaching a rope behind & holding it around a tree, our wagons & all, with a great deal of work, trouble, & fatigue, were moored safely in the valley.

We rolled up the valley one mile when we encamped, the last wagon getting in about sundown. Here we had good grass, fine water, & plenty of wood. Two gentlemen came in our camp right from the "Diggins." The road is [as] bad as ever for six miles, when we have it excellently good, but no grass, for 50 miles. On this account, for the purpose of cutting, drying, & packing sufficient grass for this expected Jornado, we determined to remain here tomorrow. Still flattering accounts from the mines.   [*Distance, 4 miles.*

Monday, August 27th.

We layed in camp all day with the usual monotony. Our camp was pleasantly & beautifully situated upon the side of the mountain facing the valley. Men were busily employed cutting & drying grass for the stretch. A great number of both "Wohaughs" & "Muros" rolled into the valley after us & layed here also today. Our scythes were in great demand by them, & had it not been for ours, I scarce know what they would have done, as they were the only ones about. There is again considerable diarrhea in camp produced by the great quantities of fresh meat we have had of late. We have had a deer a day for some time, & caution will not prevent them from indulging too much. In the evening the mules were driven up & piquetted out for the purpose of getting a very

16. Bear Creek or River rises in the Sierra Nevada and flows westward into the Feather River, which is in turn a tributary of the Sacramento.

early start in the morning to get ahead of the Wohaughs, having been delayed in our route for several days by them.

Tuesday, August 28th.

We were off this morning before the light of day. Soon after our wagons left, the whole valley seemed in a commotion, & one hundred wagons rolled in behind us. The road was still as bad as ever, with fewer hills, however, but those very rough. Two hills in particular, one to descend and the other ascend, was very steep, requiring the teams to be doubled. This was about 5 miles from the valley. We passed several springs to our left on the side of the mountain we were upon. We travelled 13 miles, the longest drive we have made for some time. Not a spear of grass could be seen along, but trees, oak & pine, had been cut down to browse the animals that had passed before us.

We met quite a number of cattle driving back to the valley which were said to have been poisoned by eating wild laurel. Where we encamped was a good spring in a ravine below us, which was ample for ourselves & stock. [*Distance, 13 miles.*]

Wednesday, August 29th.

Some of our teams left last night at 3 o'clock, & the remainder at daybreak. The road was still rolling as usual. In 9 miles we came to another "Elephant" (they are very plenty upon this road). There was a hill as steep as any we had yet had to descend, and another equally steep to ascend immediately from its base. Trees were cut & tied behind & allowed to drag, with some men riding upon them. In this way many of [the] teams came down very well. Others again, came down with ropes around trees, & lowered gradually. This however did not answer as well as the trees, as there was great risk of the rope breaking, which would have been attended with very serious consequences. This did happen to us, breaking a rope an inch & a quarter thick. Away went mules, wagon, & driver, with great velocity for a short distance, but they succeeded in stopping them. If they had not as soon as they did, there is no knowing what might have

been the result. After a time all were safely landed below &
Here for the First time we saw the "Gold Diggings."

I suppose we must *at last* consider ourselves in California.
Here they were Digging, Digging.

There was a little stream running along the deep hollow
upon which they were working. There was about 50 men at
work, & their average, I understand, was one ounce to one
[ounce] & a half a day. They were using what they call the
rocker. They are about the size of a common cradle with
just such rockers. Half way upon the top is a seive upon
which the stone & dirt is thrown, & a man rocks or jolts it
with one hand & with the other pours water upon it. The fine
dirt & sand is washed down in the bottom where there is
clefts, seperated a foot apart & a few inches high, to catch
the heaviest of the sand & with which the gold is mixed.
When it gets full up to the clefts, a hole being bored in the
bottom of each, the dirt & sand is drawn off in a pan &
washed, by shaking, rubbing, & washing the dirt, stone, &
gravel out, the gold remaining in the bottom. This is the
most tedious part of the operation but yet it is attended
with considerable interest. To one of these ordinary washers,
four men generally work, one to dig, one to carry the dirt,
the other to rock, and the last to wash.

Many were using their pans alone, & with equal success.
Bread pans, wash bowls, tin pans, & plates of every description were in use & demand. The most of those that we found
here were emigrants whose teams had so far given out as not
to be able to ascend the steep hill from the hollow, & they
had stopped here & sent their mules to Sacramento valley,
distant 40 miles, to recruit & bring provisions back to them.
I borrowed a basin from a gentleman who was working,
scraped it up full of dirt, & washed it out, getting about one
dollar's worth of gold. In the afternoon we rolled up the big
hill by doubling teams. Some teams were much stronger
than others & they rolled faster, consequently when night
came on, the teams behind did not come up, but coralled
where they best could. We fed the last grass today at noon,
& this evening we commenced upon oak leaves.

[*Distance, 14 miles.*

Thursday, August 30th.

We started early again this morning, the mules right well filled although they had nothing but leaves. After rolling 4 miles we came to a small branch upon which they were also digging, & with satisfactory results.

Our teams are now so very weak that they can scarcely pull up the slightest hill. We kept along this creek a half mile, all along which they were digging. One large washer had got out 1 lb. in two hours this morning.

We here ascended another of *those* hill[s] & passed over in a valley where once there had been grass, but alas, alas.

Our teams were so far given out now that we determined to *hold a talk* to determine to do something for them. After considerable discussion,[17] it was thought best to leave half of our wagons & to take half on with all of the mules, & after they recruited to come back after the remainder. Six men were left with the wagons, to watch them. The principle reason for haste is the melancholy fact that we had not provisions enough to last three days. Our meat has been out for 10 days, bread & coffee without sugar, & coffee & bread without salt or grease or sugar.

This arrangement was finally made. Half of the wagons were taken, hitching 8 mules to them; the extra mules were packed, provisions divided, & after so long a time we rolled, each wagoner to make the best time he could under the circumstances. We encamped in about 1 mile distance along the road after travelling 5 miles. Oak leaves was our only provender for our already broken down antelope mules.

[*Distance, 10 miles.*[18]

---

17. Hoffman says, ''After a great deal of wrangling.''

18. Hoffman's diary continues for two days longer. For Aug. 31, it says, ''We proceeded this morning, leaving several mules through the day that could not travel further.''

For Sept. 1, ''Made another effort today after having travelled twelve miles yesterday with practically no food for man or beast, and by bringing all the energy and courage which both men and beasts possessed, and putting same into action, we succeeded in making a march of sixteen miles, reaching the first or Johnston's Settlement in the territory of California, about night, where both man and beast were well fed and taken care of.''

After a few days of much needed rest we [that is Hoffman and his associates, but not the entire company] proceeded to Sacramento and from there to San Francisco.''

APPENDIX A

CONSTITUTION OF THE CHARLESTOWN, VIRGINIA, MINING COMPANY

[From *The Spirit of Jefferson*, February 20, 1849.]

ARTICLE I

Object and Title of Association.

SECT. 1. The members of this association have united in organization and do hereby acknowledge and recognize a joint Co-partnership for the purpose of proceeding to the Territory of California to acquire Gold and other valuable minerals by mining, &c., and to better their pecuniary condition in the most practicable and laudable manner.

SECT. 2. The name and style of this Co-partnership shall be "The Charlestown (Va.) Mining Company."

ARTICLE II

Period of Organization.

SECT. 1. The company shall continue its Co-partnership for and during the time, from 10th of February, 1849 to the 1st of April, 1850.

SECT. 2. The Company may, after the 1st of April, 1850, reorganize, for such period as may be deemed practicable. Nevertheless, nothing in this shall be construed as binding on those to remain and continue in the co-partnership, who may be members at the expiration of the original co-partnership, April 1st, 1850.

ARTICLE III

Officers of the Company.

SECT. 1. The Officers of the Company shall be a President, and three Commanders—known as 1st, 2nd, and 3d, and rank accordingly—a Treasurer, Quarter Master, and a Secretary, who shall be chosen by the Board, and serve as one of its members.

SECT. 2. The Officers of the Company shall constitute a Board of Directors, for the general and supreme regulation and government of the Company—in all cases unprovided for in this Constitution.

ARTICLE IV

Duties of the President.

SECT. 1. The President shall preside at all meetings of the Board of Directors, and decide all questions of order.

SECT. 2. He shall appoint all Committees to carry out the views of the Company or Board of Directors.

SECT. 3. He shall draw all drafts on the Treasurer after the Board of Directors shall have passed upon and ordered such disbursement.

SECT. 4. At the "Diggings," he shall, by and with the advice and consent of the Board of Directors, divide and sub-divide the Company into such parties as may be deemed practicable, and give such general instruction or direction as may be deemed advisable.

SECT. 5. The President shall be considered as the General Commander of the Company, except at such times—either on the route to California, or after arrival—as the Board of Directors may deem it advisable to place the Company under military discipline—at which time his authority shall be temporarily suspended.

SECT. 6. In case of a sudden attack, or other emergency, the President shall, immediately, resign, temporarily, into the hands of the Commanders, the control and arrangement of the Company for attack or defence.

ARTICLE V

Duties of the 1st Commander.

SECT. 1. The 1st Commander or Captain shall be the medium through which the military orders of the Board of Directors shall be carried into effect.

SECT. 2. The 1st Commander shall have entire and complete control in any such emergency as to prepare for an attack or to act on the defensive.

SECT. 3. The 1st Commander shall, when invested with command on the route, appoint such guard and so officered as his judgment may dictate.

SECT. 4. The 1st Commander shall preside at all meetings of the Board in the absence of the President—and may be called to the Chair temporarily.

ARTICLE VI

Duties of the 2d and 3d Commanders.

SECT. 1. In the absence of the 1st Commander, the 2d Commander or 1st Lieutenant shall assume his functions of Office, and be fully invested with all the powers delegated to the 1st Commander.

SECT. 2. The 3d Commander or 2d Lieutenant is vested with authority to assume command in the absence of the 1st and 2d Commander—if the Company shall be under military discipline.

SECT. 3. The 1st and 2d Lieutenants shall assist the Captain according to their several ranks when the Company shall be under military duty.

ARTICLE VII

Duty of the Secretary.

The Secretary shall keep exact and plain minutes of the proceedings of the Board as well as that of the Company, when in general meeting assembled.

ARTICLE VIII

Duties of the Treasurer.

SECT. 1. The Treasurer shall receive all monies or mineral substances, or other valuables, and receipt therefor to the President.

SECT. 2. He shall keep an exact and true account of all money or mineral substance or other valuable, which shall have been paid into his hands, in a book which shall be provided for that purpose, as also a book in which shall be entered all sums that may have been disbursed.

SECT. 3. He shall make no disbursements unless authorized so to do by the Board of Directors, attested by the order of the President.

SECT. 4. It shall be the duty of the Treasurer to receive from each member and detachment who may have been engaged in mining, washing, or otherwise, in acquiring gold, or other valuable substance, at the close of each day—or the earliest practicable period thereafter—all, and every valuable mineral, of whatsoever quality, gold, &c., of which said member or detachment shall have become possessed.

SECT. 5. The Treasurer shall keep the joint funds of the Company in common, to be held and accounted for, and in no wise to be returned or paid over, except in such cases duly made and provided.

ARTICLE IX

The Quarter Master.

The Quarter Master shall superintend the Commissary Department. He shall provide and furnish, from time to time, the necessary food for the company, and discharge all such duties usually pertaining to his office.

ARTICLE X

The Surgeon.

The Surgeon shall have exclusive jurisdiction over the Sanitary Department, and shall appoint all Committees connected with his department for the care of the sick.

ARTICLE XI

Time of Election, Duration of Office, &c.

SECT. 1. The elective officers of the Company shall be chosen on the 10th of February, 1849, and serve for the entire term of its organization.

SECT. 2. In case of resignation or death, or in any other way, the vacant office shall be filled after notice is fully given, at a general meeting of the Company.

SECT. 3. All the elective officers shall be chosen by ballot—and it shall require a majority of all the votes cast to elect.

ARTICLE XII

Qualifications for Membership.

SECT. 1. No person shall be admitted to membership unless his application shall have been reported upon favorably by a Committee of Examination.

SECT. 2. Each member shall pay to the Treasurer, as [*sic*] such times as may be demanded, by resolution in general meeting, such sums as shall be specified, not to exceed, in the aggregate, $300.

ARTICLE XIII

Duties of the Board of Directors.

SECT. 1. The Board of Directors shall have the exclusive management and control of the civil, military, and monetary operations of the Company—except in such cases as heretofore provided.

SECT. 2. All disputes, grievances, or other matters affecting the harmony of the Company, shall be laid before the Board of Directors —and their decision shall be final.

SECT. 3. They shall call such general meetings of the Company as they may deem practicable.

SECT. 4. They shall have power to pass on all claims and demands, and draw on the Treasurer for all sums of money that may be necessary to defray the Company's expenses, and ensure its welfare and prosperity.

SECT. 5. The Board of Directors shall determine upon the civil and military operations of the Company.

SECT. 6. The orders and decisions of the Board of Directors shall be announced by the President, if in civil service, and by the 1st Commander if under military duty.

SECT. 7. The Board is vested with full power to detail members as teamsters, and make such appointments for other service as may be required.

SECT. 8. If the Company determine to return with their funds uncoined, the Board of Directors, together with the Treasurer, or such as shall be appointed a Committee by them, shall proceed with the same to the United States Mint at Philadelphia, and after it shall have been coined, they shall convey the same to the town of

Charlestown, Jefferson County, Virginia, and appoint a day for the distribution of the same, in such proportions as may be due to each member of the Company.

ARTICLE XIV

Of the Funds.

SECT. 1. No funds shall be drawn from the Treasury, either in its mineral or other state, by any member of the Company, without authorization for and an order given on the Treasurer.

SECT. 2. It is hereby enacted, that a book shall be kept by the Treasurer, in which the name of each member of the Company shall be registered, immediately opposite which shall be placed the name or names of those [who] may have advanced such member money for the expedition, together with conditions; and it shall be the duty of the Board of Directors so to consider the applications of members for funds, as to have a guarantee that such person or persons who may have advanced monies, shall not be defrauded under any pretences. Provided, nevertheless, that this Company do not hold themselves legally or morally bound to supply any deficit or fraud that may occur.

SECT. 3. By the aforesaid enactment, the Board of Directors acknowledge themselves specially bound, so far as they may have the ability and jurisdiction, to see that a fair apportionment shall be made between the contracting parties, and should the Company return in a body, as is contemplated, they will be in attendance in the town of Charlestown on a given day, and award justice to all interested.

SECT. 4. All the minerals, gold, silver, piatina, or ore, or valuable[s] of whatever character, which may be gathered, procured, or acquired, shall be paid over by each member or detachment, into the hands of the Treasurer, to go into the joint funds of the Company.

SECT. 5. The general fund of the Company, embracing all that may have been acquired by the entire membership, shall be equally divided among the members, at such times and places as may be determined upon—subject to such restrictions and regulations as already provided.

SECT. 6. Should any member of the Company die, either on the route to California or whilst there, the heirs of the same shall draw one full half share; and if he shall have been engaged in mining or other service for any time, there shall be awarded the heirs a full proportion for all such time that the member may have been engaged, together with a half share in all such sums as shall be gathered after his demise and before the date of dissolution of the Company; and the Board of Directors are hereby enjoined to see that this covenant shall be well and truly executed.

ARTICLE XV

Of the Members.

SECT. 1. Each member of the Company shall be, and he is hereby bound and duly obligated, to engage in mining, washing and cleansing the ore; or such other employment as may be assigned him by the Board of Directors: and no member of the Board shall be excused from any branch of service, which may be assigned him, by reason of his office.

SECT. 2. There shall be no exemption from any service, on any plea or excuse—sickness or other disability excepted—in which case the verbal or written certificate of the Surgeon shall be necessary.

SECT. 3. Each member of the Company hereby recognizes the power and pledges himself to sustain the authority of the Board of Directors, and the commands and orders of the President, Captain, or commanding officer.

SECT. 4. Each member acknowledges himself solemnly bound to hand over to the receiving officer at the earliest practicable time, each and all of each and every valuable, mineral, ore, gold, silver, platina, quicksilver, &c., of which he may have become possessed, whilst engaged in digging, washing, gathering, or which he may have otherwise acquired.

ARTICLE XVI

Moral Statutes.

SECT. 1. The Christian Sabbath shall be duly recognized and its observance enforced, by refraining from all other than works of necessity; and any member who shall so far violate its observance as to engage in mining, or other work of a profitable character, shall forfeit all and entire that which he may thus have acquired, together with the average of a two days' income—all of which shall go into the joint fund for the general use of the company.

SECT. 2. Gambling of each and every character, whether by cards, dice, or in any other way, shall be, and is hereby distinctly and expressly prohibited, between the members of this Company; and for each and every violation of this article, the member or members so offending, shall forfeit and cause to have deducted from their share of the joint profits of the Company, the average yield of a member's gathering in one day, for the first offence; for the second offence the proportion that he might be entitled to for one week's partnership with the Company; and for the third offence he shall be expelled— a majority of the members in general meeting so determining.

SECT. 3. The Board of Directors in this, as in all other cases where fines may be affixed, as penalties, [is] to determine upon the average value of a day's income—and the said sum or sums to be charged up on the Treasurer's book, as monies actually drawn from the Treasury.

SECT. 4. Any member guilty of intoxication, shall be fined for the first offence the average yield of a member's gathering in one day; for the second offence the proportion that he might otherwise be entitled to receive for one week's partnership with the Company; and for the third offence he shall be expelled—a majority of the members in general meeting so determining.

SECT. 5. It shall be the duty of the Board of Directors to select a suitable member, who shall read on each Sabbath morning a portion of the Scriptures, and engage in devotional exercises.

SECT. 6. The provisions of the seventeenth article shall be and continue in full force and operation, from and after the Company shall leave St. Louis, Mo. until the 1st day of April, 1850.

ARTICLE XVII

Penalties.

SECT. 1. Any member who shall fail to perform the duty assigned him, or shall refuse or neglect to engage in mining, washing, or other duty of whatsoever character, shall be fined in such sum as the Board of Directors may determine—to be charged up against the delinquent member in the books of the Treasurer, and deducted from his joint share: and should he continue thus injurious to the interests of the Company, he shall be expelled—a majority of the members so determining.

Sect. 2. In all cases of expulsion, the President shall announce, in general meeting, the name of the person accused, and the cause of complaint, when a vote shall be taken by ballot. A majority voting in favor of such expulsion, the President shall announce that as the decision, and the accused's connection with the Company shall thereupon cease.

Sect. 3. In case of expulsion, the member shall receive such proportion of the joint stock fund as the Board of Directors may decide to be his full share for the time in which he shall have been engaged in the co-partnership. He shall, however, forfeit all right in any and all the joint property, except such provision as the Board of Directors may provide, and the funds which may be in the hands of the Treasurer at the time of his dismissal.

ARTICLE XVIII

Miscellaneous.

Sect. 1. Any member may leave the Company, after its arrival in California, with the consent of two-thirds of the members, and shall be allowed such proportion of the provisions as the Board of Directors may provide—forfeiting, however, all right and title to any and all other joint property, except a rifle, revolver, and blankets.

Sect. 2. Any member leaving the Company without the consent of two-thirds of its members, shall forfeit, all and entire, his interest in the joint stock, property, provisions, or other things belonging to the Company—as well as all his interest in whatever funds may be in the hands of the Treasurer.

Sect. 3. Any member who shall attempt to defraud the Company by secreting any portion of his gains, or in and by any means or false pretences, shall be expelled by a vote of the majority of the members. And on his expulsion, [he] shall forfeit his entire right, title and interest, to each and every article, as well as the general fund which may belong to the Company.

ARTICLE XIX

[no title]

The provisions, &c., that may be shipped, shall be invoiced in the name of the President and Directors of this Company, and shall be subject to their order, after arrival in California.

ARTICLE XX

[no title]

The Constitution shall not be altered or amended, unless one week's previous notice shall have been given, and the same be passed by two-thirds of the members, in general meeting.

APPENDIX B

ROSTER OF MEMBERS OF THE CHARLESTOWN COMPANY

THIS roster is based upon a list in the *Spirit of Jefferson*, February 13, 1849, with additions and corrections derived from later issues of the same periodical, and from Edward McIlhany, *Recollections of a 49er*.

OFFICERS

FRANK SMITH, Guide

BENJAMIN F. WASHINGTON, President.

ROBERT H. KEELING, First Commander.

SMITH CRANE, Second Commander.

JOSEPH E. N. LEWIS, Third Commander.

EDWARD M. AISQUITH, Treasurer.

NATHANIEL SEEVERS, Quartermaster.

J. HARRISON KELLY, Secretary.

DR. WAKEMAN BRYARLY, Surgeon.

MEMBERS

Allen, John
Barley, Richard
Bender, Jacob
Blakemore, R. M.
Boley, John T.
Bowers, John William
Bradley, Thornton C.
Burwell, Walter J.
Clevinger, Asa
Cockrell, Daniel
Comegys, George W.
Conway, Hugh
Cribs, James S.
Cunningham, Charles
Cunningham, George
Cunningham, James
Daugherty, Enos
Davidson, James
Davidson, Samuel
Davis, Joseph C.
Duke, F. W.
Engle, Jacob H.
Engle, Joseph
Fagan, Daniel
Ferrill, Milton
Gallaher, John W.
Garnhart, John H.
Geiger, Vincent E.

Gittings, Charles F.
Hardesty, T. P.
Harrison, Hamilton C.
Hayden, Charles A.
Herbert, Noble T.
Hoffman, Benjamin
Hooper, Edward
Humphries, J. Thomas
Humphreys, Dr. Joseph D.
Lock, Elisha
Lupton, John M.
McCurdy, James
McIlhany, Edward
Mackaran, William H.
Marmaduke, A. J.
Marshall, George
Miller, Andrew R.
Miller, Morgan
Milton, Taliaferro
Moore, Henry H.
Moore, James H.
Moore, John, Jr.

Moore, Thomas C.
Murphy, John H.
Poland, John T.
Purcell, John
Riely, Edwin A.
Rissler, William
Rohrer, Elisha
Seevers, Benjamin F.
Showers, John S.
Showman, P. B.
Simpson, Francis R.
Slagle, Charles F.
Small, James B.
Stonebraker, G. C.
Strider, Isaac Keys
Strider, Jesse A.
Tavener, Newton
Thomas, Charles G.
Wagner, Andrew
Walpert, John C.
Washington, Lawrence
Washington, Thomas F.

Young, Joseph C.

APPENDIX C

VINCENT E. GEIGER'S DIARY FROM STAUNTON, VA., TO ST. JOSEPH, MO.

LEFT Staunton, Va. Thursday night Feby 8th 1849, at about 12 o'clock—left Stevenson, McClung, Tanquary, Cushing, & Currie in good spirits—after taking a farewell drink. Hired two horses of Mr. Miller & took Kinney's [boy] Anthony along to take the horses back. Anthony got drunk & fell off—I went to sleep riding along & woke up, my horse & I standing in a fence corner. Stopped at Mr. Eidsen's & told him a cock & bull story about the grand pe.[?], gambling &c. Got to Gaily's (Mr. Crawford) about 3 o'clock in the morning & stopped for breakfast. Hired a buggy on Friday, 9 & went to Harrisonburg. Waited there for the stage & was joined by R. H. Keeling. Went on to Winchester—12 miles from there (west). Stage broke down & I rode one of the horses into town. Took the cars there & reached Charlestown at 11 o'clock A.M., (on the 10th—Saturday). Joined the C.V.M.C.[1] & paid in $110, the first instalment. Keeling admitted & elected captain. Remained there until Sunday, 4th of March, & then took cars for Cumberland, Md., & thence on to Pittsburg, Pa., by stage & steamboat. Arrived there on the 5th, stopped at the St. Charles. Met with W. B. Dorman & others from Rockbridge Co[unty], Va.—also C. Gailer of Keokuk. Left Pittsburg on Tuesday morning, on board the steamboat HIBERNIA NO. 2 & reached Cincinnati, Ohio about daylight on Thursday the 8th & took lodgings at the Broadney Hotel. Keeling, Dorman, & others in company. On Saturday, 3rd March, paid in $190 to the company—my last instalment.

Thursday, March 8th.

In Cincinnati—went to the National Theatre—rather a poor performance—House not good.

---

1. *i.e.*, Charlestown, Va., Mining Company.

Friday, March 9th.

Met with Alex. Fisher & Geo. Ribble of Staunton, Va.—the latter of whom came to this city in September last with me.

Friday 9th—In City—nothing of moment occurred—went to the Theatre—better than it was last night.

Saturday, March 10th.

Doing nothing. At the American Theatre. Play, California Gold Seekers.[1] Pretty good.

Sunday, March 11th.

Visited the Catholic Cathedral. A splendid edifice—large crowd —good music. The pews have locks & each one is locked up. A party of Californians from Shenandoah Co[unty], Va., reached here today—rain & continuing cloudy. Wrote to J. M'Clung & S. Churchman.

Monday, March 12th.

Left Cincinnati in company with W. B. Dorman, on board S. B. CAMBRIA—A large company on board, most for California, among them about 30 real live yankees from Maine—some of them exceedingly verdant—always shooting guns, pistols, &c. Today before I started, met with Gallagher, Cockrell, & Engle of our mule committee. Keeling returned up the river to Pittsburg.

---

1. The Cincinnati *Enquirer*, Feb. 2, 1849, carried an advertisement of a new play, "Buckeye Gold Hunters," or "Dutchley in California" to be presented at Rockwell's new American Theatre, 6th and Vine Streets. The cast included Mr. Gaylor as Harry Harding, Mr. Lewis as Hans Dutchenheimer, Mrs. Kent as Betsey, and Mrs. Wilkinson as Tarclosa. On March 4, the *Enquirer* stated that the play had been written for the American Theatre by Mr. Charles Gaylor, and that it had filled the house for twenty successive nights. On March 10, another notice in the *Enquirer* announced that the play was to be revived for one night, "at the request of several members of different companies bound for California now in the city en route for the Diggins [*sic*]." "La Tour de Nesle" was offered as part of the same program.

If this play was written specifically for the Cincinnati theatre, it would seem to be an entirely different play from "The Gold Seekers," which appeared at the Bowery Theatre in New York, Dec. 28, 1848. T. Allston Brown, *A History of the New York Stage* (New York, 1903) I, 124.

Tuesday, March 13th, Wednesday, March 14th.

On the river. Some black-legs fleeced a young fellow of $150— at Poker—4 eights & 4 fours the hands. Nothing else of note occurring.

Thursday, March 15th.

Reached St. Louis about 12 o'clock at night[2]—remained on board until next day.

Friday, March 16th.

Went ashore & put up at the Missouri Hotel on Main Street.[3] Met with Jno. Brown of Fisherville and with him looked about the city—took several cocktails & had some fun. St. Louis is a place of great business & is daily growing—I like it better than Cincinnati.

Saturday, March 17th.

Moore, & the remainder of the committee reached here this morning—also P. McKay & Mr. Cockrell & a lady from Va. Looked about the city—priced mules & horses—which were very high. Found J. B. Jost & C. Clarke of Rockingham Co[unty], Va. at 49 Locust Street publishing a family paper & keeping a job office. At night attended the Democratic Mass meeting—remained a short time—found some fellow making a free-soil speech.[4] Went on board the S. B. KIT CARSON for Lexington Mo., on the Missouri River. It is a full bold stream—full of snags—some beautiful country & many little turns on the river. Boonville, Jefferson City & other towns on the river were visited.

2. The St. Louis *Republican*, March 17, announced the arrival of the steamboat *Cambria*, from Pittsburgh; it had left Cincinnati on Monday, March 12.

3. The St. Louis *Republican*, March 17, listed W. B. Dorman of Illinois and V. E. Gaiger *(sic)* of "ditto," as having arrived at the Missouri Hotel on March 16. On March 20, it carried an advertisement of the Missouri Hotel, at Main and Morgan Streets, "opposite the most active part of the steamboat landing."

4. The St. Louis *Republican*, March 19, carries a full account of a Democratic mass meeting at the Rotunda on March 17, at which resolutions were adopted advocating exclusion of slavery from the territories. Apparently the Benton faction was in control of this meeting.

Sunday, March 18th, Monday, March 19th,
Tuesday, March 20th, Wednesday, March 21st.

Arrived at Lexington Mo. at 2 o'clock P.M., and took up board at the City Hotel. Met with Wilson & Kise of Augusta. H. Sheets & M. Fitzpatrick also reside here. A row took place in the bar-room between some drunken men—threats of knives &c., but no damage done.

Thursday, March 22nd.

Looking about the town—it is a very pretty place of about 2500 inhabitants. The town is well laid off & has been built up in the last 10 years. The buildings mostly brick, & good. A Masonic College near the town is a very pretty building. The country surrounding is beautiful & the land exceedingly rich. A good many emigrants in town—mules in the hands of speculators & are held at 70 to 100 dollars—most exorbitant prices. Weather very pleasant—quite like spring.

Friday, March 23rd.

In Lexington. Met with Sheets & others & Col. Geshen formerly of Greenbrier. Cockrell bought 30 mules for our company of W. H. Hay, for $2,000.

Saturday, March 24th.

Left the City Hotel and took up lodgings at Mr. Jno. Clawson's formerly of Jefferson Co[unty], Va. Pilot McKay got here about 9 o'clock at night.

Sunday, March 25th.

In Lexington. Moore arrived with 60 mules. Cold & stormy.

Monday, March 26th.

In Lexington.

Tuesday, March 27th.

In Lexington. Moore & McKay & G. Cockrell left.

Wednesday, March 28th.

In Lexington. Dorman & Boydkin arrived today. Took a chance for a watch & *lost, of course.*

Thursday, March 29th.

In Lexington. Dorman & Boydkin left. A rowdy & drunken company from Pittsburg Pa., numbering about 300 passed up the river tonight.

Friday, March 30th.

In Lexington.

Saturday, March 31st.

Left Clawson's & went to Monroe House.

Sunday, April 1st.

Up to Wednesday 11th at Monroe House. D. Cockrell who has been sick with small pox got out today. I have been very unwell myself for several days. Keeling was here on Thursday last & left Saturday for Independence. Moore left for the same place on yesterday.

APPENDIX D

TABLES SHOWING TRAVEL SCHEDULE OF VARIOUS EMIGRANTS OF 1849 BY WAY OF THE SOUTH PASS

NEITHER the diaries nor the routes were at all times precise enough to afford a basis for the exact comparison of time schedules. For instance, all diarists who followed the south bank of the Platte were certain to mention reaching Fort Kearney, but those who followed the north bank might not record their arrival at a point on the river opposite the Fort. Consequently, it is sometimes necessary to estimate the date, on the basis of the context. No inferences have been drawn except where they were strongly substantiated, but I have indicated all estimated dates by placing them in brackets. For a discussion of the time element in overland travel, and of the factors involved in making such a comparison as is attempted in these tables, see above, pp. 51–53.

TABLE I.

Dates of departure on the journey, of reaching important points along the trail, and of arrival at the settlements in California.

	Place of departure	Date of departure	Arrival Fort Kearney	Arrival Fort Laramie	Arrival South Pass	Arrival Fort Hall	Arrival Sink of Humboldt	Approximate arrival in California
Kelly	Independence	Apl. 16	May 8]	May 27	[June 8]	via Salt Lake	......	July 26
Long	Independence	Apl. 23	May 14	June 7	June 22	June 11	Aug. 2	Aug. 14
Isham	St. Joseph	Apl. 26	May 13	June 3	June 19	July 4	July 28	Aug. 11
Love	Independence	Apl. 27	May 18	June 5	June 22	July 9	Aug. 13	......
Johnston	Independence	Apl. 28	May 15	May 28	June 10	via Salt Lake	July 15	[July 28]
Dundass	near Ind.	Apl. 30	May 26	June 16	July 6	via Salt Lake	Sep. 4	[Sep. 13–15]
Delano	St. Joseph	May 2	May 23	June 12	June 29	July 18	via Lassen's	Sep. 17
Tiffany	St. Joseph	May 3	May 18	June 6	June 22	July 9	Aug. 3	Aug. 25
Wistar	Independence	May 3	May 30	June 16	June 30	July 20	Aug. 10	......
B. C. Clark	Westport	May 3	May 22	June 10	June 24	July 10	Aug. 2	[Aug. 24]
Hale	St. Joseph	May 5	May 24	June 15	July 3	July 23	via Lassen's	Oct. 15
Page	St. Joseph	May 6	May 24	June 13	July 2	July 20	Aug. 21	Sep. 12
McCall	St. Joseph	May 7	May 29	June 18	July 5	via Salt Lake	Aug. 26	Sep. 15
S. B. F. Clark	St. Joseph	May 8	May 26	[June 18]	July 5	via Salt Lake	Aug. 10	Aug. 23
Backus	St. Joseph	May 11	May 25	July 1	July 14	July 17	Aug. 11	Sep. 5
Brown	Independence	May 12	June 9	June 28	July 14	via Hudspeth's	via Lassen's	Sep. 7
Caldwell	......	......	May 28	June 16	July 8	July 30	via Lassen's	Oct. 23
GEIGER-BRYARLY	St. Joseph	May 14	May 28	June 14	June 29	July 14	Aug. 8	Sep. 1
Lewis	St. Joseph	May 14	June 1	June 17	July 5	via Salt Lake	Aug. 22	Sep. 10
Doyle	near Ia.–Mo. line	May 15	May 28	June 19	July 10	via Hudspeth's	Aug. 26	Oct. 14
Searls	Independence	May 15	June 8	June 27	July 19	via Hudspeth's	via Lassen's	Oct. 1
Swain	Independence	May 15	June 13	July 5	Aug. 1	via Salt Lake	via Lassen's	Oct. 30
Badman	Council Bluffs	May 17	[June 4]	June 25	July 17	via Hudspeth's	via Lassen's	Sep. 24
McCoy	Independence	May 19	June 10	July 2	July 25	via Salt Lake	via Lassen's	Oct. 20
De Wolf	Westport	May 20	June 14	July 7	Aug. 3	via Salt Lake	Sep. 27	[Oct. 22]
Foster	Council Bluffs	May 22	May 31	June 16	July 4	via Hudspeth's	via Lassen's	Sep. 30
Sedgley	near Ind.	May 22	June 13	July 1	July 16	via Hudspeth's	via Lassen's	Sep. 22
Webster	Independence	May 26	June 19	July 8	Aug. 1	via Hudspeth's	via Lassen's	Oct. 17
Orvis	Council Bluffs	May 27	[June 4]	June 14	June 28	via Salt Lake	date not given	Aug. 12
Bruff	above, St. Jos.	June 4	June 17	July 10	Aug. 1	Aug. 24	via Lassen's	Oct. 21
Royce	Council Bluffs	June 8	[June 23]	July 11	Aug. 4	via Salt Lake	Oct. 5	Oct. 24

TABLE II

Number of Days in travel between certain specified points.

	Point of Departure to Ft. Kearney	Ft. Kearney to Ft. Laramie	Ft. Laramie to South Pass	South Pass to Fort Hall	Fort Hall to Sink of Humboldt	Humboldt to Settlements in California	Total from departure to arrival in California
Kelly	22	19	12	...	?	...	101
Long	21	24	15	19	22	12	113
Isham	17	21	16	15	24	14	117
Love	21	18	17	17	35	...	...
Johnston	17	13	13	35 ↓	↑	13	91
Dundass	26	21	20	60 ↓	↑	11	138
Delano	21	20	17	19	25	...	138
Tiffany	15	19	16	17	21	22	114
Wistar	27	17	14	20	23	...	...
B. C. Clark	19	19	14	16	...	22	[113]
Hale	19	22	18	20	...	...	163
Page	18	20	19	18	32	22	129
McCall	22	20	17	52 ↓	↑	20	131
S. B. F. Clark	18	21 ?	19 ?	36 ↓	↑	13	107
Backus	14	20	17	16	25	25	117
Brown	28	19	16	...	...	...	[126]
Caldwell	...	19	22	22	...	...	...
CHARLESTOWN COMPANY							
Lewis	14	17	15	15	25	24	110
Doyle	17	16	18	48 ↓	↑	19	118
Searls	13	22	21	...	...	...	152
Swain	24	19	22	...	...	...	139
Badman	29	22	27	...	...	...	168
McCoy	18	21	22	55 ↓	↑	25	130
De Wolf	22	22	23	...	...	...	154
Foster	25	23	27	...	...	...	155
Sedgley	9	16	18	...	...	...	131
Webster	22	18	15	...	...	...	123
Orvis	24	19	24	...	...	...	144
Bruff	8	10	14	...	...	...	77
Royce	15	18	24	62 ↓	↑	19	138

BIBLIOGRAPHY

FOR many aspects of this study, the pertinent sources are indicated in the footnotes. This is true, for instance in the discussion of the lives of Geiger and Bryarly, and in the treatment of the various routes. The purpose of this bibliography, therefore, is not to list all sources used but (I) to indicate the principal sources of information on the Charlestown Company, (II) to list as completely as possible the published journals, and also the manuscript journals in the Coe Collection, which deal with overland journeys to California by way of the South Pass in 1849—that is, journeys which parallel that of the Charlestown Company, and (III) to offer a selective list of secondary materials which are of outstanding importance in the study of the Gold Rush.

I. THE CHARLESTOWN COMPANY

ASIDE from the Geiger and Bryarly journal, there are three sources which give important information on the Charlestown Company. First, the weekly newspaper of Charlestown, the *Spirit of Jefferson,* published full accounts of the organization of the company; and, after the journey had begun, it printed a number of letters from various members of the company, both while in transit and after arrival in California. Second, another member of the company, Benjamin Hoffman, kept a brief journal which Charles H. Ambler edited as a part of his study of "West Virginia Forty-niners" in *West Virginia History,* III (1941), 59–75. Third, another member, Edward Washington McIlhany, published his autobiographical *Recollections of a 49er* at Kansas City in 1908. On many details his memory was at fault, and only a small portion of his narrative was concerned with the overland journey. Nevertheless, his record helps to round out the story at certain points. In addition to these three primary sources, Millard Kessler Bushong, *A History of Jefferson County, West Virginia* (Shepherdstown, 1941), contains a useful summary, with references.

II. OTHER JOURNALS AND NARRATIVES BASED UPON JOURNALS.

A GREAT many of the Forty-niners wrote, at some later time in their lives, reminiscent accounts of their experiences during the Gold Rush. Undeniably, such accounts have a certain value as history, but they often betray lapses of memory, and they are also unreliable because of the selective tendency of the memory to recall certain aspects of the experience and to forget others. Therefore, I have attempted to rely, as far as possible upon accounts which were written at the time, or were based upon records made at the time. All of the wholly contemporary records were in the form of diaries, or of sets of letters which, in content, were almost like diaries. In addition, one occasionally meets with a later account such as that of Mrs. Sarah Royce, which is evidently based upon a day-by-day record, and I have included such accounts as these also. Applying these restrictions to accounts of the journey to California by way of the Oregon and California Trail in 1849, I have found twelve manuscript records which are pertinent, in the William Robertson Coe Collection in the Yale University Library, and some twenty-five printed accounts. Since all of these items are repeatedly cited in the footnotes merely by the last name of the diarist, it seems desirable to list the manuscript accounts, and after them, the printed accounts, in alphabetical order, as a means of facilitating reference from the footnotes to the bibliography.

(A) MANUSCRIPT ACCOUNTS. I have not attempted to include manuscript journals which are to be found at various important libraries, but have confined myself, so far as unprinted materials are concerned, to the Coe Collection in the Yale University Library. All of the manuscripts listed below, therefore, are from that collection. The routes of travel and the travel schedules of the journeys described in these diaries are shown more fully in Appendix D.

BACKUS. The manuscript journal of G. Backus of Burlington, Vermont, from departure from Vermont to arrival in California, with notes of life in California, March 14, 1849–October 12, 1850. About 9000 to 10,000 words.

BADMAN. The manuscript journal of Philip Badman of Warren, Pennsylvania, from departure from Pennsylvania to arrival in California, with an itinerary of distances. About 11,000 words.

> Badman started out with a company known as "Captain Collyer's Company." His writing is barely more than literate, but the terse saltiness of some of the comments is outstanding.

B. C. CLARK. The manuscript journal of Bennett C. Clark has been published, and is included in list below of printed journals.

DELANO. The manuscript journal of Alonzo Delano in its published form, is one of the classic items of Gold Rush history. See list below of printed journals.

DOYLE. Manuscript journal and letters of Simon Doyle of Rushville, Illinois, on two trips to California in 1849 and 1854, with a thirty-two page table of distances, and with letters to his parents in Rushville, April 2, 1849–June 22, 1856. The journal of the trip in '49 extends to about 18,000 words.

> Doyle, a Mexican War veteran, was a man of some education and of a thoughtful turn of mind. His comments are consistently full, and the journal is unusually valuable.

LEWIS. Manuscript journal of John F. Lewis of Huntsville, Randolph County, Missouri, from Missouri to California, May 12–December 31, 1849.

> Lewis was relatively unlettered. His journal contains about 9,000 words on the journey, and about 2,000 more on experiences in California.

LONG. Manuscript journal of Charles L'Hommedieu Long of Cincinnati, Ohio, on the journey to California, March 10–September 1, 1849. About 15,000 words.

> Long was a superior observer, and his journal is quite literate, with entries that are reasonably full. Long used pack animals from Bear River and made the later portion of the journey on foot. His journal is a striking example of a rapid and efficient trip.

LOVE. Manuscript journal of Alexander Love of Leesburg, Pennsylvania, from his departure from Leesburg, with some interruptions, until his return by way of Panama in 1852, March 20, 1849–March 5, 1852.

> The portion of this diary dealing with the overland journey includes about 9,000 words. Love was 39 years old at the time of the Gold Rush. The trip was rather a slow one, but was a well-organized and successful endeavor.

LYNE. Letters of James Lyne of Henderson, Kentucky, sent to his family in Henderson from various points along the way to California, April 22, 1849–January 30, 1850.

> There are ten letters. They show that Lyne travelled with the company of one, Colonel Wilson. Two supplementary letters relate to the fact that Lyne was drowned in the Sacramento River, early in 1850.

ORVIS. The manuscript journal of Andrew Orvis of Lake Marie, Wisconsin, from his departure from his home until his arrival in California and at the Diggings, March 12, 1849–June 8, 1850.

> This brief record (about 3,000 words) is of especial interest because it is the account of a man who was deserted by his companions, was left without rations, and almost lost his life on the desert. Many suffered similar hardships, but those who suffered most were too preoccupied with their survival to write observations. Orvis covered the period July 10–August 12, in one continuous account, but even so, this is almost an unique record of his type of experience. Orvis was born in 1819 in Arcade, Wyoming County, N.Y., and died in China, N.Y., in 1895.

SWAIN. The manuscript journals and letters of William Swain of Youngstown, New York, from his departure from his home until the arrival in California, and while he was at the Diggings, April 11, 1849–August 10, 1851.

> Swain made the journey as a member of the ''Wolverine Rangers.'' He was a man of superior education and superior perception, and with a gift for writing. As a consequence, his 30,000 word diary is one of the best as well as one of the fullest of overland records. In addition to the diary, there are 14

letters to his wife, Sabrina, and to other members of the family; another diary, with another set of letters, covers the period spent in California.

TIFFANY. The manuscript journal of P. C. Tiffany of Mt. Pleasant, Iowa, of his journey from his home, to California, and during the period spent in California, with a log of the return by way of Panama in 1851, April 7, 1849–March 13, 1851.

This is an unusually full account, with about 30,000 words on the overland journey alone.

(B) PRINTED ACCOUNTS. In the section below, the purpose is not to list books, but to list diaries. Thus, if one book contains more than one diary, as does, for instance, *Gold Rush,* edited by Read and Gaines, I have listed the two diaries separately, in their normal alphabetical order, with the appropriate bibliographical information for each, or with a cross-reference to the information.

BROWN. "Memoirs of an American Gold Seeker," by Honorable John Evans Brown, in *Journal of American History,* II (1908), 129–154.

Brown was born in Lewiston, Pennsylvania, in 1827, but moved with his family to North Carolina, and set out on the overland journey in 1849 from Asheville, in that state. He later made a second trip to California by sea, and later still moved to New Zealand, where he became a member of Parliament and Minister of Education. He returned to America, and died at his home "Zealandia," in Asheville, in 1895.

BRUFF. Georgia Willis Read and Ruth Gaines, editors, *Gold Rush, The Journals, Drawings, and Other Papers of J. Goldsborough Bruff, Captain, Washington City and California Mining Association, April 2, 1849–July 20, 1851* (2 vols. New York, 1944).

This is by far the most extensively and thoroughly edited of all overland journals. Bruff, born in Washington, D. C., in 1804, graduated from the Military Academy at West Point, and was assigned to the Department of Topographical Engineers. In 1849, having resigned his commission, he was elected Captain of the Washington City and California Mining Company. He led this company of 66 men slowly, but successfully, to California, maintaining strict discipline and preventing the usual disintegration. He made many sketches, and wrote a diary from which a more lengthy and more finished record was prepared soon afterward. The editors publish both versions, labelling the earlier record as P 2, 3, 4, 5, 6, and the final one as P 1 and H 1. All of my citations are to the latter version.

CALDWELL. A diary kept by Dr. T. G. [?] Caldwell, is published by Read and Gaines in *Gold Rush,* II, 1247–1268. See Bruff, immediately above.

B. C. CLARK. Ralph P. Bieber, editor, ''Diary of a Journey from Missouri to California in 1849,'' in *Missouri Historical Review,* XXIII (1928–29), 3–43.

> The diarist, Bennett C. Clark, was born in Boonville, Cooper County, Missouri, in 1819. He later became Clerk of the Circuit Court of that county. In 1849, he was elected captain of a party of twenty-three gold-seekers from the region near his home, and it was as leader of this company that he kept his diary. Severe illness caused him to discontinue it just after crossing the Humboldt Desert. Ably edited, with footnotes of especial value. The original manuscript is in the Coe Collection.

S. B. F. CLARK. *How many miles from St. Jo? The Log of Sterling B. F. Clark, a Forty-niner, with Comments by Ella Sterling Mighels* (San Francisco, Privately printed, 1929).

> Clark was born in Rutland, Vermont, in 1825. He travelled with a wagon train to Fort Laramie, and with pack animals from that point. A brief journal.

DELANO. Alonzo Delano, *Life on the Plains and Among the Diggings; Being Scenes and Adventures of an Overland Journey to California* (Auburn, N. Y., 1854).

> Delano, son of Dr. Frederick Delano of Aurora, New York, was a resident of Ottawa, Illinois, when his physician advised a change of climate for his health. This advice led him to join the migration of '49, to work for a short while in the

diggings, and later to become a prosperous merchant in San Francisco. During the journey to California, he kept a journal which described the overland journey fully and vividly. This diary, the original manuscript of which is now in the Coe Collection, was published in 1854, and has become, without doubt, the best known participant's account of the Gold Rush.

De WOLF. "Diary of the Overland Trail, 1849, and Letters, 1849–50, of Captain David De Wolf, with an introduction and notes by Edwin E. Cox," in Illinois State Historical Society, *Transactions for the Year 1925*, pp. 183–222.

De Wolf was born in 1822 in Yarmouth, Nova Scotia. He returned from California *via* Panama in 1851. During the Civil War, he became a captain in the Union Army and was killed at the Battle of Corinth, in 1862. At the time of his trip, De Wolf's family lived in Springfield, Ohio. The journal and letters are both reasonably full, and distinctly useful.

DUNDASS. *Journal of Samuel Rutherford Dundass, formerly auditor of Jefferson County, Ohio, including his entire route to California as a member of the Steubenville Company bound for San Francisco in the Year 1849* (Steubenville, 1857).

Almost all companies resolved not to travel on Sunday, but Dundass was with one of the few groups which held to the resolution. The diary tends to be sententious. Dundass, who was travelling for his health, died of typhoid in 1850.

FOSTER. Lucy A. Foster Sexton, *The Foster Family, California Pioneers of 1849* (San Jose[?], 1889).

Contains the overland journal, with letters, of Rev. Isaac Foster. Foster, a native of Connecticut, was born in 1790, and was a resident of Illinois at the time of the Gold Rush. He became judge of the mayor's court in San Jose and died there at the age of 78. He started on the overland trip as a member of the Iowa Company of California Emigrants, but this association was soon dissolved. Foster was a man of superior judgment and practicality, and his comments on the mismanagement of many of the emigrants are illuminating.

HACKNEY. Elizabeth Page, editor, *Wagons West, a Story of the Oregon Trail* (New York, 1930).

> Although this volume consists primarily of the story of Henry Page (*q.v.*), with his letters, it also contains the complete text of the diary, by Joseph Hackney, of his overland journey as a member of the Green and Jersey County Company. Although Hackney was scarcely literate, his journal forms a superior record of the trip.

HALE. "Diary of a Trip to California in 1849, written by Israel Foote Hale," in *Quarterly of the Society of California Pioneers*, II (1925), 59–130.

> Israel Foote Hale, born in 1804, made the overland trip in 1849, carrying his seventeen-year-old son Titus with him. His home is not identified, but it is stated that he returned to it in 1851, after finding a fair amount of gold dust, and he lived until 1891. The diary, written for his family, is reasonably full.

HIXSON. Owen C. Coy, *The Great Trek* (Los Angeles and San Francisco, 1931).

> This narrative history of the Gold Rush contains extracts from the journal of Jasper Hixson. The portions dealing with the crossing of the Humboldt Desert are especially good.

ISHAM. *G. S. Isham's Guide to California and the mines and return by the Isthmus with a general description of the country. Compiled from a journal kept by him in a journey to that country in 1849 and 1850* (New York, 1850).

> A brief itinerary. This is an unusually rare item of which but two copies are known, one being in the Coe Collection.

JOHNSON. John McCoy, editor, *Pioneering on the Plains* (privately printed, 1924[?]).

> This volume, consisting primarily of papers of the McCoy family, also contains the letters of John A. Johnson to his wife. Johnson was an Ohio lawyer who went to California because he was threatened with tuberculosis. These letters, principally from Independence, are superior to any other

source I know of, in depicting the conditions and problems of getting started on the journey.

JOHNSTON. *Experiences of a Forty-niner, by William G. Johnston, a member of the Wagon Train first to enter California in the Memorable Year 1849* (Pittsburgh, 1892).

This, one of the better known journals, is the account of an unusually successful and rapid trip. Despite the claim in the title, it seems to be a debatable question whether this party, or that of William Kelly was first to reach California in 1849, but both reached there about a month in advance of the bulk of the migration.

KELLY. William Kelly, *An Excursion to California over the Prairie, Rocky Mountains, and Great Sierra Nevada* (2 vols. London, 1851).

Although not printed in diary form, this is in fact a day-by-day record, and a careful analysis will make it possible to assign the correct date for most of the events described. Kelly was a prosperous Englishman who appears to have made the journey for the sake of the adventure; literally, it was "an excursion to California." With ample funds, and splendidly outfitted, Kelly's company, of which he was captain, made the journey with unusual rapidity. See Johnston, immediately above.

McCALL. A[nsel] J[ames] McCall, *The Great California Trail in 1849. Wayside Notes of an Argonaut* (Bath, N. Y. [reprinted from the Steuben *Courier*] 1882).

McCall was a resident of Bath, New York. His journal reflects very humane feelings, dogmatism, and an enthusiasm for current fads. It is highly readable, the observations are acute, and the value of the work is greater than that of many diaries issued in much more pretentious format.

McCOY. John McCoy, editor, *Pioneering on the Plains* (privately printed, 1924[?]).

Contains the diary of Samuel F. McCoy of Chillicothe, Ohio. McCoy's brother, John, had just returned from Santa Fé, and Samuel travelled with his outfit. The diary entries are brief, and are full of pious moralizing. See Johnson, above.

MORGAN. Mrs. Martha M. Morgan, *A Trip Across the Plains in the Year 1849* . . . (San Francisco, 1864).

Mrs. Morgan travelled only as far as Salt Lake City during 1849. In 1850, she continued her journey to California. Her route followed the Mormon Trail along the north bank of the Platte.

PAGE. Elizabeth Page, editor, *Wagons West, a Story of the Oregon Trail* (New York, 1930).

Contains excellent letters of Henry Page of Woodburn, Illinois, to his wife, Mary, while on the overland journey. Also contains the constitution of Page's company, and a complete narrative by the editor.

PLEASANTS. W[illiam] J[ames] Pleasants, *Twice Across the Plains 1849* . . . [sic] *1856* (San Francisco, 1906).

Pleasants and others who travelled with him lived at Pleasant Hill, Cass County, Missouri. The record is not in diary form, but it appears to be based upon notes made while the party was in transit.

ROYCE. Ralph Henry Gabriel, editor, *A Frontier Lady, Recollections of the Gold Rush and Early California by Sarah Royce* . . . (New Haven, 1932).

Sarah Royce was the mother of Josiah Royce, the philosopher. She was born in Stratford on Avon in 1819, but was brought to New York State as an infant. She married Josiah Royce, and with him made the journey to California. Her husband apparently understood nothing of overland travel, and their trip was hopelessly mismanaged. Her account of the grim experience shows extraordinary perception, and it is on a different level from most of the personal accounts. She wrote this account for her son, during the eighteen eighties, but the evidence shows that it was based upon an earlier written record.

SEARLS. *The Diary of a Pioneer, and other Papers, Being the Diary Kept by Niles Searls on His Journey from Independence, Missouri, to California* (San Francisco, 1940).

> This is an important item because it constitutes almost the only record of an emigrant who travelled with one of the companies which undertook to transport passengers to California for a stated fare. Searls took passage with the Pioneer Line. The officers of the company made great efforts to fulfill their contract, but this form of transportation proved, at that time, a disastrous failure. Searls, born in 1825 in Coeymans, New York, was admitted to the bar in 1848, and opened a law office in Cass County, Missouri, but in the following Spring he joined the Gold Rush, paying the Pioneer Line $200 for his passage.

SEDGLEY. Joseph Sedgley, *Overland to California in 1849* (Oakland, 1877).

> Sedgley started out as a member of the Sagamore and California Mining and Trading Company of Lynn, Massachusetts, with 52 members, but he left the company fairly early in the journey. Sedgley and Bruff are more diligent than almost any other diarists in recording the names of persons whose graves they pass along the trail.

WEBSTER. Kimball Webster, *The Gold Seekers of '49, a Personal Narrative of the Overland Trail . . . with an Introduction by George Waldo Browne* (Manchester, N. H., 1917).

> Webster was born in Pelham, New Hampshire in 1828. Before the Gold Rush, he worked in a granite quarry, and he later returned to New Hampshire where he was a surveyor, engineer, and justice of the peace. He lived until 1916. He travelled to California with the Granite State and California Mining and Trading Company. The diary occupies pages 23–99.

WISTAR. *Autobiography of Isaac Jones Wistar, 1827–1905* (2 vols. Philadelphia, 1914).

> The first volume of the autobiography of this distinguished physician contains a full, and unusually well written diary of his journey from Independence, Missouri, to California.

III. SELECTED LIST OF SECONDARY MATERIALS.

AMONG historians of a past generation, there were four especially, who made basic contributions to the history of the overland migration. These four were Hubert Howe Bancroft, Reuben Gold Thwaites, Archer Butler Hulbert, and William James Ghent. Bancroft, in Volume VI of his *History of California* (San Francisco, 1888), gave a long account of the Gold Rush, based upon a vast number of references, which were shown in the footnotes to his text. This was, apparently, the first extensive account based upon genuine research. Thwaites' contribution is to be found primarily in the footnotes to his thirty-one volumes of *Early Western Travels, 1748–1846* (Cleveland, 1904–1907). These notes identify thousands of persons, place names, Indian groups, *et cetera*, which were significant in the history of the West. Neither Bancroft nor Thwaites, however, had attempted to trace the exact routes of overland travel, and this aspect of the subject remained to be developed by Hulbert. His results were presented, for popular reading, in his volume, *Forty-niners* (Boston, 1931), and for more scholarly purposes in the elaborate *Crown Collection of American Maps*, Series IV, *The American Transcontinental Trails* (1925–1928). W. J. Ghent contributed the best single volume on the Oregon Trail in his *The Road to Oregon, a Chronicle of the Great Emigrant Trail* (New York, 1929).

There are a number of contemporary writers who have made and are making valuable contributions in this field. Without being invidious, however, it is quite safe to say that the most extensive editorial notes on the Gold Rush are to be found in Georgia Willis Read and Ruth Gaines, editors, *Gold Rush, The Journals, Drawings, and Other Papers of J. Goldsborough Bruff* (2 vols., New York, 1944). These notes, a monument of thoroughness, deal exhaustively with many points which are of interest to all students of the trail. A recent book, designed for the general reader, but nevertheless providing an excellent history of the Oregon and California Trail, is *The Wake of the Prairie Schooner*, by Irene D. Paden (New York, 1943). In addition to its other merits, this contains the best sketch maps that have yet been published. Another treatment, which similarly combines historical accuracy with literary skill, is *The Great Trek* by Owen C. Coy (Los Angeles and San Francisco, 1931).

If illustrations are desired, nothing compares with the reproductions of photographs of points along the trail, by Louis Palenske, in Rufus Rockwell Wilson's edition of Alonzo Delano's *Life on the Plains and Among the Diggings* (New York, 1936).

One of the best and most scholarly treatments of the Gold Rush is Ralph P. Bieber, editor, *Southern Trails to California in 1849* (Glendale, Cal., 1937). Although dealing, as the title implies, primarily with the southern routes, this volume contains an indispensable account of the arrival of the news of gold in the East, and the development of the Gold Fever. Professor Bieber has recently completed plans for writing a history of the Gold Rush as a whole, to be published in 1949, and it is safe to anticipate that this will be the standard work.

INDEX